LIBERIA IN MAPS

LIBERIA IN MAPS

LIBERIA IN MAPS

edited by
Stefan von Gnielinski, D.Sc. (Hamburg)
formerly Professor of Geography
University of Liberia

AFRICANA PUBLISHING CORPORATION · NEW YORK

Published in the United States of America
by Africana Publishing Corporation
101 Fifth Avenue
New York, N.Y. 10003

Library of Congress Catalog Card No. 72-80411

ISBN 0 8419 0126 0

First published 1972

Printed in Great Britain

CONTENTS

LIST OF CONTRIBUTORS

Austin Amagashie, BA (UL) *Teaching and Research Assistant, Department of Geography, University of Liberia.*

Stefan von Gnielinski, DSC (HAMBURG), MRSV (AUSTRALIA) *formerly Professor and Head of Department of Geography, University of Liberia.*

J W A Jansen, AGRICULTURAL ENGINEER (WAGENINGEN) *Associate Expert, FAO, College of Agriculture and Forestry, University of Liberia.*

Abeodu Bowen Jones, PHD (NORTHWESTERN UNIVERSITY, ILLINOIS) *Research Specialist, Department of Education, Republic of Liberia.*

A E Nyema Jones, PHD (UNIVERSITY OF CHICAGO) *Chief, Liberian Geological Survey, Bureau of Natural Resources and Surveys, Monrovia.*

Martin Sieh Karpeh, MD (HAMBURG) *Physician and Surgeon, Executive Mansion, Monrovia.*

Werner Korte *University of Giessen (W Germany); formerly Research Fellow, Department of African Studies, University of Liberia.*

W Ernst Kuhn, PHD (ST GALLEN) *Professor of Economics, University of Nebraska; formerly Fulbright Professor of Economics, University of Liberia.*

Andreas Massing, DIP SOCIOLOGIST, UNIVERSITY OF FRANKFURT *formerly Research Fellow, Department of African Studies, University of Liberia.*

Hon Bai T Moore *Under Secretary, Department of Information and Cultural Affairs, Republic of Liberia, Monrovia.*

Clive W Pearson, BA (OTAGO) *Lecturer in Geography, University of Liberia.*

Charles Steiner *Curator and Taxidermist, University of Liberia; formerly National History Museum, Basel.*

Janet Bartley Williams, BSC (LONDON) *Lecturer in Geography, University of Liberia.*

Armahrue N Woods, BA (UL) *Teaching and Research Assistant in Geography, Department of Geography, University of Liberia.*

Unless otherwise stated, maps were compiled and drawn by Stefan von Gnielinski.

INTRODUCTION

During my five years assignment as chairman of the Department of Geography, University of Liberia, Monrovia, the lack of a comprehensive textbook describing the Liberian environment and its people made work difficult for me and my students. Of course, there is a great number of publications dealing with many special subjects and various aspects of the country, but however valuable and informative they may be, most of them do not provide a great number of maps, if any. The absence of maps is not only regretted by the geographer, whose most important tools they are, but also by readers who want to provide themselves with an overall picture at first glance.

Liberia in Maps is a combined effort of a number of past and present members of the Department of Geography, University of Liberia, to fill this gap and furnish an informative textbook interpreting the Liberian setting through the medium of the map. The volume contains 50 maps of Liberia, each accompanied by a brief analytical text. It aims to be a geographical appraisal, providing the student as well as the general reader with information about the complexity of the Liberia of today in terms of continuity and changes which have taken place during the past decades. It is also intended to provide some basic facts about those natural and human resources of the country in a way which can be best interpreted by a plan or map. However, it should be kept in mind that, although the map can vividly delineate the land, some of the important social, cultural, economic and political aspects of the country cannot be presented in map form and therefore could not be considered in this publication.

From the beginning it was understood that the task of editing this book would not be an easy one. Except for weekends and vacations, there was little time for field investigation because of the heavy teaching load placed upon a small staff. Furthermore, as noted above, the selection of maps is not comprehensive. Some topics, especially in the social field, could not be included because of inadequate information; others await the availability of data.

Most of the maps are based on the planimetric map of Liberia (scale 1 : 500 000) compiled from aerial photographs and published in 1957 by the Government of Liberia through the joint Liberian–United States Commission for Economic Development. Although the new coverage made by photo-planimetric methods from aerial surveys started in 1966 and completed during 1970 by the US Army is not yet available, the use of these airphotos has been most helpful. For the Monrovia region a topographic map, published by the government in co-operation with the Federal Republic of Germany, based on air photos taken by Hansa Luftbild, Muenster, at a scale of 1 : 20 000 proved very useful as did the city map of Monrovia at a scale of 1 : 7500 completed in 1970 by the US Army Corps of Engineers in co-operation with the Liberian Cartographic Service.

It should be pointed out that, although the maps have been compiled and drawn according to the latest information available, they do not necessarily have the same affirmative level. Some are the results of lengthy investigation and research; others are more tentative and therefore have to be understood as mere generalizing sketch-maps. However, this should not obviate their utility. The international boundary of Liberia was plotted from the best available data but must not be considered authoritative. Name spellings are approved by the Liberian Board of Geographic Names.

The editor would like to express his sincere thanks to his colleagues for their contributions and for their patience in considering editorial suggestions. Special thanks are due to the colleagues outside the department who have co-operated most wholeheartedly and thus have allowed us to fill some of the gaps in our appraisal.

The editor is particularly grateful to all the authorities, government bodies, e.g. the University of Liberia, the Department of Planning and Economic Affairs, the Department of Agriculture, the Department of Information and Cultural Affairs, the Bureau of Mineral Resources including the Liberian Cartographic Survey and the Liberian Geological Survey and many others for the aid and information they have provided. My friends and colleagues from the Liberian and US Geological Survey especially were extremely helpful and co-operative, making available their equipment and facilities for my work. Agencies like US AID, private concessions, and mining companies were also helpful in many ways as were my students and the many Liberian people interrogated through the country. But for their kind co-operation *Liberia in Maps* could not have appeared.

I was very fortunate to count on both patient encouragement and discerning criticism from my wife, Anneliese, who helped me with the cartography and put the bibliography in its final form.

STEFAN VON GNIELINSKI

1 LIBERIA IN AFRICA

The establishment of the Republic of Liberia, the first and oldest in Africa, dates back to 1847. The country lies on the west coast of the continent along the wide south-west curve north of the equator called the Upper Guinea Coast. The exact position is:

longitude: 7° 18′ – 11° 30′ West,
latitude: 4° 20′ – 8° 30′ North.

The extreme south-east of the country is closer to the equator than any other coastal part of Africa west of the Niger delta and, with a distance of some 1600 miles (2570 km.) to Brazil, it is closer to the South American continent than any other African state, a fact which proved of great strategic importance during the Second World War. Because of its longitudinal position which is similar to that of Ireland and Portugal, the official time is 45 minutes earlier than Greenwich Mean Time.

Liberia comprises an area of 43 000 square miles (111 370 sq. km.)*; that means it would fit into the African continent some 268 times. Compared with other African states Liberia is only a small country. Only seven independent African states are even smaller in area, namely Gambia (4000 sq. miles; 10 400 sq. km.), Swaziland (6700 sq. miles; 17 350 sq. km.), Rwanda (10 200 sq. miles; 26 500 sq. km.), Burundi (10 700 sq. miles; 27 800 sq. km.), Lesotho (11 800 sq. miles; 30 700 sq. km.), Togo (21 800 sq. miles; 56 700 sq. km.) and Sierra Leone (27 900 sq. miles; 72 400 sq. km.). Compared with other parts of the world Liberia is the size of Pennsylvania, Ohio, or Tennessee, a little bigger than Iceland and roughly equivalent to the area Germany lost after the Second World War.

The country has 350 miles (563 km.) of coastline and extends inland on the western side to about 170 miles (274 km.) near Voinjama, while on the eastern side the distance from Greenville to the northern border on the Cavalla River is only 110 miles (177 km.). The access to the sea is an important advantage. In Africa there are 14 countries including three in Western Africa – Mali, Niger and Upper Volta – which do not have this advantage and therefore have to negotiate with their coastal neighbours for trade outlets.

Since the foundation of the republic, Liberia has played a very important role in the emergence of Africa because at all times she has represented the aspiration to self-determination and independence. Never having been a colonial possession Liberia was consequently an obstacle in the eyes of the colonial powers during the partition of Africa. It is indeed remarkable that she was able to preserve her independence, although she lost substantial parts of her territory to France and England.

* Measurements made with the polar planimeter indicate that the area of Liberia is approximately 38 250 square miles or 99 068 sq. km.

Because of Liberia's origin her relations with the United States of America have been cordial and marked by close public and private association. The official language is English and the US dollar has been the country's basic monetary unit and legal tender since 1943. Even the constitution of the republic was modelled on that of the United States. This constitution enacted a comprehensive Bill of Rights; it restricts ownership o land to citizens of the Republic and confines the right of citizenship to Negroes only.

In modern times the significance of Liberian history for Africa lies in the fact that the newly independent states face many of the problems and in many cases are following paths similar to those which Liberia pioneered between 1822 and 1914. Liberia has been an outspoken advocate of African unity. She was one of the eight countries to attend the Accra Conference in April 1958, at which dependent African countries, in their efforts to attain self-government, sanctioned schemes of mutual assistance. Two important meetings on Liberian soil followed: the Saniquellie Conference in 1959 and the Monrovia Conference in 1961. Both were initiated by President Tubman, an ardent supporter of Pan-Africanism. The Monrovia Conference was of special significance for the course of African unity. Twenty states from north and south of the Sahara were represented, agreed on a series of resolutions, and formed a community: the Monrovia Group. This group actually served to launch a larger and more significant conference in Addis Ababa in 1963. Here the Organization of African Unity (OAU) was born, and now includes all independent states in Africa except South Africa. The OAU Charter, one of the historic documents of this century, states that the purpose of the organization is to promote unity, solidarity and international co-operation by co-ordinating political, economic, educational and cultural policies. It was truly no coincidence that this charter was almost identical with the one drawn up by the Monrovia Group. Emperor Haile Selassie honoured this by bringing into special prominence the merits of President Tubman, who 'for his role in the drive for African Unity has earned the respect and admiration of his colleagues'.

Along with other African states Liberia firmly opposes the South African apartheid policy. She stopped trade relations with South Africa in 1961, subsequently banned South African aircraft from landing in and ships from calling at the country, and maintains a similar attitude towards the Portuguese administration in African territories.

Liberia was a charter member of the League of Nations and is proud of being a charter member of the United Nations. In 1961 she became the first African member of the Security Council and holds membership in almost all the special agencies of the United Nations. More pro-Western than some African states, Liberia has no diplomatic relations with the communist block. Nevertheless, she maintains a policy of strict neutrality.

STEFAN VON GNIELINSKI

LIBERIA IN AFRICA

20° 10° 0° 10° 20° 30° 40° 50° 60°

30°

MOROCCO
SPAN. SAHARA
ALGERIA
LIBYA
EGYPT
Tropic of Cancer

MAURITANIA
MALI
NIGER
CHAD
SUDAN
FR. SOMALILAND

SENE-GAL
GAMBIA
PORT. GUINEA
REP. OF GUINEA
UPPER VOLTA
NIGERIA
CENTRAL AFRICAN REPUBLIC
ETHIOPIA
SOMALIA

SIERRA LEONE
IVORY COAST
GHANA
TOGO
DAHOMEY
CAMEROON
UGAN-DA
KENYA

LIBERIA
SPAN. GUINEA
Equator
GABON
CONGO (Brazzaville)
Rwanda
Burundi
ZAIRE
TANZANIA

London
New York
Lisbon
Dakar
Monrovia
Recife
Lagos
Rio de Jan.
Buenos Aires
Cape Town

ANGOLA
ZAMBIA
MALAWI
MOZAMBIQUE
MALAGASY REP
RHODESIA
SOUTH WEST AFRICA
BOTSWANA
Tropic of Capricorn
REPUBLIC OF SOUTH AFRICA
SWAZILAND
LESOTHO

Scale
0 500 1000 Miles
0 500 1000 Km

9

2 LIBERIA AND HER NEIGHBOURS

Liberia has three neighbouring states—Sierra Leone in the west, Guinea in the north and the Ivory Coast in the east. Since the country has a compact shape and a coastal position, its borders are fairly short, having an overall length of about 860 miles (1400 km.): 158 miles (254 km.) with Sierra Leone, 320 miles (515 km.) with Guinea and 382 miles (615 km.) with the Ivory Coast. The border with Sierra Leone is well defined by two prominent water courses, the Mano and the Morro Rivers, to some 90 miles (145 km.) from the coast. Thereafter, the frontier runs north-east until it reaches the Makona River. Here at approximately 8° 30′ north latitude is Liberia's most northerly place. The borderline with the Republic of Guinea has a very irregular course. It follows the Makona River to a few miles north of Voinjama, cuts across some ridges and river valleys, follows the Nianda River in a southerly direction, and thereafter describes a big arc towards the Nimba Mountains to reach eventually the boundary between Liberia and the Ivory Coast. This frontier is the most extensive and well defined, and follows the Nimba Mountains south along the River Nuon (Cestos) for about 70 miles (113 km.) before it cuts across the main divide reaching the Cavalla River, whose course it follows until it reaches the coast.

The nucleus of Liberia comprises a piece of land on and around Cape Mesurado some 130 miles (209 km.) long and 40 miles (64 km.) wide acquired by the immigrants from the tribal chiefs on 15 December 1821. After initial struggles the settlers were able to expand their little colony, and the newly elected legislature in 1848 defined the territorial limits of the republic as running from Moffi Creek to the Grand Cess River extending approximately 40 miles (64 km.) inland. The colony of Maryland continued to remain independent until 1857, when it joined Liberia as a new county increasing the coastal area from River Cess to the San Pedro River 60 miles (97 km.) east of the Cavalla. During this time the country enjoyed the greatest coastwide extent of her territory. However, when the colonial scramble of the European nations started, Liberia soon found herself pushed back out of areas lawfully acquired by purchase or by exploration, and the map showed some shrinkage of the coastline. The trouble ironically started with Britain, the first state to extend diplomatic recognition to Liberia in 1848. Under the pretence that Liberia could not keep law and order in the area east of the Sewa River, the British took possession of it in March 1883. After some lengthy disputes the Liberian British Treaty in 1885 established the boundary with Sierra Leone along the Mano River. The French, noticing the failure of Liberia to resist the British successfully made extensive claims as far as Gaware including Cape Palmas, and only a sharp protest from the USA prevented the annexation. Liberia was helpless and had to agree on the Cavalla River boundary at the convention in Paris 1892. Provisions were made to settle all questions between Liberia and French Guinea, but because of the fact that at this time the geographical knowledge about the hinterland concerned was vague, no agreement could be reached. During 1911, however, the Makona River became the line of demarcation between the two countries, and Liberia again found herself deprived of a large area of her territory. In an attempt to bring rivers more consistently under the control of the respective countries a minor exchange of land with Sierra Leone took place in 1911. After that the attitude of Britain toward Liberia underwent a complete change to cordial relations. Only the Guinean border was subject to further negotiations as recently as 1958, but the independence of the Republic of Guinea during the same year put an end to further talks.

All in all the losses of territory were quite substantial. Consideration of the losses, however, should not obscure the fact that Liberia, which only in 1908 belatedly began to organize a border force, saved a larger hinterland for further development than for instance the British in Sierra Leone. Because of this, independence even for a weak country proved more effective than colonial status under a great power.

The Liberian boundaries resulting from French and British colonial expansion are not drawn according to tribal distribution. Consequently, many of the tribes are divided by these borders, and the boundaries may have interfered with their activities, but generally certain quantities of goods get across and many of the tribal people still have close kinship with contiguous groups in Sierra Leone, Guinea and Ivory Coast. There are in fact no sharp cultural or historical differences between the adjacent neighbours. The people have much in common and live side by side without friction. It is not surprising that Liberia and Sierra Leone have even discussed the possibility of a union which would bring many advantages for both countries and could be an excellent example for the whole of Africa.

Compared with her neighbours Liberia is only sparsely peopled with some 27 inhabitants per square mile (10 per sq. km.) while Sierra Leone has about 78 persons per square mile (30 per sq. km.), Guinea has 40 (15), and Ivory Coast 33 (13). Since 1960 motor roads connect Monrovia with all three neighbouring states, and during the last year ingress and egress have been considerably simplified. The official crossing points are:

Liberia–Sierra Leone at Kolahun–Kailahun
Liberia–Guinea at Ganta–Nzérékoré
Liberia-Ivory Coast at Tobli–Toulépleu

All the capital cities are connected by telephone and regular air services.

Although the complementarity of the major natural products have been a factor inhibiting the expansion of economic co-operation between the neighbouring countries, the Heads of State of Guinea, Ivory Coast, Liberia and Sierra Leone, on the initiative of President Tubman, met in Monrovia to discuss steps toward West African Economic Integration. Whatever the outlook is, Liberia is willing to co-operate with her neighbours. The envisaged mining of iron ore across the border in Guinea provides an excellent opportunity for co-operation, and for Guinea to save the expenses of railroad construction by transhipping iron ore through Liberia using the existing railway line of the LAMCO Mining Company.

Liberia's relations with her neighbours since their independence have been friendly and cordial, and are marked by mutual respect and esteem, although political views may not be shared on all subjects.

STEFAN VON GNIELINSKI

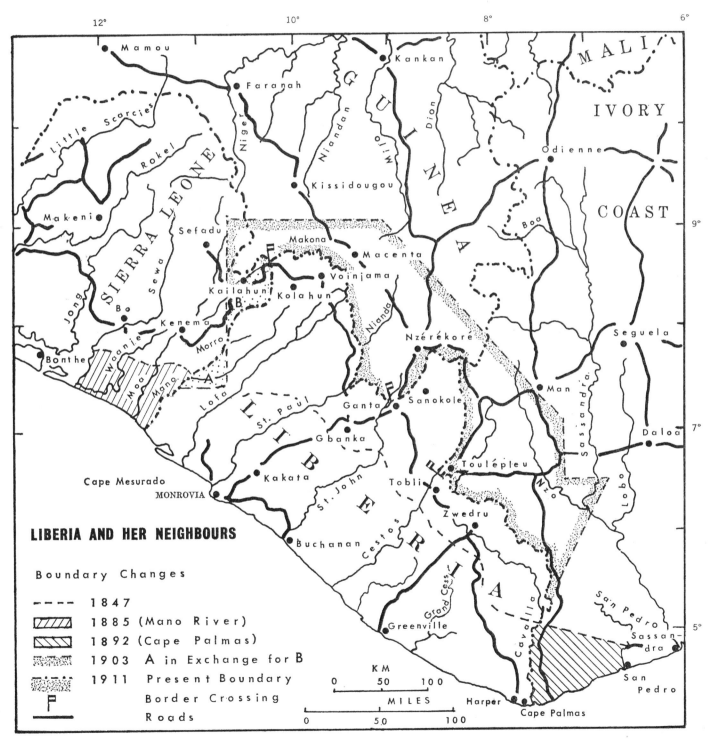

LIBERIA AND HER NEIGHBOURS

Boundary Changes

- – – – – 1847
- 1885 (Mano River)
- 1892 (Cape Palmas)
- 1903 A in Exchange for B
- 1911 Present Boundary
- Border Crossing Roads

3 HISTORICAL BACKGROUND

Liberia is a unique country in West Africa, essentially because of its non-colonial background, and few books on Africa consider its place in the main stream of African literature.

The Liberia of today is the home of 1·5 million indigenous Africans grouped into fragmentations of several of the major West African ethnic groups and the descendants of the Negro immigrants from the United States and the West Indies in the first half of the nineteenth century. Although the coast of Liberia was already well known and frequented in the fifteenth century under the name of 'Grain Coast' or 'Malagueta Coast', its political history started with the declaration of independence in 1847 with Joseph J Roberts as first president and father of the republic. Since then it has had a colourful and changeable history as the oldest independent African republic.

The history of the indigenous population of Liberia has not yet been fully investigated. It appears fairly certain that these peoples arrived between the twelfth and sixteenth centuries from the north, north-east and east; many came from the savanna areas near the Sahara Desert fleeing from the Islamic Jihad (Moslem Holy War); many were looking for new living space. The coastal people were primarily fishermen and hunters, while the people of the interior had brought with them some inheritance from Islamic contact in agricultural, cultural and religious practices. Nevertheless the Poro and Sande native African educational institutions developed without alien contact.

The earliest information about the territory that is now Liberia was given by a number of seafarers and explorers. In 520 BC Hanno of Carthage sailed along the West African coast but the first European ship ever to come to its shore carried the Portuguese flag. Pedro da Cintra arrived in 1461 and opened the Portuguese trade monopoly which lasted up to 1515. Chief items of trade were ivory and malagueta pepper, which later gave the coast its name. During the first hundred years of their adventures the Portuguese had named nearly every cape, inlet, river and mountain on the west, south and east coasts of Africa. Their nomenclature in West Africa has been lasting, for instance: River Gallinhas, Cape Mount (Gabo do Monte), Cape Mesurado (Moderate), Rivers St Paul and St John (discovered on the feast days of these biblical saints), Cestos River (*cestos* = basket, after the fish baskets used here), Sangwin from *sanguinho* = bloody, denoting the blood-red colour of the stream after floods. Cape Palmas received its name from the abundance of palm trees, and the Cavalla River from the Portuguese word *cavala*, meaning a big fish, mackerel. The Portuguese taught the Vais and Krus their language and brought the orange, coconut, pineapple, tobacco, the European domestic ox, the hog and Muscovy duck into the country.

After 1518 the French renewed their interest in Atlantic voyages and from 1553 the English also frequented the Liberian coast.

The first extensive descriptions of the country were given by the German Samuel Braun and the Dutchmen Olfert Dapper and John Snoek. Braun touched the Grain Coast on three voyages in 1611–13, 1614–16, and 1617–20. His descriptions, especially of Cape Palmas, were published by the German geographer Levinus Hulsius at Frankfurt (between 1615–50). Dapper gave some information about trade on the St Paul and the St John Rivers, and about the Kru, the Vai, the Gola and other tribes. Snoek visited the regions of Cape Mount and Monrovia at the beginning of the eighteenth century and gave a sympathetic description of the friendly people at the mouth of the River Cestos which, during this time, was the centre of the pepper trade. In the seventeenth century the chief commodity of trade changed from pepper and ivory to slaves and brought in its wake a number of intertribal wars.

In 1816 the American Colonization Society was founded to find a solution to the Negro problem in the United States by resettling the freed and captured slaves in the country of their forefathers. In December 1821 Ayres and Stockton of the Colonization Society made a sales agreement with the chiefs of the De and Mamba tribes for a strip of coast land 130 miles (208 km.) long and 40 miles (64 km.) broad as well as the future site of Monrovia. Nevertheless the tribal chiefs were reluctant to give up the land in question and the colonists had to brave many weeks of attack on Providence Island before they moved to the Mesurado Promontory. The little colony did not have an easy start. Besides tribal attacks, diseases and lack of technical and financial assistance marked its way.

In 1825 Liberia received its first constitution and its name. From 1830 onward other small colonies were founded: all of them joined the Commonwealth of Liberia except Maryland which followed in 1857. A dispute over non-payment of harbour dues with the British Government which was unwilling to accept a private commercial enterprise as a sovereign government led to the Declaration of Independence on 26 July 1847. Until 1865 about 15 000 American settlers came to Liberia besides 5000 slaves recaptured from ships and 300 Negroes from the West Indies.

With the industrial revolution and the following colonial expansion Liberia went through very difficult decades. Countless border disputes with England and France and a desperate financial position make it surprising that the republic was able to survive and retain its sovereignty.

The turning point ending the struggle for survival in the dramatic and often stormy history of Liberia dates back some three decades only. (See Chapter 32: Economic History.) Since this time the country has gained a remarkable political, social and economic stability, facing the challenge of progress.

A B JONES

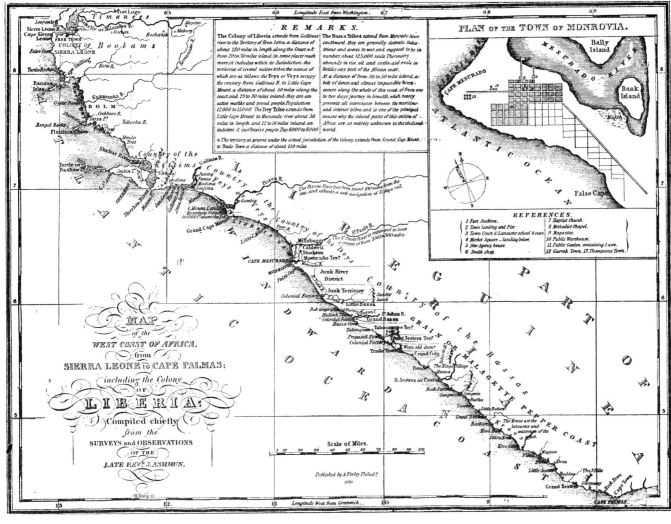

MAP of the WEST COAST OF AFRICA, from SIERRA LEONE to CAPE PALMAS; including the Colony of LIBERIA; Compiled chiefly from the SURVEYS and OBSERVATIONS OF THE LATE REVd J. ASHMUN.

Published by A. Finley Philada 1830

REMARKS.

The Colony of Liberia extends from Gallinas river to the Territory of Kroo Settra, a distance of about 280 miles in length, along the Coast, &c. from 20 to 30 miles inland, in some places much more; it includes within its Jurisdiction, the territories of several native tribes, the names of which are as follows, the Feys or Veys occupy the country from Gallinas R. to Little Cape Mount, a distance of about 50 miles along the coast, and 25 to 30 miles inland; they are an active warlike and proud people. Population 12,000 to 15,000. The Dey Tribe extends from Little Cape Mount to Mesurado river about 30 miles in length, and 12 to 16 miles inland; an indolent & inoffensive people. Pop. 6000 to 8000.

The Bassa Tribes extend from Mesurado river southward; they are generally dense, industrious and averse to war, and supposed to be in numbers about 125,000 souls. The country abounds in rice, oil and cattle, and rivals in fertility any part of the African coast.

At a distance of from 30 to 50 miles inland, a belt of dense and almost impassible forest occurs along the whole of this coast, of from one to two days journey in breadth, which nearly prevents all intercourse between the maritime and interior tribes, and is one of the principal causes why the inland parts of this section of Africa are so entirely unknown to the civilised world.

☙ The territory, at present under the actual jurisdiction of the Colony, extends from Grand Cape Mount, to Trade Town, a distance of about 150 miles.

PLAN OF THE TOWN OF MONROVIA.

REFERENCES.

1 Fort Stockton.
2 Town landing and Pier.
3 Town Court & Lancaster school house.
4 Market Square — landing below.
5 New Agency house.
6 Smith shop.
7 Baptist Church.
8 Methodist Chapel.
9 Magazine.
10 Public Warehouse.
11 Public Garden, containing 1 acre.
12 Gurmh Town. 13. Thompsons Town.

Scale of Miles.

Longitude East from Washington.

Longitude West from Greenwich.

4 GEOLOGY

Very little was known about the geology of Liberia until the last decade when teams of geologists from the Liberian Geological Survey, the US Geological Survey and the mining companies began to conduct systematic geological mapping activities in various parts of the country and within concession areas. Results of these investigations have shown that nearly all of Liberia is underlaid by Precambrian crystalline rocks which form a part of the West African Shield, a large region consisting predominantly of ancient crystalline rocks.

The rocks forming this crystalline shield are a series of granite, gneiss and schist beds which have resulted from metamorphism by tectonic forces acting on a regional scale. Some structural features in these rocks are uniform over relatively large areas. Gneissic structure and schistosity dip at high angles in most places and are often vertical. The predominant or regional strike is NE–SW.

Unmetamorphosed sedimentary rocks exist along the coastal area of western Liberia. These rocks consist predominantly of laminated sandstone and smaller units of arkoses, siltstones, mudstones and conglomerates which are probably of Cretaceous age.

With the exception of these sedimentary beds, the rocks comprising the basement complex are of Precambrian age. Iron-bearing formations (itabirites) are interspersed in the basement complex and appear to be a part of the Precambrian formation. Bands of amphibolite which follow the trend of foliation in the gneiss are also common. A belt of rocks belonging to the granite facies, as much as 15 miles (24 km.) wide and trending parallel to the coast, extends north-west from Monrovia to the Sierra Leone border. The original sediments of the iron-bearing formation have undergone great physical and chemical changes resulting in metamorphosed and migmatized rocks.

Basic intrusive rocks (diabase and gabbro) exist along the coast, forming promontories at Cape Mount (Robertsport) and Cape Mesurado (Mamba Point, Monrovia). These rocks also form numerous dikes in the interior and coastal area of Liberia.

The igneous and metamorphic rocks of Liberia have been intensely deformed and metamorphosed by tectonic and metamorphic forces acting on a regional scale.

Age determinations of Liberian rocks by the K-Ar method in laboratories of the Massachusetts Institute of Technology (MIT) and the US Geological Survey (Menlo Park, California) suggest that the diabases differ in age from about 180 million years in the coastal zone to about 400 million years in the interior zone, while the majority of the granitic rocks fall into the range of 2500–3400 million years.

More knowledge about the geology and mineral resources of Liberia will be obtained during the course of the joint mapping and exploration activities of the Liberian Geological Survey, the US Geological Survey and the United Nations Mineral Survey which are now in progress. A preliminary geological map of western Liberia, shown opposite, has been published in colour, and it is anticipated that a complete geological map of the country will be available by the end of 1972.

A E N JONES

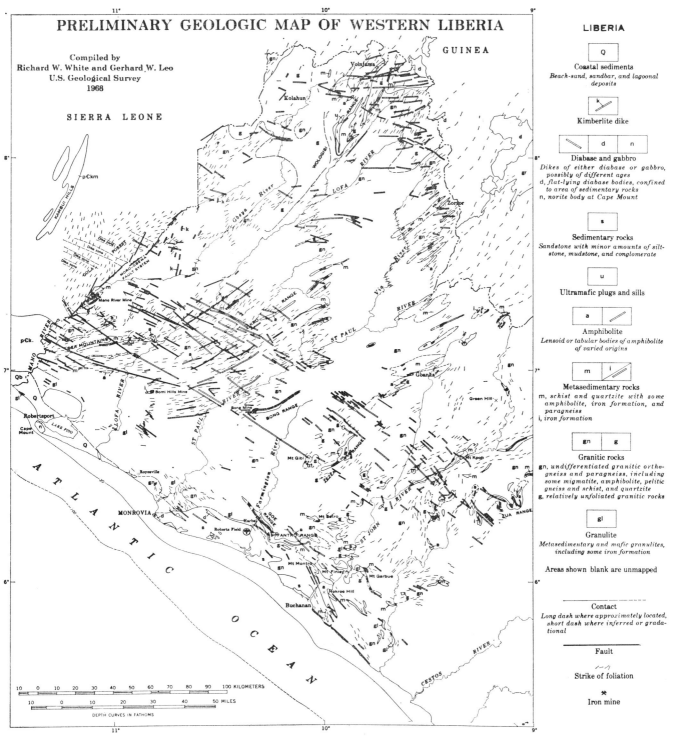

PRELIMINARY GEOLOGIC MAP OF WESTERN LIBERIA

Compiled by
Richard W. White and Gerhard W. Leo
U.S. Geological Survey
1968

SIERRA LEONE

GUINEA

ATLANTIC OCEAN

LIBERIA

Q
Coastal sediments
Beach-sand, sandbar, and lagoonal deposits

k
Kimberlite dike

d **n**
Diabase and gabbro
*Dikes of either diabase or gabbro, possibly of different ages
d, flat-lying diabase bodies, confined to area of sedimentary rocks
n, norite body at Cape Mount*

s
Sedimentary rocks
Sandstone with minor amounts of silt-stone, mudstone, and conglomerate

u
Ultramafic plugs and sills

a
Amphibolite
Lensoid or tabular bodies of amphibolite of varied origins

m **i**
Metasedimentary rocks
*m, schist and quartzite with some amphibolite, iron formation, and paragneiss
i, iron formation*

gn **g**
Granitic rocks
*gn, undifferentiated granitic ortho-gneiss and paragneiss, including some migmatite, amphibolite, pelitic gneiss and schist, and quartzite
g, relatively unfoliated granitic rocks*

gl
Granulite
Metasedimentary and mafic granulites, including some iron formation

Areas shown blank are unmapped

Contact
Long dash where approximately located, short dash where inferred or grada-tional

Fault

Strike of foliation

Iron mine

10 0 10 20 30 40 50 60 70 80 90 100 KILOMETERS

10 0 10 20 30 40 50 MILES

DEPTH CURVES IN FATHOMS

5 LANDFORMS AND RELIEF

The physical contrasts between various parts of the country are above all a function of the relief. Viewed from the sea the smooth and unbroken coastline changes gently to a central belt of undulating hills, which gradually rise to a dissected table-land, ascending finally towards the north to over 4500 ft (1371 m.) in the Nimba Mountains. Therefore, according to their physiographic features, four different natural regions can be distinguished.

The map opposite shows the four belts described, and also the major mountain formations. Three cross sections demonstrate the gradual ascent from the coast to the interior in different parts of the country.

1. *The coastal belt* extends inland for 20 to 25 miles (32 to 40 km.). It is a region of gently undulating low plains with an altitude generally not exceeding 50 ft (15 m.). The coastline itself is noted for its straight and regular sand-dune beach, dissected only by several river estuaries, lagoons and mangrove swamps formed by the tidal movement of the sea. The sandy shoreline is indented at several points by rock outcrops and three promontories that appear as landmarks from the sea. Cape Mount, the highest one in the north-west, not far from the border with Sierra Leone, rises steeply to an elevation of over 1000 ft (305 m.). It overlooks Fisherman's Lake, a broad tidal lagoon, which partly separates it from the mainland. The second promontory is Cape Mesurado, the site of Monrovia; it rises to 300 ft (91 m.) and shows a very similar picture on a smaller scale. Finally, Cape Palmas, rising to only 100 ft (30 m.) above sea-level, breaks the monotony of the low shore in the south-east near the mouth of the Cavalla River.

The continental shelf is narrow, scarcely exceeding 50 miles (80 km.) in width. A strong surf, the Kalema, with a notorious undertow prevails all along the shore, increasing the tidal movement, which can be observed by changing water-levels of river courses and lagoons several miles upstream. The tidal action dams up the water from several rivers, forming some beach ridges and submerged bars and thereby inundating parts of the shore. By this action of uprush and backwash quantities of sand are abraded and slowly transported from the wash zone along the coast and deposited again at different places. The prevailing direction of transportation is from south-east to north-west. This process is called *longshore drift*. The absence of natural harbours and islands is a remarkable feature of the Liberian coast.

2. *The belt of rolling hills* runs parallel to the coastal plains. These peneplained foot-hills with rounded ridges, interspersed by wide and rather shallow valleys and numerous watercourses, hardly reach an altitude of 300 ft (100 m.). The relief is characterized by a great number of hills, some discontinuous ranges and occasional escarpments, e.g. Bomi Hills, Goe and Fantro Ranges (Bassa Hills). They may be regarded as the out-liers of the dissected table-lands which cover the larger parts of the Liberian hinterland.

3. The third belt is called the *dissected plateaux*. It is separated from the former belt by a number of steep escarpments that rise rather suddenly in the western and central parts, but show a more gradual inclination in the east. These table-lands cover the larger part of the Liberian hinterland. Their average elevation ranges between 600 and 1000 ft (2–300 m.), but they comprise a series of mountain chains and massifs, e.g. Bong, Bea, Kpo, Zua, Putu and Tienpo Ranges with summits between 1200 and 2000 ft (350–600 m.). These mountainous ranges and to a lesser degree those within the belt of the rolling hills generally strike from north-east to south-west.

4. The final belt along the border of the Guinea Republic can be termed the *northern highlands*. They consist of the Wologisi Range south-west of Voinjama, its highest peak – the Wutivi – reaching an altitude of 4450 ft (1350 m.), and the Nimba Range which extends across the border forming part of the more extensive Nimba complex within the Guinea Highlands with elevations above 6000 ft (1800 m.). The highest peak on the Liberian side of Nimba Range, Guest House Hill, initially measured 4540 ft (1385 m.) and therefore was the highest elevation within the country. However, since this hill has been gradually levelled by the exploitation of iron ore, it is now surpassed in altitude by Mount Wutivi. Other ranges, e.g. the Wanigisi Mountains and a number of individual hill crests – some of volcanic origin – are less rugged and usually rise 300 to 500 ft (100–150 m.) above the terrain.

STEFAN VON GNIELINSKI

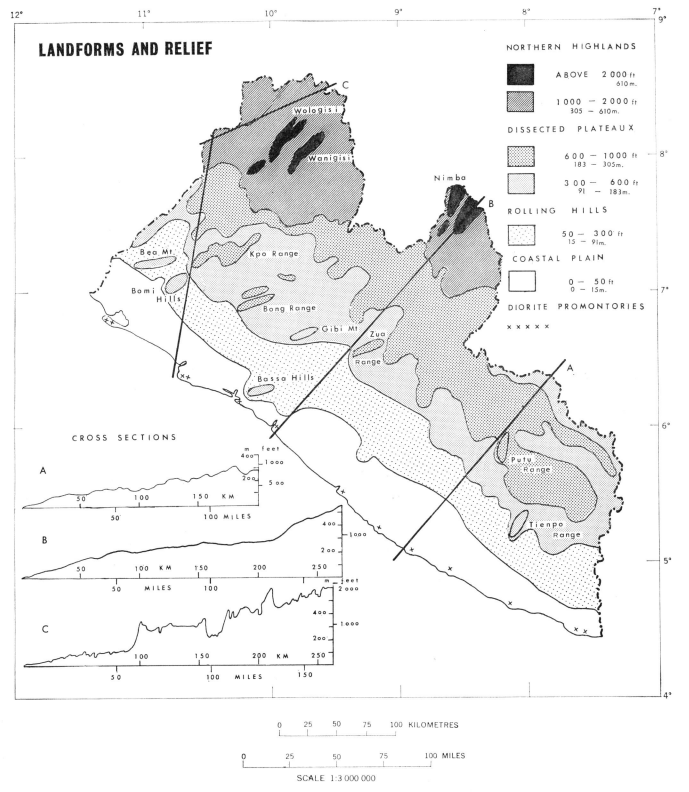

LANDFORMS AND RELIEF

NORTHERN HIGHLANDS

ABOVE 2 000 ft
610 m.

1 000 – 2 000 ft
305 – 610 m.

DISSECTED PLATEAUX

600 – 1 000 ft
183 – 305 m.

300 – 600 ft
91 – 183 m.

ROLLING HILLS

50 – 300 ft
15 – 91 m.

COASTAL PLAIN

0 – 50 ft
0 – 15 m.

DIORITE PROMONTORIES

x x x x x

Wologisi

Wanigisi

Nimba

Bea Mt

Kpo Range

Bomi Hills

Bong Range

Gibi Mt

Zua Range

Bassa Hills

Putu Range

Tienpo Range

CROSS SECTIONS

A

m feet
400
1 000
200
500

50   100   150   KM

50   100 MILES

B

400
1 000
200

50   100   KM   150   200   250

50   MILES   100

C

m feet
2 000
400
1 000
200
250

50   100   150   200   KM   250

50   100   MILES   150

0   25   50   75   100 KILOMETRES

0   25   50   75   100 MILES

SCALE 1:3 000 000

6 SOILS

Soils may be defined as the thin surface layer of the earth, formed by the weathering of rock and the decomposition of organic matter. The nature of soil depends largely on the parent rock, the relief, the prevailing vegetation and above all on the climatic conditions. In hot tropical areas, as in Liberia, the climate tends to become the dominant soil-forming factor, reinforced by the associated effects of the abundant and dense vegetation. The warm and humid climate conditions cause intensive mechanical and chemical weathering of the parent rock and leaching of the soil profile. Thus Liberian soils share many important features, even though some minor variations reflect the more local influence of relief and geology. The bedrocks from which the soils have been formed are mainly of crystalline, igneous and metamorphic origin, consisting of granites, gneisses, gneissic sandstones, schists and shales.

In Liberia three major groups of soils can be differentiated: *latosols*, *lithosols* and *regosols*.

The *latosols* or lateritic soils occur on undulating and rolling land, and occupy about 75% of the total area. They are heavily leached, and silica, nutrients and humus are mostly washed out. Iron and aluminium minerals have accumulated as permanent residual materials, forming hardpans and cemented layers within the subsoil or B-horizon, while on the surface hard and rounded iron oxides – known as iron stones or buckshot – can be observed. This process which is called *laterization* has a pronounced binding effect, making the soils impermeable and increasing the hazards of run-off and erosion. The prevalence of the iron oxides gives the laterites the characteristic brown or red colour. These latosols are zonal soils correlated to similar soil groups in West Africa. By English pedologists they are subdivided mainly on the extent of leaching, as reflected in the base saturation and acidity (pH value) of the soil profile. Liberian latosols in the wetter part of the country can be broadly correlated with the British 'oxysols' and with the French 'sols ferralithiques'. Approximately the first 8 in. (20 cm.) form the topsoil, which is brownish in colour owing to rich humus content. The topsoil is often sharply divided from the subsoil, which is red, brown or yellow in colour, and layers of gravelly concretions, iron aluminium oxides of varying thickness, are often encountered. Because of the lack of nutrients and their compact texture and impermeability, these soils are of low to medium fertility. However, adapted to tree crops and forests, they are protected against erosion and leaching and become very productive. Open cultivated crops may be produced with good success, provided lime and fertilizers are applied.

In sharp contrast to these latosols are azonal soils, classified as *lithosols*. The striking characteristic of these soils is that profile development is very slow and often subject to erosion. The lithosols represent about 17% of the total area on mostly hilly and rugged land. Because of their elevated position they are mostly very shallow and frequently show outcrops of decomposing rock. The percentage of gravel is also very high and therefore the nutrient and moisture storage capacity of the soil is greatly reduced. Because of the shallow profile and the coarse texture, these soils are of limited agricultural value.

Regosols are sandy soils which occur within the narrow coastal belt and also in several small patches farther inland. Along the coast they are mainly marine sediments consisting of more than 70% of fine to coarse sand and silt. These sands are heavily leached and bleached to an almost white colour, and the percentage of clay and organic matter is very small. Therefore they are very poor in plant food, highly acid, sterile and infertile. Coconut palms are about the only useful plants grown with success on these types of soil. Where drainage is poor, swamps develop. Soils subject to long periods of water-logging, e.g. mangrove swamps and half-bog soils, usually contain a considerable amount of plant debris and other organic matter accumulating in dark-brown or greyish-black peaty layers below the shallow water. Because of the poor drainage, these marshy soils are unproductive, but could be of some use for rice production, as practised in Sierre Leone for many years.

Alongside the stream and river beds rich alluvial soils are encountered. They contain a high amount of the necessary plant nutrients and are best for agricultural production. However, they represent only between 2 to 3% of the total area.

In general, the soils of Liberia are quite productive. Because of the dense vegetation they concentrate a rich humus layer on the top, increasing the fertility. However, the humus content and with it the fertility tends to decrease rapidly after clearing and cultivation, and its restoration is very important to maintain the soil's organic content. This is best achieved by planting tree crops, especially rubber and oil palms, which adapt themselves to the comparatively acid soils, have low nutrient requirements, and protect the land against erosion and leaching.

STEFAN VON GNIELINSKI

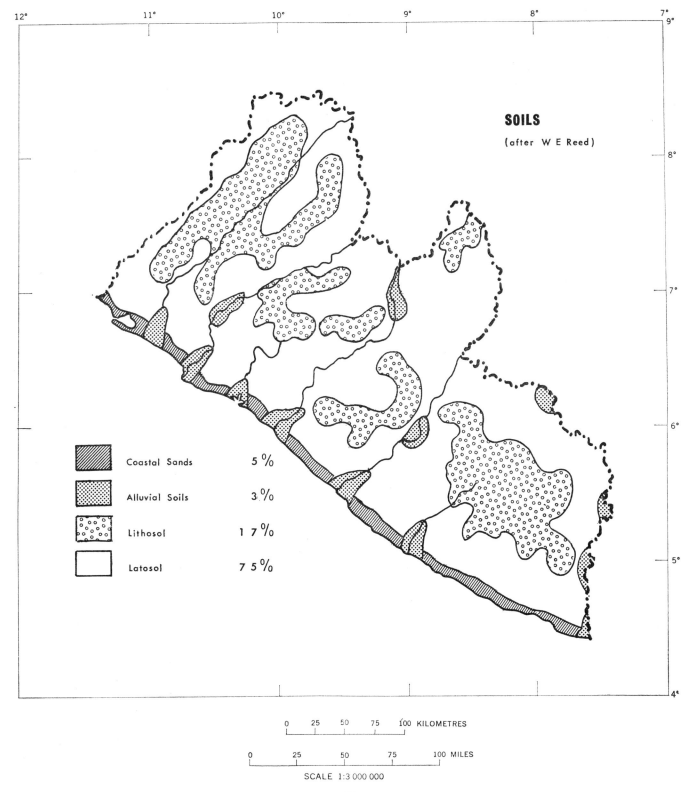

SOILS

(after W E Reed)

Coastal Sands	5 %
Alluvial Soils	3 %
Lithosol	1 7 %
Latosol	7 5 %

0   25   50   75   100   KILOMETRES

0   25   50   75   100   MILES

SCALE 1:3 000 000

7 DRAINAGE

The country is well watered by six principal streams and numerous smaller rivers. With the great number of their tributaries they have developed a dense drainage system with a dendritic pattern. This drainage system has been determined by the geological structure and by the general slope of the relief of the country and follows the direction of the mountain ranges from north-east to south-west, perpendicular to the coast. The only major exceptions are the Cavalla and its tributary, the Duobe, which flow for some distance almost due east before they ultimately turn to the sea, watering an area of some 5000 sq. miles (12 950 sq. km.), bordered by an irregular divide formed by the Putu and Tienpo Ranges. The other rivers are spaced at fairly regular intervals across the country roughly parallel to each other. Their gradients are fairly steep and irregular, the basins are mostly narrow, and valleys and flood plains are not well developed. Waterfalls and rapids are very often encountered, and bedrock quite frequently outcrops the riverbeds. Close to the coast most watercourses form wide meanders, and minor interlaced channels with small islands and sandbars usually block their entrances.

Altogether 15 river basins can be distinguished. The largest of them are:

The major river basins in Liberia

River	Tributaries	Basin area sq. miles	Basin area in Liberia sq. miles
1. Cavalla River	Duobe R., Hana R.	11 670	5 300
2. Cestos	Wono Creek	4 850	3 900
3. St John	Neye R., Ya and Zor Creek	6 650	5 700
4. St Paul	Wuni and Via R., Tuma Creek	8 460	4 950
5. Lofa	Lawa and Mahe R.	4 100	3 550
6. Mano	Morro and Zeliba R.	3 200	2 440

Along the eastern side of the country the *Cavalla River*, with headwaters in Guinea and Ivory Coast, reaches Liberia east of Tapita and from here forms the boundary with the Republic of Ivory Coast. It reaches the Atlantic about 15 miles (25 km.) east of Cape Palmas and is navigable from its mouth for about 50 miles (80 km.) inland to its first rapids. The Cavalla is the largest river in Liberia. It drains an area of about 11 670 sq. miles (30 225 sq. km.). With its two major tributaries, the Duobe and the Hana Rivers, water resources and hydro-electric potentials are quite promising, but have not yet been developed.

The next basin is that of the *Grand Cess* which comprises an area of only 770 sq. miles (1994 sq. km.). It is followed by the *Dugbe* basin (860 sq. miles; 2227 sq. km.), the *Sinoe* basin (1300 sq. miles; 3367 sq. km.), and the *Sangwin* basin (1800 sq. miles; 4667 sq. km.). These basins are rather narrow, and the headrivers are of no great length. The *Cestos River* drains the eastern side of the Nimba Mountains. Its upper course is known as the Nuon River and forms part of the border with the Ivory

Coast. The *St John River* rises in Guinea – where it is known as Mani River – north-west of the Nimba Mountains. It receives much water from the Neye River, the Zor and Ya Creeks, and drains the largest river area within Liberia (5700 sq. miles; 16 763 sq. km.). Close to the sea the basin narrows and makes some room for the minor basin of the *Timbo River* (1200 sq. miles; 3108 sq. km.), the estuary of which is only 12 miles (19 km.) west of the Cestos.

Two minor basins, that of the *Du River* (385 sq. miles; 999 sq. km.) and the *Farmington River* (1125 sq. miles; 2914 sq. km.) follow. Although the Farmington is a relatively short watercourse which rises in the Bong Ranges, it is the only inland waterway of some commercial importance. From the Firestone plantations in Harbel, some 15 miles (24 km.) upstream, rubber is transported by shallow draught barges down the river and to Monrovia for shipment overseas. A few miles north of Harbel the company has also installed a hydro-electric plant. The Farmington flows into the Atlantic some 35 miles (56 km.) west of the St John. It forms a rather large estuary together with the Junk River and its tributary, the Du River, and the little Bassa River from the east.

The *St Paul River* rises in the Guinea Mountains east of Mecenta and enters Liberia not far from Zorzor. Until then it is called Nianda River. Its estuary is badly obstructed by a large sandbar, but the Stockton Creek, a tidal watercourse which connects the St Paul with the smaller Mesurado River at Monrovia, makes the river navigable for about 20 miles (32 km.) to White Plains, the site of the hydro-electric plant and the water reservoir serving the needs of the capital city. On its wide alluvial flood-plains sugar-cane and other cash crops are cultivated. Its major tributaries include the Via and Wuni Rivers and the Tuma Creek. It is interesting to note that the Tuma Creek originally flowed into Lofa River. Its drainage pattern has been changed recently by alluvial river capture.

The *Lofa River* rises in Guinea and enters the country between Voinjama and Zorzor. It flows through sparsely populated, dense rainforest. The lower reaches are obstructed by rapids to within some 20 miles (32 km.) of the sea. In the Lofa and its tributaries diamond panning and dredging is carried out. A pumping station on the Mahe River supplies the Liberian Mining Company with water. The *Mafa River* basin drains an area of only 510 sq. miles (1320 sq. km.). It is followed by the *Mano River* which is formed by the confluence of the Morro and the Zeliba Rivers. Its headwaters also come from the Guinea Highlands and flow south-west through the Gola Forest marking the border between Liberia and Sierra Leone.

A minor basin of the *Makona River* in the north-west completes the basins. This area consists of fertile land and the presence of the river allows swamp rice production.

In comparison with the major river basins in Africa, those in Liberia are only minute. Little is known about the volume of flow of the rivers as gauge readings and data on discharges are not available. Seasonal precipitation causes considerable fluctuations of the flow of river levels. Although all of the main rivers carry a great volume of water all the year round, the upper courses are usually shallow because of the fast run-off especially during the dry season. During the rainy season most streams overflow their banks after heavy downpours, but even during this time the rivers are not navigable for any great distance, and on the whole they are not lines of travel but rather obstacles to transport. The water resources and hydro-electric potentials of Liberian rivers may provide excellent possibilities for further development.

STEFAN VON GNIELINSKI

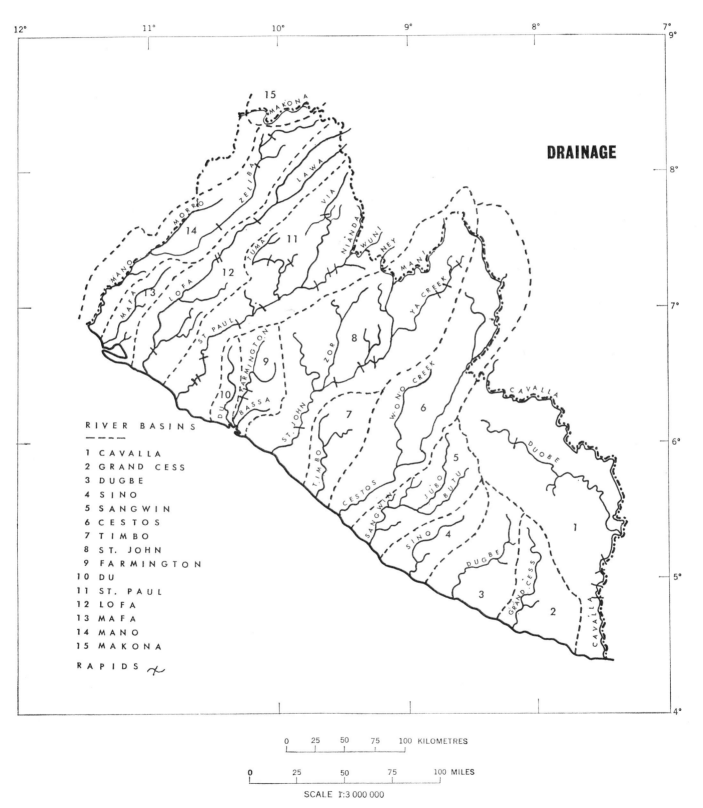

DRAINAGE

RIVER BASINS
- - - -

1 CAVALLA
2 GRAND CESS
3 DUGBE
4 SINO
5 SANGWIN
6 CESTOS
7 TIMBO
8 ST. JOHN
9 FARMINGTON
10 DU
11 ST. PAUL
12 LOFA
13 MAFA
14 MANO
15 MAKONA

RAPIDS

0   25   50   75   100 KILOMETRES

0   25   50   75   100 MILES

SCALE 1:3 000 000

8 CLIMATE: GENERAL

The equatorial position and the distribution of high and low pressure belts over the African continent and the Atlantic Ocean determine the climate of Liberia and more generally of West Africa. Because of this position and the moderating influence of the nearby ocean, the climate is marked by an even and fairly warm temperature throughout the year and above all by its very high humidity. Unlike those in the temperate zones, the seasons are not determined by changing temperatures but by the prevailing precipitation. Therefore, a rainy and a dry season with transitional periods can be differentiated.

These relatively marked seasons result from the movements of the high and low pressure belts caused by the apparent position of the sun and the subsequent wandering of the Inter Tropical Convergence Zone (ITC) from north to south according to the seasonal change in the northern and southern hemispheres. From March to September the sun is overhead in the northern hemisphere within the Tropic of Cancer and builds up a low pressure belt above the Sahara while at the same time the air masses over the South Atlantic are relatively cool. From September to March the sun is overhead south of the equator and the position is reversed. As a result of these pressure shifts, the dry continental air-mass and the moist south equatorial maritime air-mass replace each other at half-yearly intervals. The rainy season, which lasts approximately from late April to the end of October, is caused by the South Atlantic subtropical high called the South-west Monsoon or mT (maritime Tropical Air Mass). For the rest of the year the Inter Tropical Front, which is the boundary of the two air-masses, moves south, and most of West Africa comes under the influence of the North-easterly Trades (Passat) or Harmattan, which blows from the Sahara and is noted for its low humidity. Usually at the end of December, during January and sometimes until February, this dry wind sweeps across the continent with full force and may reach Liberia for a short period, bringing along a considerable amount of dust, high temperatures during the day, and low and chilly temperatures during the night.

Short convectional thunderstorms, which are called line squalls, reaching velocities of up to 60 mph (100 kph), generally introduce and close the rainy season. They appear with a remarkable suddenness, but last only a few minutes and mostly precede torrential rain.

In the immediate vicinity of the coast there is another circulation of air. This is the daily change of sea and land breeze. On sunny days the air over the land warms up rapidly, expands, rises, and flows at high altitude toward the sea where it is displaced by a fresh sea breeze. At night, as a consequence of the more rapid cooling of the land as compared with the sea, a circular flow in the opposite direction sets in and a land breeze blows out toward the sea. In this warm and tropical climate the changing land and sea breeze is felt as a big relief and wind is considered man's best friend.

In 1951 the Division of Meteorology within the Department of Public Works was established. It supervises a number of weather stations throughout the country, which measure daily rainfall and record maximum and minimum temperatures. Longer term records are available at Ganta (1927) and the Firestone Plantations at Cavalla (1936) and Harbel (1928). Apart from these, many missions and private enterprises collect and evaluate meteorological data. The Department of Geography, University of Liberia, also maintains three weather stations and records have been taken for the last eight years.

Since the various climatic factors remain very much the same year after year, the climate of Liberia follows a pattern that can be fairly well predicted. Relatively high temperatures, heavy and intensive rainfall, and an air humidity which is most of the time above 90% provide a climate which seems to be not at all invigorating. However, in spite of the atmospheric humidity which rarely remains within the limits suitable for physical and mental work and often causes fatigue and weariness to take its natural course, most people living in Liberia find the climate quite tolerable, even pleasant most of the time.

STEFAN VON GNIELINSKI

CLIMATE

JANUARY

JULY

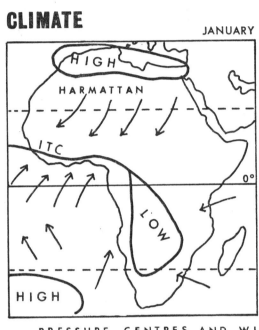

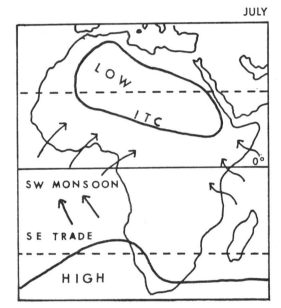

PRESSURE CENTRES AND WINDS. IN AFRICA

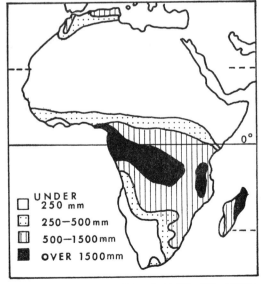

UNDER
250 mm

250—500 mm

500—1500 mm

OVER 1500 mm

DRY SEASON — NOVEMBER TO APRIL

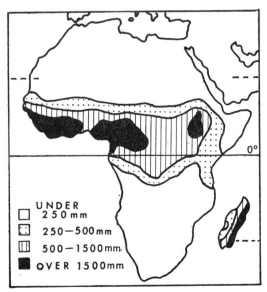

UNDER
250 mm

250—500 mm

500—1500 mm

OVER 1500 mm

RAINY SEASON — MAY TO OCTOBER

9 CLIMATE: RAINFALL

The Liberian coastline runs approximately from south-east to north-west and at right angles to the prevailing south-westerly rain-bearing winds. As the maritime air reaches the coast it is forced to rise, it cools, and condensation takes place which causes the extremely heavy precipitation. Consequently the rainfall is heavier than on any other part of the west coast of Africa except the Freetown Peninsula in Sierra Leone and a small isolated location near Buea in Cameroon. The annual rainfall near the coast amounts to nearly 180 in. (4550 mm.), but figures have exceeded this in some years. Especially in the vicinity of Monrovia averages of 190 in. (4770 mm.) have been recorded over a period of four years, and during the year 1968, 200 in. (5080 mm.) were measured. The other coastal stations have slightly less rainfall, e.g. Robertsport (169 in.; 4290 mm.), Buchanan (160 in.; 4060 mm.), and Greenville (172 in.; 4370 mm.). Beyond Greenville the rainfall decreases considerably. The average figures from Harper show only 115 in. (2920 mm.), while the figures for Tabou (Ivory Coast), which lies in the rain shadow of Cape Palmas, hardly reach more than 90 in. (2290 mm.) annually. Towards the interior the amount of rainfall decreases also, because by now the air has lost a great part of its moisture so that the rain becomes lighter in regions distant from the coast, except for the higher areas, where the air is forced to rise, causing some relief rain. Because of its high altitude the district around Mount Nimba receives much more rain (127 in. = 3225 mm.) than would be expected from its geographical position. In the north-west there is a similar situation. The hilly districts of Kolahun and Voinjama receive about 30 in. (750 mm.) more rainfall than Zorzor (82 in.; 2080 mm.) which lies 680 feet (210 m.) lower. The driest part of the country is the central interior and a narrow strip in the north-east. The wide stretch of land between Suakoko (73 in. = 1850 mm.) and Tapeta (74 in. = 1880 mm.) receives only about 70–80 in. (1780–2030 mm.) of rain during the course of the year.

The various average monthly rainfall column graphs indicate a pronounced seasonal pattern. Generally a fairly distinct dry season extends from about November to April and a wet season the remainder of the year. The months of heaviest rainfall vary somewhat in different parts of the country, but normally are June, July and September. In Monrovia a record monthly rainfall of over 53 in. (1350 mm.) was measured during July 1966. In August most stations show a marked decrease of precipitation, and a short dry season known in Liberia as the 'mid dries' sets in for a fortnight or so, while in September the rain starts with new force. The extreme south-east corner of Liberia – the Harper area – is even noted for two distinct rainy seasons, with maxima in May–June and September–October, and with a well defined short dry season in between. At Greenville, these two wet seasons are not so clearly marked, but a sharp decline in rainfall during July and August is also apparent. Similar observations can be made at all stations in the eastern parts, for instance, Tapeta, Pinetown, Zwedru (Tchien) and even at stations within the Ivory Coast.

The distribution of rain throughout the year and particularly the length of the dry periods are at least as important as the amount of rainfall. Since Liberian soils have usually only low moisture storage capacities, the amount and frequency of rainfall during the dry season becomes a limiting factor for the cultivation of many crops.

In spite of the heavy precipitation, it does not rain continuously during the rainy season. It is common to have sunny days even during the months when the rain is heaviest. In the interior heavy showers may occur, but only very rarely will it rain for the whole day. Naturally, the rain may last for a day or two without a stop. At such times the rain pours down steadily and there is hardly any visibility, and the water usually covers the ground for several inches. Some idea of the intensity of rainfall near the coast may be gained if it is realized that after a heavy cloud burst in Monrovia on 7th July 1966, which lasted for 4 hours, approximately 9·1 in. (231·6 mm.) of rain were recorded. This amount represents almost half of the annual rainfall of Berlin which is about 23·2 in. or 590 mm.

Observations concerning the diurnal distribution proved that two-thirds of the rain in Monrovia falls during the night between 6 p.m. and 7 a.m. Most of the rest usually falls during the early morning hours, while only a minimum of rain is recorded between mid-day and the early afternoon. This is one reason why the rainy season in Liberia may not be as inconvenient and disturbing as in other parts of the world.

STEFAN VON GNIELINSKI

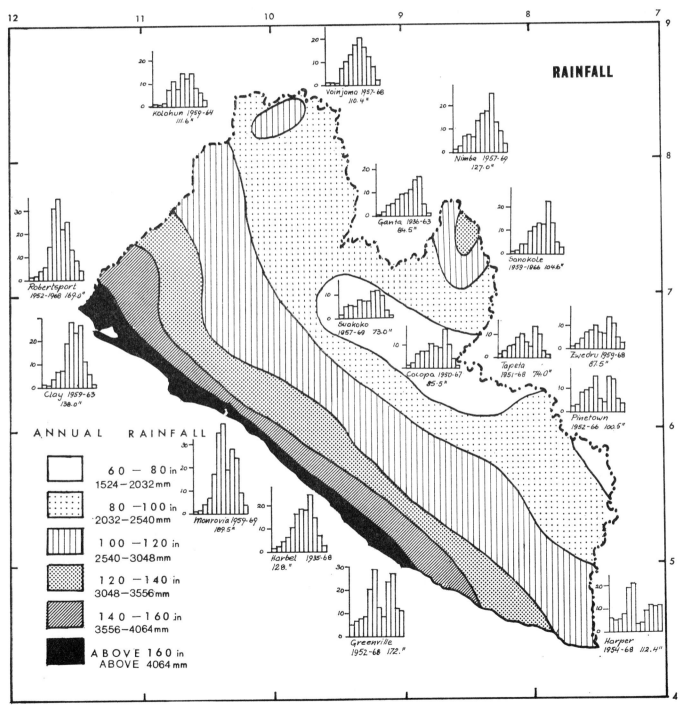

RAINFALL

Kolahun 1959-64
111.6"

Voinjama 1957-68
110.4"

Nimba 1957-69
127.0"

Ganta 1936-63
84.5"

Sanokole
1959-1966 104.6"

Robertsport
1952-1968 169.0"

Suakoko
1957-69 73.0"

Clay 1959-63
138.0"

Cocopa 1950-67
85.5"

Tapeta
1951-68 74.0"

Zwedru 1959-68
87.5"

Pinetown
1952-66 100.5"

ANNUAL RAINFALL

	60 — 80 in 1524 — 2032 mm
	80 — 100 in 2032 — 2540 mm
	100 — 120 in 2540 — 3048 mm
	120 — 140 in 3048 — 3556 mm
	140 — 160 in 3556 — 4064 mm
	ABOVE 160 in ABOVE 4064 mm

Monrovia 1959-69
189.5"

Harbel 1935-68
128."

Greenville
1952-68 172."

Harper
1954-68 112.4"

10 CLIMATE: TEMPERATURE

Because of the equatorial position of Liberia the sun is almost overhead at noon throughout the year, and insolation is very intensive in all parts of the country. Therefore, high temperatures with little monthly variations should be expected. However, since temperatures are not solely dependent on insolation, but are affected by the degree of cloud cover, air humidity, rainfall and vegetational cover, temperatures in fact are much lower than anticipated.

Along the coast the proximity of the Atlantic Ocean has a moderating effect on the temperatures, and annual and daily variations are evenly balanced, while toward the interior the continental influence becomes more dominant, the range of temperatures widens, and the variation of minimum and maximum increases markedly. It is difficult to quote figures for temperature, since they vary considerably with location and altitude, but 80° to 90°F (27° to 32°C) during the day and 70° to 75° (21° to 24°C) at night seem to be fairly representative. Because of the uniform and high humidity – the relative humidity ranges generally between 85 and 95% within the coastal area – temperatures seem much higher than they actually are. Only within the higher regions near the Guinean border, where the average altitudes are between 1800 and 2000 ft (550 and 610 m.), is the climate more pleasant, since temperatures are much lower during the entire year. At times the inhabitants of these regions even suffer from the cold nights.

The map shows the average annual temperatures of Liberia. They range in the coastal area from 75° to 80°F (24° to 27°C) while in the interior they are usually some degrees higher except for the mountain regions. Although the country is situated north of the equator, the highest temperatures occur between January and April and the lowest ones are usually recorded during the months of August and September. These low temperatures are mainly caused by the large amount of cloud cover common over much of coastal West Africa during these months.

The moderating maritime influence can be seen if temperatures at Monrovia and Greenville are compared with those of other inland stations. Monrovia, which measured an average maximum of 85·2°F (30°C) and an average minimum of 73·4°F (23°C) has only an annual variation of 11·8°F, while in Sanniquellie, 200 miles (320 km.) inland, an average maximum of 93°F (34°C) and an average minimum of 65°F (18°C) is recorded and the variation is already 28°F. In Greenville the annual variation is only 8°F, since the average maximum is 81°F (27°C) against the average minimum of 73°F (23°C).

If the average diurnal cycle of temperatures in Monrovia is observed during January and July the small and almost insignificant variation also becomes apparent.

Sunshine

Sunshine is at a minimum during the wet months, particularly June to September, with a definite minimum in August. Since early 1963 the daily hours of sunshine have been recorded at the university weather station, Monrovia. The results indicate that the days of long and bright sunshine fall on the days between December and March, and an average of 6·30 or even 7 hours per day is not exceptional. During June and September only a few hours of sunshine are recorded, and during August sunshine is particularly low, hardly exceeding an average of more than 1·30 hours per day. Sunshine and cloudiness therefore do not necessarily correlate with the rainfall; especially since August, when the 'mid dries' occur, is the time of highest cloud cover. Figures of other stations e.g. at University Farm, at Firestone (Harbel), and also in Freetown (Sierra Leone) are very similar, so they seem to be indicative of conditions in the wetter parts along the coast, while sunshine figures in the interior are generally higher.

Humidity

The influence of the equatorial maritime airmasses – the southwesterlies – cause the very high humidity of Liberia. A relative humidity of 90–100% during the rainy season is common, while during the dry season the average humidity is somewhat lower and usually in the range of 85–95%. In Monrovia the relative humidity is in close accordance with the existing air temperature and its variation depends on the prevailing season and the hour of the day. Towards midday the relative humidity may sink to 80–85% during the rainy season and, during February–March, the driest period of the year, even to 65%. However, regardless of season the relative humidity during the night and early morning hours is almost always in the range of 90–100%. Since this is also the time of lowest diurnal temperatures, it is evident that before sunrise the air is practically saturated with moisture. Again, the data from other stations, Bomi Hills, Harbel and Greenville, show very similar results, leading to the compelling assumption that the percentage and periodicity of humidity is valid within the whole sphere of constant monsoonal air-flow. Only the zone north of the Inter Tropical Front, where the continental air masses prevail from mid-December to the end of January, shows arid conditions and owing to the extreme dryness of the Harmattan the humidity may drop below 50% at times.

STEFAN VON GNIELINSKI

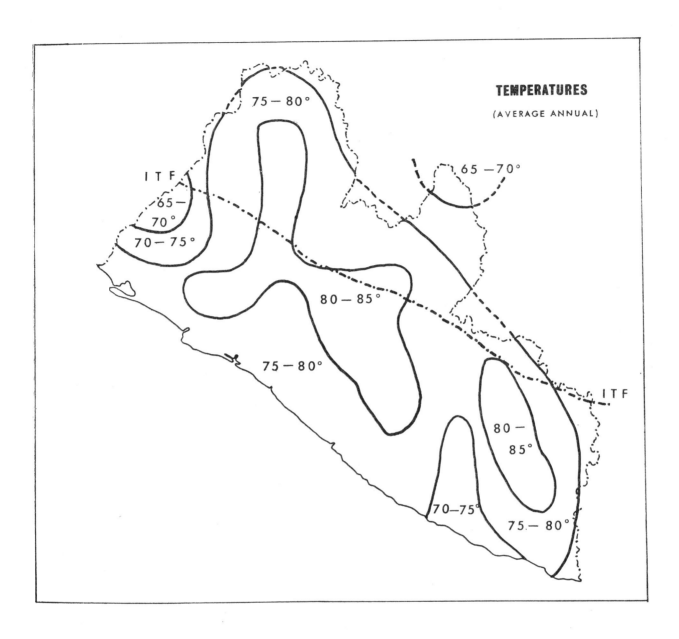

TEMPERATURES

(AVERAGE ANNUAL)

75 — 80°

65 — 70°

I T F

65 —
70°

70 — 75°

80 — 85°

I T F

75 — 80°

80 —
85°

70 — 75°

75 — 80°

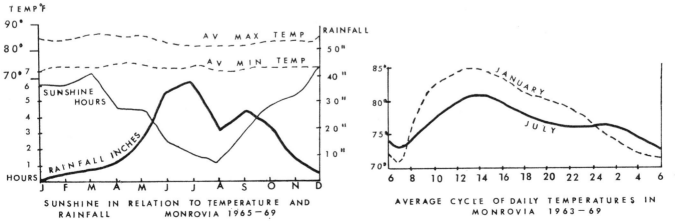

TEMP °F

90°
80°
70°
6
5
4
3
2
1
HOURS

AV MAX TEMP

RAINFALL

50"

AV MIN TEMP

SUNSHINE
HOURS

40"

30"

RAINFALL INCHES

20"

10"

J F M A M J J A S O N D

SUNSHINE IN RELATION TO TEMPERATURE AND
RAINFALL   MONROVIA 1965—69

85°

80°

75°

70°

JANUARY

JULY

6   8   10   12   14   16   18   20   22   24   2   4   6

AVERAGE CYCLE OF DAILY TEMPERATURES IN
MONROVIA 1963—69

11 VEGETATION

The *tropical rain forest* belt in West Africa extends from Sierra Leone to Ghana and comprises in Liberia most of the country except a very narrow strip along the coast where mangrove vegetation alternates with coastal savanna. The climatic conditions in the whole country allow the vegetation to develop into a tropical high forest, and most probably the entire land area was once covered with it. Nowadays the total area of tropical high forest and old secondary forest consists of only one-third of the country, while the remaining 65% is composed of forested areas such as young secondary forest and intermediate forest and further non-forested areas such as farmlands, savannas, towns, swamps, etc. The far north-west of the country and small parts in Nimba County are grass-woodlands. Although the general climatic conditions are nearly equal throughout the country, the amount of rainfall and humidity, which influence the vegetation in a large measure, decreases toward the interior. Consequently three vegetational zones can be distinguished: the *coastal savanna*, the *high forest* belt, and the *northern savanna*.

The *coastal savanna* extends 9 to 16 miles (15 to 25 km.) from the coast into the country and was in earlier times covered with high forest as forest relics indicate. The actual vegetation consists mainly of grass (*Andropogon* sp.) with scattered, often malformed trees (*Parinari macrophylla, Anthosthema senegalense, Dracaena mannii*). There are also scattered oil palms (*Elaeis guineensis*) and mango (*Mangifera indica*) indicating former human occupation. Along the rivers in the coastal zone dense thickets of mangrove vegetation may have developed with species of *Rhizophora* and *Avicennia*. Landward, beyond the tide, another type of vegetation has developed with species such as *Pandanus* and *Raphia* palms.

The *high forest belt* in Liberia can be divided into the evergreen rainforest zone and the moist semi-deciduous forest zone. The transition zone between these two belts lies in western Liberia about 43 miles (70 km.) from the coast and in the eastern part of the country up to 87 miles (140 km.) inland.

The evergreen rainforest receives an annual rainfall of 80 in. (2000 mm.) or more, and it consists of species which do not have a well marked period of leaf fall. The taller trees frequently reach over 200 ft (60 m.) and species normally reaching the upper levels of the canopy are *Gilbertiodendron preussii, Monopetalanthus compactus, Lophira alata, Heritiera utilis, Erythrophleum ivorense*, and many others. Because of the mixed character of this forest it is called *mixed evergreen rainforest*. Infrequent countings of tree species per acre show more than 40 species. Sometimes patches of the forest may be dominated by only one or two species and this type of forest is called *single dominant forest*. Species such as *Tetraberlinia tubmaniana* and *Loesenera*

kalantha frequently grow in single dominant stands. Together with young trees of the dominant species many other species occupy the lower levels of the canopy and may form one complete continuous layer of leaves, preventing the light from reaching the soil. The shrub layer is not, however, normally very thick and is easy to enter.

A forest type normally separated from the evergreen forest is the wet coastal rainforest which is found in the south-eastern part of Liberia between the Rivers Cess and Greenville and which reaches 40 to 50 miles (65 to 83 km.) into the country. The vegetation is specially characterized by the occurrence of many single dominant stands, with dominant species such as *Tetraberlinia tubmaniana*.

North of the belt of mixed evergreen forests is encountered the *moist semi-deciduous forest* which has many trees in common with the first type mentioned, but also many other species particular to this vegetation type. It may be that species are much more frequent in the mixed evergreen rainforests than in the moist semi-deciduous forests and vice versa. The climatic conditions in the north-western part of the country are characterized by an annual rainfall of 80 to 110 in. (2030 to 2790 mm.) and in the south-eastern parts by 70 to 80 in. (1780 to 2030 mm.). The long dry season (4.5 to 5.5 months) forces many species to drop their leaves during part of this period to minimize their evaporation. The semi-deciduous forest is a transition to the deciduous forest type found in the Ivory Coast but not in Liberia. It has many valuable species such as *Entandrophragma* sp., *Tieghemella heckelii, Terminalia* sp., *Triplochiton scleroxylon* and *Chlorophora excelsa*. Species which are typical for the mixed evergreen rainforests have disappeared (*Gilbertiodendron preussii, Monopetalanthus compactus*).

The three above-mentioned types of high forest are mostly closely linked, but various kinds of transition occur, which are mostly influenced by the topography and soil conditions of the country. The influence of shifting cultivation on the vegetation has been immense, and most of the high forests have at times been converted into farmland. After the farms are abandoned, the vegetation replaces itself again and gradually the high forest reappears. Several development stages can be recognized such as 'recent farmland', 'old farmland', and intermediate forest. This process of regeneration from farmland to secondary high forest takes approximately 100 to 130 years.

The *northern savanna* comprises the grass-woodlands in the far north-western parts of the country and a small part of Nimba County and is a type of manmade savanna. Continuous burning and clearing for agricultural purposes prevented the original vegetation from establishing itself again. *Pennisetum purpureum*, the so-called elephant grass which grows to a height of 10 ft, is the typical grass species and only here and there small forested areas are present.

J W A JANSEN

28

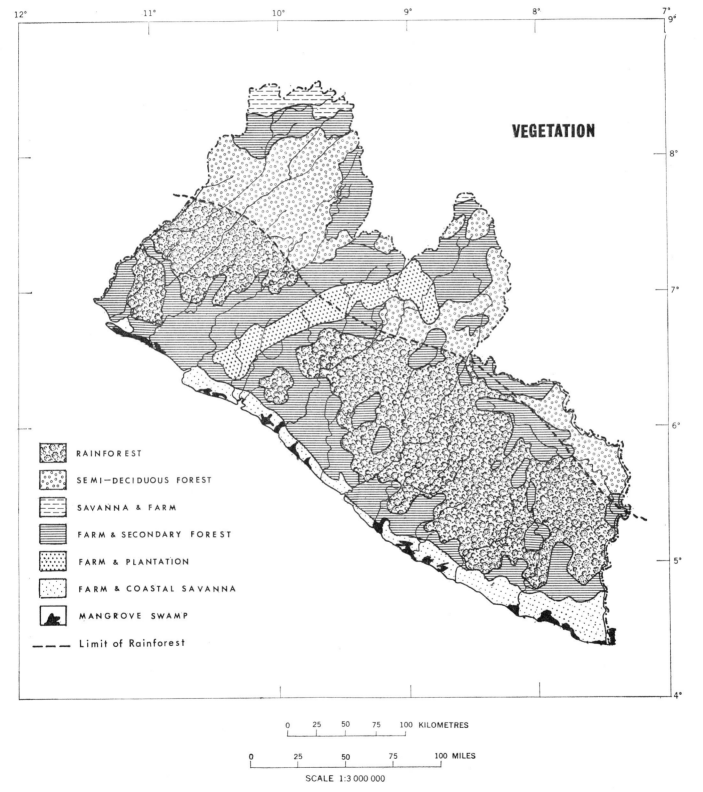

VEGETATION

RAINFOREST

SEMI−DECIDUOUS FOREST

SAVANNA & FARM

FARM & SECONDARY FOREST

FARM & PLANTATION

FARM & COASTAL SAVANNA

MANGROVE SWAMP

——— Limit of Rainforest

0   25   50   75   100 KILOMETRES

0   25   50   75   100 MILES

SCALE 1:3 000 000

29

12 WILDLIFE

Animals and especially birds are abundant in the forests as well as in the coastal regions of Liberia. Because of human activity, however, many forms of wildlife have been depleted for many years, and wherever industry (iron ore mining) moves in on virgin forest areas and where roads and new settlements have been built, wildlife is in retreat.

Scientists have made collections of animals from all parts of the country and have done research in many fields of zoology. So far the studies have mainly concentrated on mammals, and 130 species have been collected and classified, but they are far from being completed. Some 400 species of birds are believed to live in Liberia. They and most of the reptiles, amphibians, fishes and insects have still to be collected and studied.

The map is an attempt to show the approximate area of occurrence of some of the best known species.

The largest among the mammals, the elephant (*Loxodonta africana cyclotis*), is still found in the south-eastern, northern and north-western parts of the country, where they travel restlessly through the forest in small groups, occasionally damaging some farms. Within the rivercourses and freshwater swamps of the same regions the pigmy hippopotamus (*Cheoropsis liberiensis*) occurs, a rare animal solely found in West Africa. Here is also found the red river hog which is sometimes domesticated, and occasionally the red or black buffalo, known as 'bush cow'. Antelopes and duikers are represented by 11 species, of which the zebra duiker (*Cephalophus doria*), Jentink's duiker (*Cephalophus jentinki*), bongo (*Boocerous eurycerus*) and the royal antelope (*Neutragus pygmaeus*) are the most interesting. The rarest mammal is undoubtedly the manatee (*Trichechus senegalensis*), commonly called 'sea cow'. Only three or four are found annually at the mouths of the larger rivers and in lagoons.

Fifteen species of carnivorous mammals are known. The golden cat (*Felis aurata aurata*), cusimanse (*Crossarchus obscurus*), genet (*Genetta maculata*), finger otter (*Aonyx capensis*) and honey-badger (*Mellivora capensis leuconota*) are just a few of them. The leopard (*Panthera pardus leopardus*), the largest and most beautiful one in this group, has rapidly decreased during the last few years and may very soon be extinct.

The primates are represented by 12 species, ranging from the bush-baby (*Galago demidovii demidovii*) through monkeys and three species of colobus to one ape, the chimpanzee (*Pan troglodytes verus*).

Insect-eating bats as well as fruit-bats are well known throughout the country.

Liberia can boast of a very large number of colourful birds of many groups and families. In lagoons, rivers, creeks and swamps many herons, egrets, and bitterns stalk through the shallow water. Only one species of duck, the Hartlaub's duck (*Pteronetta hartlaubii hartlaubii*) lives alone or in families in forest creeks. A few other ducks and geese occasionally pass through the country. Vultures are not found, but there are several eagles, kites, hawks and buzzards. The largest eagle, with a wing-span of nearly 6 ft (2 m.), the crowned hawk

eagle (*Stephanoaetus coronatus*), pursues mainly monkeys. Among the owls are found three species of interesting fishing-owls. Francolins and quails, locally called 'bush-chicken', are found in deserted farms, while the crested guinea-fowl (*Guttera adouardi verreauxi*) and the white-breasted guinea-fowl (*Agelastes meleagrides*) live in the dense forest. Very often the grey parrot (*Psittacus erithacus timneh*) is kept in captivity, where it can be taught to whistle and to speak words. In the wild it is very shy, and lives in groups. Surely the most grotesque birds are the hornbills, of which there are seven species in Liberia. The best known bird is most probably the garden bulbul (*Pycnonotus barbatus*), commonly called 'pepperbird'. Its joyous morning chant is known to all Liberians. Like living jewels the brilliantly coloured sunbirds fly busily from flower to flower, searching for the sweet nectar. Weaver-birds, for example the village weaver (*Plesiositagra cucullatus cucullatus*), are abundant in towns and villages. Because of their never-ceasing appetite for young rice, farmers detest their nesting colonies. Other seed-eating birds are whydas, seed-crackers, finches, waxbills and mannikins. From November to March many migratory birds from Europe can be observed. The white cattle egret (*Bubulcus ibis*) is a good example.

Snakes are not as common or as dangerous as is generally believed. Only about half of them are poisonous. Most poisonous are the beautifully coloured gaboon viper (*Bitis gabonica rhinoceros*) and the rhinoceros viper (*Bitis nasicornis*), commonly called 'cassava snake'. Because of their aggressiveness the green mamba (*Dendroaspis viridis*) and the black cobra (*Naja melanoleuca*) are more dangerous. Non-poisonous snakes kill their prey by strangling. The largest and best known is the rock python (*Python sebae*), which grows up to 20 ft (6·5 m.) long. Completely harmless are all the lizards, the agamas, skinks, geckos, chameleons and the Nile monitor lizard (*Varanus niloticus*). Three species of crocodiles occur within Liberian limits, but only the Nile crocodile (*Crocodylus niloticus*) grows over 7 ft (2 m.) long.

In the thicket of the forest the hinged tortoise (*Kinixys* sp.) can be seen occasionally, while the gaboon terrapin (*Pelusios gabonensis*) prefers swamps. In larger rivers fishermen frequently catch the big soft-shelled river turtle (*Amyda triunguis*). Among the little tree frogs is one of special interest. It lays its eggs in a foam nest fixed on a leaf in a shrub directly over a patch of water. The tadpoles hatch, protected by the foam, and fall into the pool, where they continue their development. The forest giant toad (*Bufo superciliaris*) and the wormlike amphibian, the caecilian, are found only very rarely.

Insects are numerous and in evidence the year round. The moist, humid climate favours their activity. The malaria-carrying *Anopheles* mosquito is common and represented in several species. Tsetse-flies and other pests breed along the shaded swamps and watercourses in the forests. Many ants, including the aggressive driver-ants, termites called 'bug-a-bugs', as well as snails, centipedes, scorpions, including a giant scorpion (up to 6 in. or 150 mm. long) add to the abundance and multiplicity of life within the tropical regions.

G STEINER

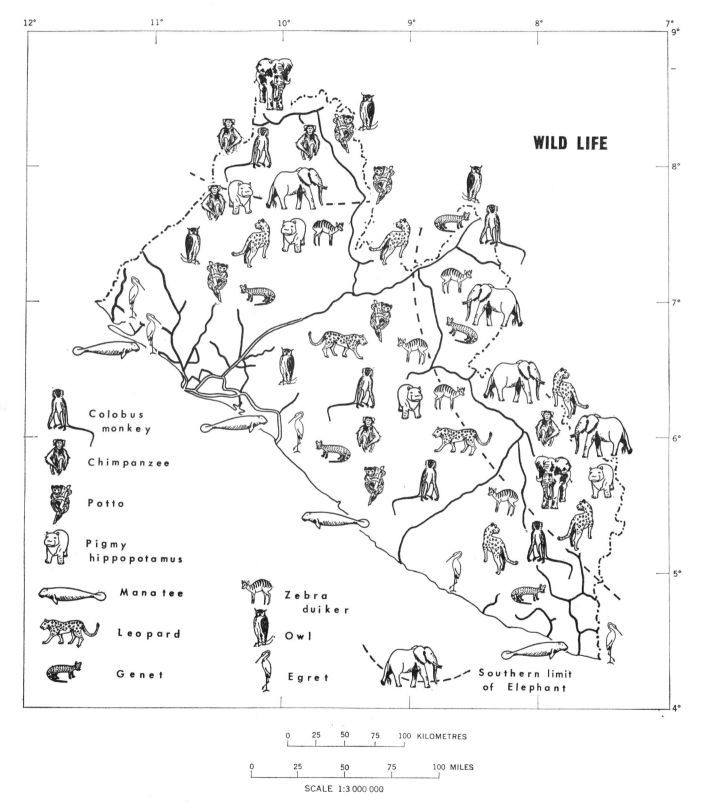

WILD LIFE

Colobus
monkey

Chimpanzee

Potto

Pigmy
hippopotamus

Manatee

Leopard

Genet

Zebra
duiker

Owl

Egret

Southern limit
of Elephant

0   25   50   75   100 KILOMETRES

0   25   50   75   100 MILES

SCALE 1:3 000 000

13 GOVERNMENT AND ADMINISTRATIVE AREAS

The Constitution of the Republic of Liberia was modelled on that of the United States of America which provides a democratic form of government. Its powers, authority and responsibilities are divided among three co-ordinate branches: legislative, executive and judicial. The Constitution was drafted in 1847 by Professor Simon Greenleaf of Harvard University. Its first article is the Bill of Rights, which lays down the principles on which the republic is founded. Citizenship is limited by this constitution to Negroes or persons of Negro descent. The government is centralized in Monrovia, the capital city of the republic.

The *legislative* branch is bicameral, consisting of the Senate, whose members hold office for six years, and the House of Representatives, whose members are elected on the basis of population for four-year terms. At present the nine counties are represented in both the Senate and the House of Representatives, while the four territories are only represented in the House. There are at present 70 members in the legislature (18 Senators and 52 Representatives) and more than half of them are direct representatives of the tribal population. The National Legislature is a body of various ethnic groups representing the many different regions into which the country is divided. It functions as the law-making body of the country. While the Vice-President presides in the Senate, the House of Representatives elects a Speaker.

The President is head of the government and is elected for an eight-year term. He can be re-elected in terms of four years. The same applies to the Vice-President. The Constitution stipulates that election shall be by ballot. Among the earliest reforms of President Tubman's administration in 1946 the right to vote was extended to every citizen of 21 years of age and over and in possession of real estate. (In the interior the payment of the hut tax is an equivalent requirement.) Women were first granted suffrage during the same year. Today they enjoy equal rights and occupy prominent roles in the political sphere of the country. The President or Chief Executive appoints his Cabinet, at present consisting of 16 members, who must be confirmed by the Senate. Together with his Secre-

taries he executes the laws of the country. Each Secretary heads a department. According to order they are: State, Treasury, Justice, Posts and Telecommunications, National Defence, Internal Affairs, Education, Public Works, Agriculture, Public Health, Commerce and Industry, Information and Cultural Affairs, Planning and Economic Affairs, the Special Commission on Government Operations, and finally Public Utilities and Co-ordinations Departments, which were instituted by act of legislature only recently.

Next to the Cabinet the President appoints the County and Territorial Superintendents and other officials including the judges of the courts and the officers of the army. He is Commander-in-Chief of the Liberian Armed Forces, which he may call to defend the Republic. Subject to the concurrence of the Senate he signs treaties with other nations. In his annual message the President reports to the legislature once every year on the state of the nation.

The third branch of the government is the judiciary which interprets the laws of the country. It comprises the Supreme Court and various courts with subordinate jurisdiction. The Supreme Court consists of the Chief Justice and four Associate Justices appointed by the President of Liberia for life. Circuit Courts have been established in all counties as well as Probate Courts which are also in the territories. A number of Municipal Courts and Justice of the Peace Courts are in the principal towns. They have jurisdiction over petty offences. Appeal from these courts is to the Circuit Courts.

For administrative reasons Liberia was initially divided into two regions: the coastal region and the interior. This system lasted until 1963. The coastal belt was delimited to a distance of 40 miles (64 km.) inland and subdivided into five counties. They are: Grand Cape Mount, Montserrado with Marshall and Bomi Territories, Grand Bassa with River Cess Territory, Sinoe with Sasstown Territory and Maryland with Kru Coast Territory. The hinterland consisted of three provinces which were subdivided into several districts: the Western Province with the Suehn-Bopolu and the Kolahun-Voinjama Districts, the Central Province with the Gbanka, Sanniquellie, Kakata and Tappita Districts, and the Eastern Province with the Tchien and Webbo Districts.

A N WOODS

ADMINISTRATIVE AREAS

(UNTIL 1963)

Kolahun
Voinjama

WESTERN
PROVINCE

Zorzor

CAPE
MOUNT
COUNTY

Bopolu

Sanokole

Ganta

Gbanka

Totota

CENTRAL

Robertsport

MONTSERRADO
COUNTY

PROVINCE

Tappita

MONROVIA

GRAND

BASSA
Buchanan
COUNTY

Zwedru

BOUNDARIES

—·—·— NATIONAL

—··—··— PROVINCE & COUNTY

———— DISTRICT

HEADQUARTERS

✪ PROVINCE & COUNTY

● DISTRICT

EASTERN
PROVINCE

River Cess

SINOE
COUNTY

Greenville

MARYLAND
COUNTY

Nyaake

Harper

```
0   25   50   75   100  KILOMETRES
```

```
0     25    50    75    100 MILES
```

SCALE 1:3 000 000

14 ADMINISTRATIVE BOUNDARY CHANGES

For more than a century the administration of the hinterland provided a dual code of laws, with tribal rules in the provinces of the interior and statutory laws operative in the coastal towns. There the settlers and other educated elements have been granted a status of local autonomy which is expressed in the different administrative status of their settlements. These are referred to as *townships* or *municipalities* and are governed by a council of citizens. While each county and territory was represented in the national legislature, the provinces of the hinterland did not share the same privilege.

After the inauguration of President W V S Tubman the emancipation of the hinterland began. From the very beginning of his state leadership he was convinced that it was of the highest national importance to call for national unity and solidarity. His personal commitment towards the unification of the Liberian people was reflected in his 'unification policy'. In this policy the President pledged to eliminate all social and political inequalities.

In 1960 the Supreme Court of Liberia declared that the political subdivisions of the country into county and hinterland jurisdiction were unconstitutional, because in fact the subdivisions did not constitute a just and fair representation of the citizens inhabiting these areas; rather there should be one law for all the people of Liberia, irrespective of cultural origin or geographic location. During its last session in the same year the Liberian legislature authorized the President to set up a national committee known as the 'National Commission on Territorial Subdivisions'. Early in 1963 President Tubman announced that the commission established to investigate the administrative reorganization of the hinterland regions had completed its work.

The President, accepting the recommendations of the commission, created four new counties, thus dissolving provincial rule and bringing the number of counties to nine. He appointed superintendents directly from the tribes to administer them.

With the foundation of the four new counties in the hinterland the entire country is now governed by a unified system of laws, and the new counties are fully represented in the legislature and enjoy all the rights and privileges long established in the other counties. On 26 July 1964, during the observance of Liberia's 117th Independence Anniversary, representatives of these newly constituted counties took seats in the legislature, increasing the members of both the House of Representatives and the Senate to a total number of seventy.

The reorganization of Liberia's administrative areas can be best seen by comparing the two administration maps. The names of the new counties from west to east are: Lofa, Bong, Nimba and Grand Gedeh. The names of the five older counties along the coast remained unchanged, but their areas, except for Maryland County, were enlarged slightly, extending the new boundaries farther inland and including smaller parts of the former hinterland.

According to size Lofa County with an area of 7475 sq. miles (19450 sq. km.) is the largest county, followed by Grand Gedeh with some 6575 sq. miles (17100 sq. km.) and Grand Bassa with approximately 5100 sq. miles (13260 sq. km.). While Nimba and Sinoe Counties are over 4000 sq. miles (10000 sq. km.), Bong County has 3650 sq. miles. Montserrado and Cape Mount are almost equal in size with 2550 and 2250 sq. miles (6600 and 5830 sq. km.) respectively. The smallest county is Maryland with only 1675 sq. miles (4340 sq. km.).

The administrative change is a step forward in the development of the whole country. The hinterland, until recently isolated by poor communications with the capital city, lacking many facilities, has markedly improved its infrastructure. The road network has been extended so that communications have made substantial progress during the last few years. Major development in health and sanitation, education, trade and commerce as well as in agriculture can be observed in all counties. There is no question that the unification policy has been a success, bringing manifold benefits to the nation. The dismantling of the social and political barriers between the various people in Liberia is the achievement of President Tubman. **STEFAN VON GNIELINSKI**

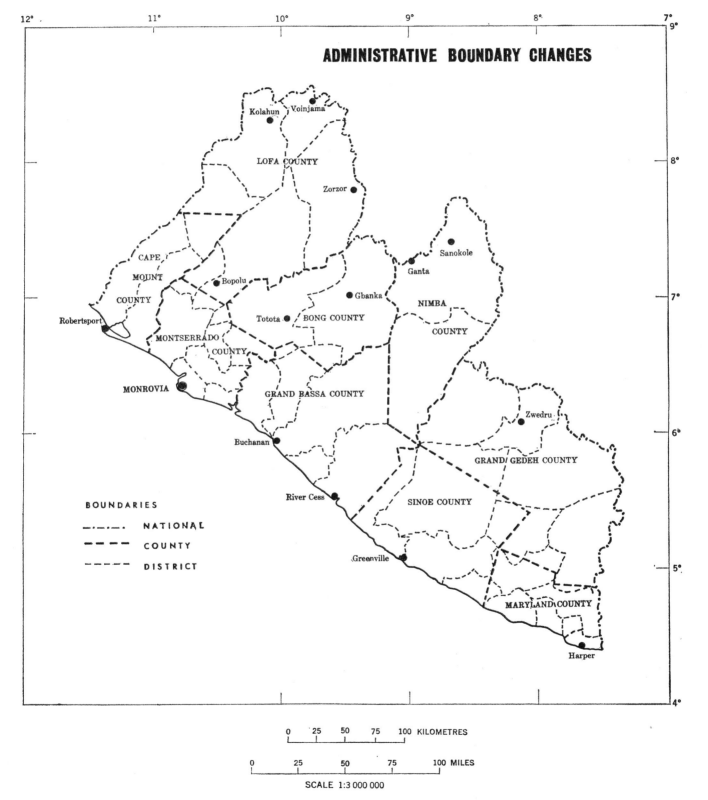

ADMINISTRATIVE BOUNDARY CHANGES

Kolahun
Voinjama

LOFA COUNTY

Zorzor

Sanokole

Ganta

CAPE
MOUNT
COUNTY

Bopolu

Gbanka

NIMBA

COUNTY

Robertsport

Totota
BONG COUNTY

MONTSERRADO

COUNTY

MONROVIA

GRAND BASSA COUNTY

Zwedru

Buchanan

BOUNDARIES

—·—·— NATIONAL

— — — COUNTY

– – – DISTRICT

River Cess

SINOE COUNTY

GRAND GEDEH COUNTY

Greenville

MARYLAND COUNTY

Harper

0   25   50   75   100 KILOMETRES

0   25   50   75   100 MILES

SCALE 1:3 000 000

15 CHIEFDOMS

The traditional life of Liberian tribes centred around kin-based groups. These groups were located in a village, half-town or village quarters, while a town and several half-towns constituted a chiefdom. Such a chiefdom did not necessarily represent a unified political entity. Certain groups or clans merely joined in relatively short-lived confederacies and often ignored ties of kinship. Intertribal movements, warfare and the slave trade were usually the reasons to pledge allegiance to a chief. These chiefdoms were mostly very small, generally representing units of some 5000 people.

The first attempt to integrate the tribal chiefdoms into the administrative system of the hinterland was made by President W D Coleman (1896–1900). He had broad ideas for the opening up of the interior, which he felt was of the utmost importance for the wealth of the whole nation. President Arthur Barclay (1904–12) took measures to raise the political status of tribal authority and improve the government of the provinces and districts. In fact, the present system of tribal administration of chiefdoms is based on a legislative act of 1905, passed during his term in office. The system was extended during the administration of President Daniel Howard (1912–20) as well as President Charles D King (1920–30). It provides for the appointment of tribal rulers with whom the government could deal in case of tax collections, the supply of public labour and recruitment of soldiers. Thus the highest tribal authority, the Paramount Chief, is at the same time the highest administrative and political official of the chiefdom. In 1923, a conference at Suehn laid down the rules and regulations of the hinterland administration in a legal form. They provided for the election of Paramount Chiefs by a council of elders and lower tribal chiefs, subject to the approval of the President of Liberia. This modified the traditional political tribal system, especially of those tribes with a more segmentary lineage organization such as the Kissi, Bassa, Grebo and Krahn, where the political leaders were the lineage elders.

Next to the administration and supervision of his chiefdom the Paramount Chief is also responsible for the improvement of agriculture, trade, sanitation and for the general welfare of his people. Since it is the policy of the government to administer tribal affairs through tribal chiefs the Paramount Chief is in charge of the tribal court. He enforces the interior regulations and tribal customary laws, settles disputes over land tenure and property rights, and executes such lawful instruction as may be given to him by the District Commissioner.

The Paramount Chief receives no salary, but is entitled to 10% of the taxes he collects for the government within his administrative area. If, however, after honourable service he retires because of illness, old age, etc., he is granted an annuity for the rest of his life. Serving under him are several clan chiefs and under each of them several town chiefs. Chiefdom headquarters are usually the residence villages of the elected chiefs, but there is a tendency for the Paramount Chiefs to have another residence in the district town or the capital.

In 1969 the Department of Internal Affairs registered 126 chiefdoms with some 508 clans. The size of the chiefdoms varies considerably, and those in the interior are much larger than those in the coastal counties. Especially large are the chiefdoms situated in areas of low population density. The largest one, the Komgba Chiefdom, with some 1242 sq. miles (3230 sq. km.) lies within Lofa County, but extends into Cape Mount County. During the census in 1962, 1650 people were recorded within its boundaries, showing an extremely low population density. In comparison the chiefdoms with the largest population are Zo-Ge with 35 784, Sagleipie with 30 966, and Gbandi with 25 800 inhabitants. Even Garawe (Maryland), the smallest chiefdom in Liberia with only 4·3 sq. miles (11·2 sq. km.), has a population of over 1830. Maryland County has the largest number of chiefdoms (32), but they are all very small in area. The largest is Wedabo (97 sq. miles, 250 sq. km.), whereas the average size is approximately 52 sq. miles (135 sq. km.). The following table shows the number and size of the chiefdoms within the different counties.

Number and size of chiefdoms (1970)

County	Area sq. miles	Number of chiefdoms	Largest chiefdoms		Smallest chiefdoms		Average
1. Lofa	7475	12	Komgba	1242	Wai-Woniglomai	151	623
2. Grand Gedeh	6575	17	Konobo	783	Niabo	53	386
3. Grand Bassa	5075	13	3-B	1067	Rock Cess	203	390
4. Nimba	4650	9	Sanokole	765	Kpeaple	214	517
5. Sinoe	4350	18	Wedja	882	Bolo	43	242
6. Bong	3650	10	Jokole	1033	Panta	225	365
7. Montserrado	2550	9	Lofa Gola	428	Kaba	86	220
8. Cape Mount	2250	6	Pokpa	567	Kone	138	270
9. Maryland	1675	32	Wedabo	97	Garawe	4·3	52
Liberia	38 250	126					

A MASSING

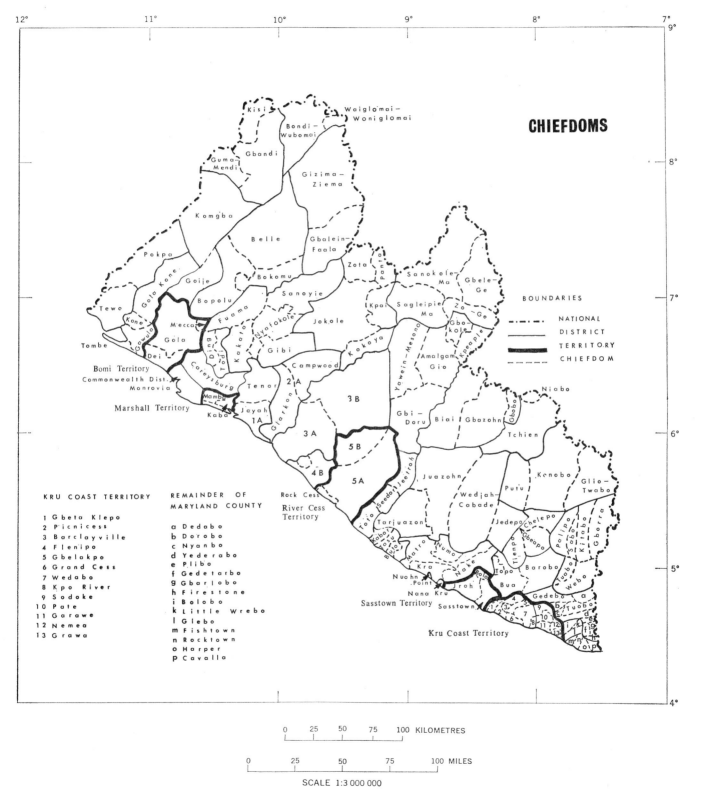

CHIEFDOMS

Kisi

Waiglomai—
Woniglomai

Bondi—
Wubomai

Guma—
Mendi

Gbandi

Gizima—
Ziema

Komgba

Belle

Gbalein—
Faala

Zota

Pokpa

Gola Kone

Goije

Bokomu

Sanoyie

Sanokole—
Ma

Gbele—
Ge

Tewo

Kone

M'ecca

Bopolu

Fuama

Nyofokole

Jokole

Kpai

Sagleipie
Ma

Zo—Ge

Gbo—
kole

Gola

Kakata

Gibi

Kokoya

BOUNDARIES

NATIONAL
DISTRICT
TERRITORY
CHIEFDOM

Tombe

Dei

Goula

Bui

Du

Campwood

Yawein—Mesono

Amalgam Kpeaple
Gio

Niabo

Bomi Territory
Commonwealth Dist.
Monrovia

Careysburg

Tenor

2 A

3 B

Gbi—
Doru

Biai

Gbazohn

Gbobo

Tchien

Marshall Territory

Mamba

Kaba

Joyah

1A

Glarkon

3 A

5 B

5 A

Juazohn

Putu

Kenobo

Glio—
Twabo

Wedjah—
Cabade

4 B

Rock Cess

River Cess
Territory

Jeeroh

Seedor

Tarjuazon

Jedepo

Chelepo

Gbeapo

Pollipo

Sabo

Kiitabo

Gborra

Toio

Kobo

Numo

Moiro

Kra

Nake

Tienpo

Topo

Barobo

Tuobo

Webo

a

Nuohn
Point

Boloi

Iroh

Bua

Gedebo

Tuobo

b

Nana Kru

Sasstown Territory

Sasstown

4

5

6

c

d

Kru Coast Territory

1

2

3

7

8

9

10

11

12

13

e

f

g

h

i

k

l

m

n

o

p

KRU COAST TERRITORY

1 Gbeta Klepo
2 Picnicess
3 Barclayville
4 Flenipo
5 Gbelakpo
6 Grand Cess
7 Wedabo
8 Kpo River
9 Sodoke
10 Pate
11 Garawe
12 Nemea
13 Grawa

**REMAINDER OF
MARYLAND COUNTY**

a Dedabo
b Dorobo
c Nyanbo
d Yederabo
e Plibo
f Gedetarbo
g Gbarlobo
h Firestone
i Bolobo
k Little Wrebo
l Glebo
m Fishtown
n Rocktown
o Harper
p Cavalla

```
        0    25   50   75   100 KILOMETRES
        |    |    |    |    |
```

```
    0       25       50       75      100 MILES
    |        |        |        |        |
```

SCALE 1:3 000 000

Besides the descendants of the American colonists, who total approximately 27 000, can be distinguished sixteen indigenous ethnic units, locally referred to as tribes. These indigenous ethnic groups may be classified on the basis of two different criteria, by language or social structure. According to their linguistic relationship they can be subdivided into three main groups:

1 The *Kru*-speaking peoples which include the Grebo, Krahn, Kru, Bassa, Dei (De) and Belle. (Gbi and Doru, small subgroups, are officially not counted as tribes.)
2 The *West Atlantic* or *Mel*-speaking peoples which include the Gola and Kissi.
3 The *Mande*-speaking peoples which include the Mende, Loma, Gbandi, Kpelle, and as an eastern branch the Gio (Dan) and Mano as well as the Vai and Mandingo in the southwest.

The *Kru*-speaking people cover the largest area of settlement, in fact, more than half of the Liberian territory encompassing the coastal area from Harper to Monrovia extending to the northeastern border. The *Mande* group initially subdivided in 'Mande-tan' and 'Mande-fu', a division rejected by Welmers in 1961 (W E Welmers, *The Mande Languages*, Washington 1961), consists of eight different tribes. This group is greater in number than the Kru and includes the Kpelle, Liberia's largest tribe, but the area of settlement which is situated almost entirely within the central and northern parts of the country is much smaller in size. The Vai people have settled along the western coast in Grand Cape Mount County. According to one of the old manuscripts written in the Vai language, their ancestors were Mandingo who migrated from the Sudan and who, as a result of intermarriage with the Gola, formed a new tribe. (Compare: Department of the Interior, *Traditional History*, 'Customary Laws, etc. of the Vai Tribes', pp. 10–11.) The Mandingo, who are also called Malinke, are encountered in most West African countries. They are well known as traders and Muslim diviners, having infiltrated Liberia in small groups from the north following the main trade routes. Hence, it is not surprising that most of them have not settled in large groups, but are scattered, living in the bigger towns and marketplaces. Only at Bopolu – in the late eighteenth century the Mandingo-dominated kingdom of Kondo – and in the area of Voinjama near and across the Guinean border are there some larger Mandingo settlements. The *West Atlantic* or *Mel* language group formed by the Gola and the Kissi numbers less than 100 000 residents who inhabit a comparatively small area roughly along the north-west Liberian border.

With the exception of the Bassa, Belle and Dei, who are found solely in Liberia, all other tribes are represented in the neighbouring countries. The Grebo and Krahn live in large numbers within the Ivory Coast, probably the area of their origin. The Kru have settlements along the coast in Sierra Leone and Ivory Coast. The Gio in the north-eastern parts are very numerous in Ivory Coast where they are known as Dan. The Mano people extend from Liberia to Guinea and are also represented in the Ivory Coast. The Kpelle also reside in Guinea in great numbers; there they are called Guerzé. The Loma have many links across the Guinean border where they are known as Toma, as do the Gbandi and Kissi. The Mende number over half a million in Sierra Leone; only a few of them (5000) inhabit the Liberian side of the Mano River. Kissi, Gola and Vai are also found in Sierra Leone.

The tribal links across the neighbouring countries cause some small-scale movement, but apart from this minor mobility back and forth across the borders to Ivory Coast, Guinea and Sierra Leone, there is actually no significant international migration. In recent times the economic development of the country has caused considerable population movement within Liberia. A high proportion of long distance migration from all parts of the hinterland towards the city of Monrovia as well as into the concession and mining areas has been observed. This migration has created some zones of mixed population, especially in the vicinity of Monrovia, Harbel and Buchanan.

As stated above, it is also possible to classify the indigenous people of Liberia on the basis of their social structure. Two types can be distinguished. First there are those peoples who have political authority based on ruling families and secret societies which may be termed as belonging to the *Poro cluster*. Here the male initiation society, generally called *Poro*, acts as the agent for social and political control. In this group the following peoples are included: the Mende, Gbandi, Loma, Kpelle, Gola, Belle, Vai and Dei, as well as parts of the Mano, Bassa and Mandingo.

The second type of social structure is distinguishable in those societies where political rule is mainly exerted by elders of larger kinship groupings and may be termed the *segmentary type*. This type includes the Grebo, Kru, Krahn, Bassa, Kissi and Gio (Dan). Most of these names, however, do not refer to ethnic entities in the same sense as those of the Poro cluster, but rather to groups composed of smaller individual tribes which are culturally and linguistically related.

As can be seen in comparing the two bases for classification of Liberian indigenous peoples, there is only a partial congruence between the linguistic and social structure classifications. It is clear that social structural influences have not always spread in the same directions or with the same degree of penetration as have linguistic influences.

According to the latest population census carried out by the Bureau of Statistics, Office of National Planning, in 1962, the population figures of the tribes are:

1. *Kru* Group		3. *Mande* Group	
Bassa	166 000	Kpelle	211 000
Kru	81 000	Gio (Dan)	83 000
Grebo	77 000	Mano	73 000
Krahn	53 000	Loma	55 000
Belle	5 500	Gbandi	30 000
Dei	5 500	Mende	5 000
2. *Mel* Group		Vai	30 000
Gola	47 000	Mandingo	30 000
Kissi	35 000		

STEFAN VON GNIELINSKI

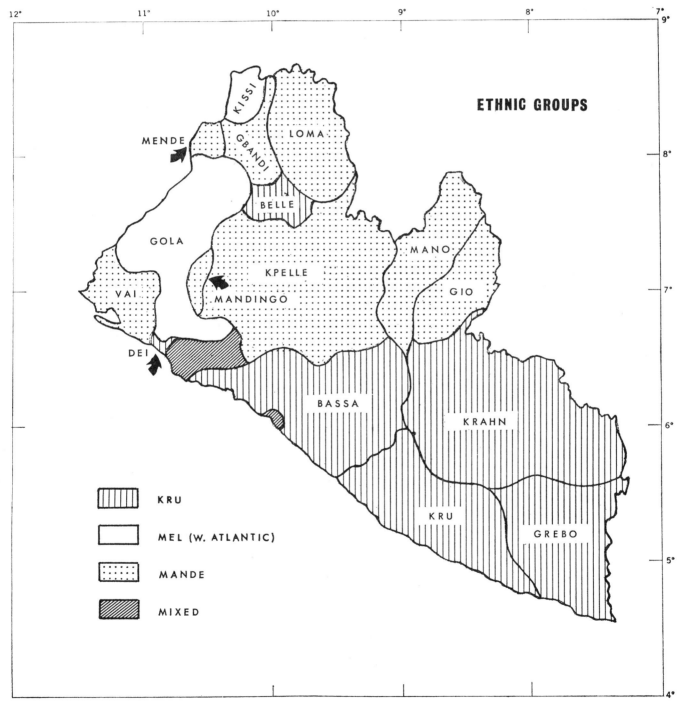

ETHNIC GROUPS

KISSI

MENDE

GBANDI

LOMA

BELLE

GOLA

KPELLE

MANO

VAI

MANDINGO

GIO

DEI

BASSA

KRAHN

KRU

GREBO

KRU

MEL (W. ATLANTIC)

MANDE

MIXED

17 LANGUAGES

According to recent classifications there are three major linguistic divisions in Liberia: the Southern Mande, the Mel languages (formerly the West Atlantic), and the Kru language group. They all are sub-families of the Niger-Congo language family.

These three language groups include the following tribes:

Southern Mande: Gbandi, Gio (Dan), Loma, Kpelle, Mende, Mano, Vai and as a subdivision the Mandingo (Malinke).
Mel: Gola and Kissi.
Kru: Bassa, Belle, Dei, Grebo, Krahn, Kru.

In the Kru group, however, there are no distinct languages which could be called Kru, Grebo and Krahn, but rather a multitude of more or less related dialects spread over southeastern Liberia. They are referred to by the name of their speakers, e.g. Kabor = Kru group, Jedepo = Grebo group, Wedjah = Sapo group. So far no research on linguistic similarities within these groups has been made, but at present, at least, comparative word lists are analysed by some students. Gola and Kissi are class languages with 8 and 9 noun classes respectively; these classes are formed by suffixes in Kissi and pre- and suffixes in Gola. The term Mel has been proposed by D Dalby denoting 'tongue' in the relevant languages which show sufficient lexical relationships to be included in a common group. The term 'West-Atlantic', introduced by Koelle, is therefore abandoned. In the Mande group, the division into Mande-tan and Mande-fu, established by Westermann and Delafosse, has been rejected in recent years by Welmers. He classifies them into North-Western Mande and Southern Mande. All of the Liberian Mande languages belong to the Southern Group.

Mande and Kru languages are non-class languages; however, lexical relationship with the Mel-class languages as well as with other West African class languages can be discovered.

Language distribution

These languages are distributed on the basis of tribal territories, i.e. the majority of its speakers live on the territory of the established ethnic groups. Only secondarily do these languages spread into territories of neighbouring tribes which, in that case, is due to the fact that they are mutually intelligible or historical and actual relationships between their speakers are present. The only exception are the Mandingo (Malinke): they belong to a group of migrant traders from Guinea or Mali, partly to descendants of a Mandingo confederacy in the area of Bopolu in the mid nineteenth century who are today interrelated with other tribes and rely on agricultural activities. Both groups have no actual tribal territory: they form minority groups, mainly in the tribal areas of the Mande groups, but enjoy superior status resulting from economic wealth, their history as a superior caste of warriors, and their religion, which is considered superior. Thus they retain their language rather than use the language of their host tribes. Only mixed-Mandingos engaged in agriculture speak Kpelle and Gola to a larger extent.

Multilingualism

Despite linguistic diversity there is a high degree of multilingualism in Liberia which may be a result of long-standing interrelations, geographical proximity and common political history. Some languages like Vai and Mandingo are widely spoken as a result of early dominance and superior status of their speakers. In areas of linguistic diversity – as it is the case within the boundary zones between the Belle, Gola, Gbandi, Kpelle, or between Gbandi, Kissi, or Dei, Vai and Gola – third languages are used as means of communication between speakers of mutually unintelligible languages, e.g. Mende, Mandingo. Some languages such as Dei and Belle are still used, but only in situations involving individuals familiar with the languages; otherwise the language of the partner is adopted. This means that the speakers of the smaller language groups speak far more languages than those of a larger group. For example, most of the Belle speak Loma, Gbandi, Kpelle and sometimes even Gola besides their own language. Multilingualism is more marked in western Liberia with its traditional trading relations than in eastern Liberia, where it refers to mutually intelligible dialects.

English serves as the official language of the country used in administration, education, law and commerce. It becomes increasingly dominant also in the tribal areas in the form of the local Liberian substandard which shows considerable homogeneity in phonology, lexicology and semantics over the whole country. In ethnically diverse settlements it tends to replace the tribal languages as a means of communication between different tribesmen. A lingua franca like Krio, the mother-tongue of the Creole community in Sierra Leone, is not known in Liberia.

The data on the plot maps are based on information obtained from questionnaires and personal inquiries done by the author during a year of research in 1968–9. This information mainly refers to the tribes of western Liberia, including the Gio (Dan). Complete shading shows the main areas where a language is spoken; broken shading indicates areas of overlap and of multilingualism. Dots show linguistic minorities in villages and towns outside the language area. These maps are intended to be purely linguistic maps, but are provisional as no linguistic survey has been done.

A MASSING

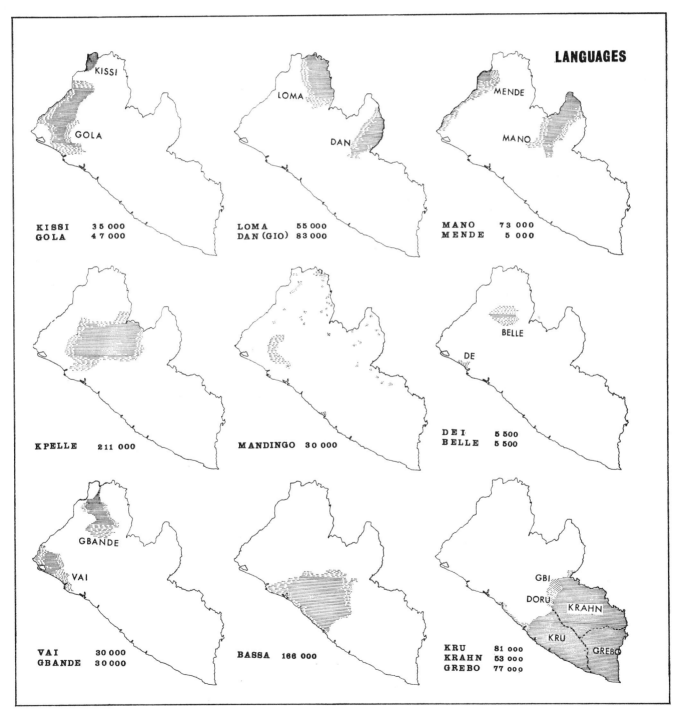

LANGUAGES

KISSI
GOLA

| KISSI | 35 000 |
| GOLA | 47 000 |

LOMA
DAN

| LOMA | 55 000 |
| DAN (GIO) | 83 000 |

MENDE
MANO

| MANO | 73 000 |
| MENDE | 5 000 |

KPELLE 211 000

MANDINGO 30 000

BELLE
DE

| DEI | 5 500 |
| BELLE | 5 500 |

GBANDE
VAI

| VAI | 30 000 |
| GBANDE | 30 000 |

BASSA 166 000

GBI
DORU
KRAHN
KRU
GREBO

KRU	81 000
KRAHN	53 000
GREBO	77 000

41

18 ART AND CRAFTS

Examples of African art in wood, ivory, brass or stone have found their way to Europe and America for many years. Already in the sixteenth century the Portuguese commissioned ivory sculptors from Sherbro Island and Benin to create ivory salt-cellars and other artifacts. Then, in the beginning of the twentieth century African art inspired many European painters and sculptors. Cézanne had just recognized that works of art could be constructed out of plastic elements – cones and spheres – and that they could or should be independent from visual reality. African art is essentially an abstract art and the cubists, upon seeing examples, found to their astonishment that what was new to them had been familiar to African artists for many hundreds of years. Modigliani, Ensor, Barlach and Klee may well have been directly influenced by the formal aspects of African work. Since that time the tremendous impact, the involvement and vitality of African art have generally been recognized and appreciated. The rise of independent African nations has stimulated a growing interest in the creative achievements of the African peoples among the general public, as the growing number of art exhibitions and a considerable amount of literature show.

It is commonly accepted that the best African carving comes from West and Central Africa, an area that extends eastward from Senegal and south to the Congo regions, and thereby also including Liberia. The art-forms are usually stylistically subdivided in the Western Sudanese, Guinea Coast and Congo regions.

African art was never the work of an individualistic artist expressing his own ideas about the universe: it consisted of objects of practical use as dwelling-places of spirits, or instruments for ceremonies of initiation or death or ancestor worship. The dense forest areas of Liberia did not lead to the building up of large empires. The people lived in small groups, but developed an elaborate social organization, some of them dominated by the secret societies, the Poro and Sande. These societies were responsible for all social law and order and their strength lay in the integration of the present with the past, the spiritual with the material. The most interesting examples of art in Liberia come from the Gio or Dan, the Krahn, the Loma and Mano and also the Kissi. Artistic activity seems to have been taken over by the Poro society and it acted as a unifying agent in the field of art, which explains the great similarities in the masks of the tribes mentioned above. The African sculptor was a highly trained workman who started his apprenticeship with a master when a child, and he learned the tribal styles and the use of tools and the nature of woods so thoroughly that his carving became almost a habit.

Although no two works of art are exactly the same and considerable room is left to the personality and individual talent of the artist, there are distinct tribal styles adhered to with strict discipline and a distinct vocabulary for abstractions with which the members of the tribe were familiar and that they could interpret.

Two groups of masks predominate in Liberia. One especially associated with the Dan (Gio) tribe represents the human face in a rather restrained naturalistic but subtly simplified way. Typical in these masks is a simplification of the face in two broad planes inclined inwards to intersect on the line of the eyes. These planes may become further subdivided, but the nose always remains in the mean plane. The other group, typically the Krahn, shows the human features strongly stylized, animalized and distorted in expressionist images of power and violence. The spirit world of Africa makes less distinction between animal and human, and features abstracted from several species are frequently compounded with the human in the same mask to add their power to it. Similar masks are found with the Mano and Loma. Statues and masks were instruments to enforce and maintain tribal traditions, but carvings were also used to identify the authority of living rulers and enhance their prestige. Examples are the ceremonial spoons of the Dan and Loma, carved drums also of the Bassa and Grebo and embellished musical instruments.

It is interesting to note that the Dan also used the lost wax process, a procedure for which the Benin culture is famous, in casting brass and bronze figurines and jewellery, especially the anklets and bracelets, sometimes weighing over 10 kg. They were an expression of wealth and power, since the woman wearing them must have found it extremely difficult to move and had to be waited upon for every trifle. Brass casting is now an almost extinct art, but curiously enough spoils from Second World War abandoned aircraft have resulted in minor casting of aluminium bracelets, anklets, etc.

Especially Liberian is the iron money of the Gbandi and Kissi, which was not cast as currency but represented one item in the bride price (usually two bars of iron money and one cow). The Kissi in ancient times also practised soapstone carving, but it is now a lost discipline, and authentic pieces are only rarely found among more recent works from Nigeria and Sierre Leone.

The dance masks of the Gola, Mende, Kpelle and Dei are intricately carved, cover the entire head of the dancer and often end in a stick. Stylistically they belong to related tribes in Sierra Leone.

BAI T MOORE

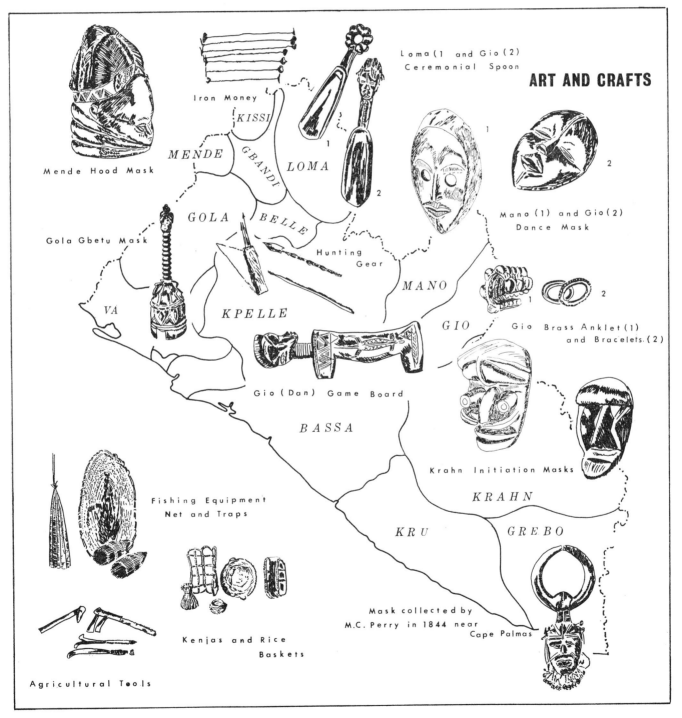

ART AND CRAFTS

Mende Hood Mask

Iron Money

KISSI

MENDE

GBANDI

LOMA

Loma (1 and Gio (2) Ceremonial Spoon

1

2

1

2

Mano (1) and Gio (2) Dance Mask

Gola Gbetu Mask

GOLA

BELLE

Hunting Gear

MANO

VA

KPELLE

1

2

GIO

Gio Brass Anklet (1) and Bracelets. (2)

Gio (Dan) Game Board

BASSA

Krahn Initiation Masks

Fishing Equipment Net and Traps

KRAHN

KRU

GREBO

Kenjas and Rice Baskets

Mask collected by M.C. Perry in 1844 near Cape Palmas

Agricultural Tools

43

19 DENSITY OF POPULATION

Many parts of the African continent, especially its vast desert zones and the dense rainforest belt are very thinly populated. Liberia, situated within this rainforest belt, has only a small population which, according to population estimates by different sources, varies between 800 000 and 2·5 million people. According to the first national census undertaken in 1962 by the Liberian Government and assisted by foreign experts from UNESCO, the country had 1 016 443 inhabitants, of whom 500 588 were males and 512 855 were females. These figures correspond roughly with those derived from a previous hut count made from aerial surveys.

The United Nations Organization assumes a population increase for Africa of 52% in the next 25 years. The highest growth rate is expected for Nigeria with somewhat more than 2% per year. The rate for Liberia is not as high. According to estimates made by the Department of Planning and Economic Affairs the average increase of population ranges between 1·6 and 2% a year. High infant mortality is the main cause of the low rate of population growth. The average life-expectancy is less than 40 years, and only 4% of the population reaches the age of 65 years. The population estimate of 1967 indicates that 40·8% of the population consists of children under 15 years. Liberia thus has a very young population.

On the basis of the 1962 census the overall population density during that year was about 27 persons per sq. mile (10 per sq. km.) exceeding the average density of Africa (25 per sq. mile) only slightly and much below the average density in neighbouring Sierra Leone (78 per sq. mile). Spatially, the distribution of population is irregular in Liberia as in many other African countries. This uneven distribution is vividly portrayed by the map. It reveals that large areas of western and southeastern Liberia are only thinly populated, especially in regions designated as national forests. In contrast, the density exceeds 200 per sq. mile in the area surrounding Monrovia, 100 per sq. mile (80 and 40 per sq. km. respectively) in the concession areas of the mines and plantations, and in some coastal towns, such as Buchanan and Harper. This is characterized by internal migration from the interior to the urbanized areas in search of employment, educational opportunities, better health facilities, and due to the sheer attraction of city life itself. The dereliction of the rural areas is a problem of far-reaching consequences. Approximately 18 to 20% of the indigenous tribal population is enumerated outside the county or place of origin. In Montserrado County, where the nation's capital is located, about 64% of the population consists of people from other counties and territories.

To meet the urgent need for demographic data, the Department of Planning and Economic Affairs initiated the Liberian Population Growth Survey. A sample survey was designed to provide current and accurate estimates of births, deaths and population mobility on an annual basis. In addition, estimates of the current population, age and sex distribution as well as many other demographic characteristics are determined. In November 1970 the first bulletin of the Population Growth Survey was published. It revealed that the population of Liberia had increased to 1 523 050. The findings were computed from data collected by household sampling. The survey covered 100 randomly selected villages located in 50 clans, and 100 sample blocks – each comprising approximately 200 households – in the urban areas (all in all nearly 70 000 people or roughly 5% of the current estimated population of the country). On the assumption that the annual growth rate is 1·6%, underenumeration during the 1962 census becomes apparent.

According to these new figures the average overall population density now reaches 39 persons per sq. mile (15 per sq. km.). Although these figures are more impressive, it still means that Liberia is not densely populated and one may therefore conclude that Liberia is one of the few countries in the world that does not have to cope with population pressure. Her problems are of a different nature. It takes an optimum number of people to develop resources. Prospects for accelerating population growth are good. To provide maximum manpower, adequate health facilities coupled with a nation-wide education campaign for alleviating mass illiteracy were introduced.

Number of inhabitants, per cent distribution and density of population by major administrative area

County	Population 1962	1970	% distribution	Area in sq. miles	Density 1962	1970
Liberia	1 016 443	1 523 050	100	38 250	27	(39)
Grand Bassa	131 840	(198 000)	13·0	5 075	26	(39)
Bong	131 528	(196 400)	12·9	3 650	36	(56)
Cape Mount	32 190	(48 700)	3·2	2 250	14	(21)
Grand Gedeh	59 275	(88 300)	5·8	6 575	9	(13)
Lofa	123 165	(184 300)	12·1	7 475	17	(25)
Maryland	62 786	(94 500)	6·2	1 675	37	(56)
Montserrado	258 821	(388 500)	25·5	2 550	101	(152)
Nimba	160 743	(240 600)	15·8	4 650	35	(52)
Sinoe	56 095	(83 650)	5·5	4 350	13	(19)

Figures for 1970 are estimates on the per cent distribution and population density of 1962

A N WOODS

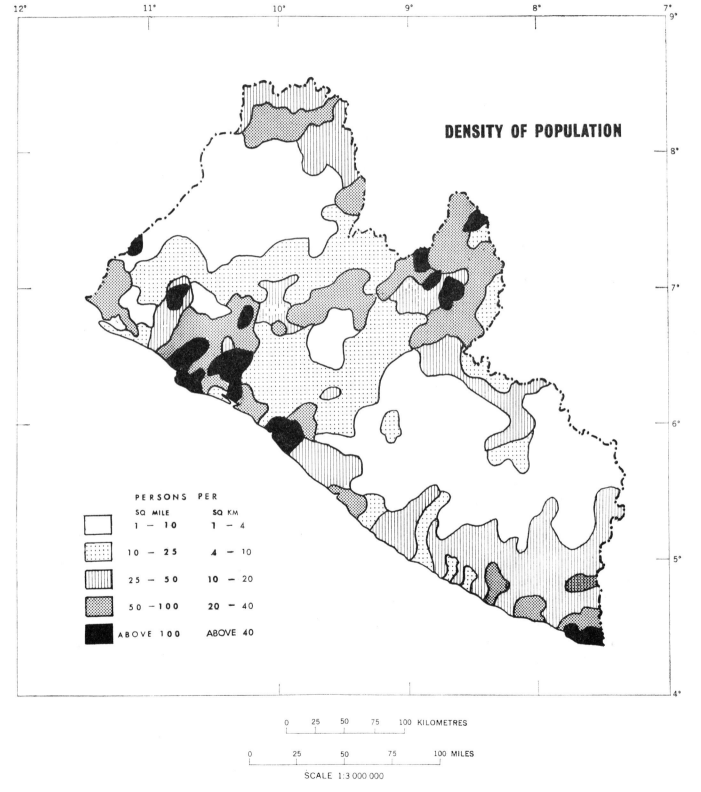

DENSITY OF POPULATION

PERSONS PER

SQ MILE	SQ KM
1 — 10	1 — 4
10 — 25	4 — 10
25 — 50	10 — 20
50 — 100	20 — 40
ABOVE 100	ABOVE 40

0 25 50 75 100 KILOMETRES

0 25 50 75 100 MILES

SCALE 1:3 000 000

45

Settlements form such distinctive features in the landscape that they can be described as fundamental signs of the relationship of man to his environment. There are strong links between the physical environment, e.g. vegetational cover, relief, water supply and soil, and the pattern of settlement distribution.

In Liberia the general inaccessibility of much of her territory makes for a low overall population density. Early maps of West Africa marked the entire region of the rainforest as almost completely uninhabited, and only within the marginal lands toward the savanna and along the coastal fringes a few scattered settlements were recorded. Apart from the physical conditions of the environment, the existence of the variously sized population clusters within the country is also an inevitable feature of the spatial organization of human activity. The traditional settlement pattern consisted of a vast number of small and scattered villages. However, soon the necessity for mutual defence against slave-traders and other enemies forced the people to form larger communities, which nevertheless hardly exceeded 2000 inhabitants. However, settlements differ greatly in size, varying from places with two to five huts to towns with several hundred houses. The larger ones are usually found in the northern parts, where occasionally up to 600 huts can be encountered, but generally speaking villages with 40–100 huts are the normal type. In the eastern parts most villages are even smaller and the majority of them have fewer than 50 huts. The towns of the paramount chiefs are usually larger, 150 to 200 dwellings being the most frequent size. So the Liberian villages lie unevenly distributed within the high forest or on its margin. The larger ones are known as towns, the smaller ones as half-towns or hamlets. There are also shelters and small huts on or near the fields, usually referred to as rice-kitchens where families live during the harvesting season. During the last century the settlers from America developed the coastal areas and founded coastal towns, which became clusters of mixed population that attracted trade and commerce from the hinterland. The establishment of large plantations, the opening of the iron ore mines, and the construction of all-weather roads in the interior induced the growth of new settlements and a migration towards these areas. However, apart from this the traditional and ethnic distribution of rural population, e.g. the settlement pattern, remained basically unchanged and the bulk of the people are still attached to the areas they consider their ancestral homes.

The map shows the distribution of settlements. It is based on the planimetric map of Liberia at a scale of 1:500 000. Use has been made of the aerial photos taken in 1966–69 by units of the US Army Corps of Engineers in co-operation with the Liberian Cartographic Survey. By evaluating these air photos and considering the results of the 1962 census, it was possible to plot the individual towns and villages. There are approximately 10 000 settlements in the country. According to their size, the number of dwellings, and their degree of locational permanence they can be divided into five categories. The first category comprises the 39 townships or settlements of more than 2000 inhabitants which, owing to their size and functions may be considered urban. The second group includes 175 settlements of 200 and more dwellings which remain basically rural. The third category comprises some 700 villages with 50–200 buildings, while the fourth category consists of more than 1500 settlements of 10–50 dwellings, and shows a decreasing locational stability. The last category includes mainly temporary settlements, including hamlets and half-towns of 1–3 huts, but frequently up to 10 huts. Since they are very numerous, estimated at more than 7500 and of semi-permanent position, they were omitted from this map. However, it is felt that in spite of this omission the general settlement pattern is particularly noticeable.

Areas of high settlement density

The important regions of high settlement density are found within the coastal areas, especially around Monrovia. Comparable concentrations of population exist close to the larger coastal towns such as Buchanan, Greenville, and Harper. High settlement densities occur within the broad band that extends along the main road, leading from Montserrado County northeast to the Guinea border and spread out to Lofa and Nimba Counties. The road, providing better transportation and market facilities, facilitated increased settlement. While in the north-west the high density is associated with areas of better soil fertility (important cash crop regions of coffee, cocoa, etc.), the high density in Nimba County is mainly due to the mining activities of Lamco, and also to the diamond prospecting within the Bahn District.

Areas of low settlement density

The areas devoid of settlement are easily detected on the map. They comprise the vast areas of dense rainforest, especially the National Forest Reserves (see forest map), the coastal mangrove swamps, some of the higher mountain ranges, and parts of the dissected plateaux. These are mainly the western central regions close to the border of Sierra Leone, and the forest lands in the south-east which are renowned as the most inaccessible areas in Liberia. Here the scarcity of settlement and people has proved to be a major factor limiting general development.

STEFAN VON GNIELINSKI

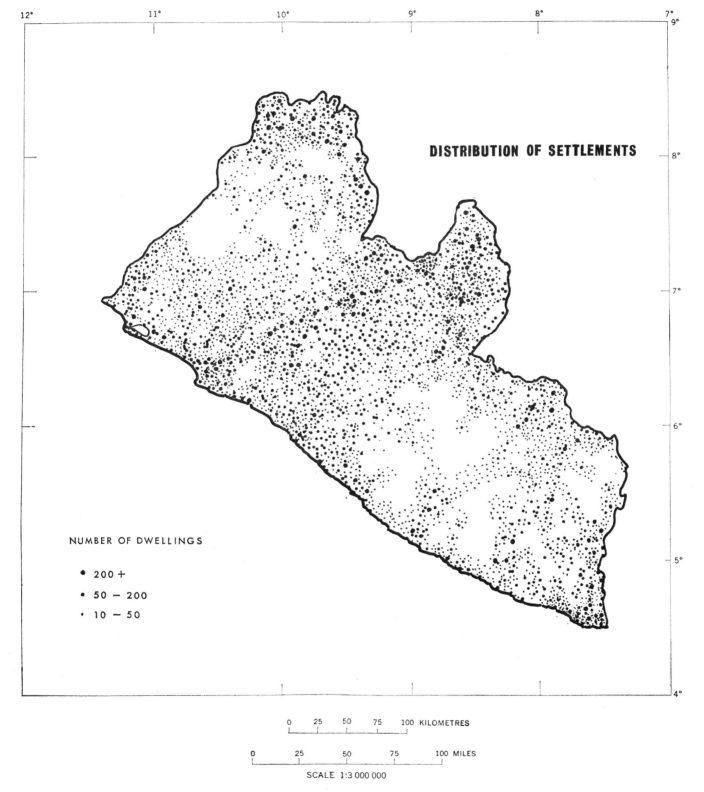

DISTRIBUTION OF SETTLEMENTS

NUMBER OF DWELLINGS

● 200 +

● 50 — 200

· 10 — 50

0   25   50   75   100 KILOMETRES

0   25   50   75   100 MILES

SCALE 1:3 000 000

47

21 TOWN SIZE AND TOWN SITES

Settlements may be classified as rural and urban. According to this broad subdivision Liberia is certainly basically rural, because the dominant settlement pattern is the village or 'rural town', and nearly 80% of the population live in these rural settlement units.

However, there are many different definitions for the term 'rural' and 'urban', and they are variously used according to the purpose for which they are required. In Liberia most settlements – even those with fewer than 40 to 50 huts – are called 'towns'; the name 'village' is hardly ever used. However, 'town' is really not justified in its proper sense in most cases. Urban settlements are economically integrated and internally specialized places, usually with an administrative status and a minimum population of some 2000 to 3000 inhabitants. This is true to some degree for all coastal towns founded by the early settlers from America. Towns like Monrovia, Buchanan, Harper, Greenville, Robertsport, and even Marshall may vary considerably in size, but the urban environment of all these places is obvious by a certain administrative function, a concentration of services and supplies. They are also meeting places and centres for trade and commerce where educational institutes, churches and hospitals are provided.

Another more recent type of town was created by foreign investment. Within the large plantations of Firestone in Harbel and Cavalla, of Goodrich in Kle and other concession areas, centres developed which, according to their density, employment opportunities, amenities and facilities, have to be considered as urban. This goes also for the mining towns. The beginning of the iron ore mining industry stimulated urbanization and resulted in the growth of towns like Bomi Hills (Liberian Mining Co., population 9000), Yekepa (LAMCO, population 14 000), Mano River (National Iron Ore Co., population 6000) and Bong Town (Bong Mining Co., population 9000). Here the industrial function is most clearly discernible. A similar development, although to a much lesser extent, can be noticed within the diamond mining region of the Bahn district. The occurrence of diamonds attracted people rapidly, and Bahn has become one of the major 'towns' of the interior with a population of some 4000 people. However, after the mineral resources are exhausted these towns may lose their significance and the urban pattern may change.

Since 1945 the growth of towns has been remarkable. The construction of ports and the increased overseas trade accentuated the rapid development of the capital city Monrovia and also of Buchanan. In the interior the urbanization was accelerated in recent years by the construction of roads. Connected with the capital city and other central places, the town within the rural area became a centre of various new functions. It provides the rural land with a commercial complex, a market, with an administration, and extends its services to the smaller settlements within its sphere of influence. Kakata, for example, enjoys its nodal position with excellent road links to Monrovia, Bong Mine, Firestone and into the interior and has become the largest rural town in the country with an estimated 9–10 000 inhabitants. Voinjama and Kolahun gained importance, because their hinterland consists of very prosperous cash crop areas for which they established ready markets. Zorzor and Ganta are mission headquarters, the activities of which are reflected in the social and economic structure of these towns. Another flourishing town is Gbanka, the capital of Bong County. Because of its nodal position it has become a very important market town, a centre of trade and education (Cuttington College). The growth of Zwedru was not so remarkable, but steady also. Other towns not interconnected with the road system show signs of stagnation and even experienced depopulation, e.g. River Cess, Hartford, Belle Yalla and Marshall and to some extent Robertsport. A decline of population can also be noticed in some of the older towns in the proximity of Monrovia, e.g. Royesville, Virginia, Louisiana, caused by migration to the capital city.

Number and Size of Liberian Towns 1962 and 1970

Population size	Number of towns census 1962	estimate 1970	Total population 1970	% of urban population
2 000– 3 000	10	14	30 400	9·3
3 000– 4 000	5	9	31 000	9·5
4 000– 5 000	2	6	26 500	8·1
5 000–10 000	3	6	41 500	12·7
10 000–20 000	1	1	12 000	3·7
20 000–50 000	1	2	70 000	21·5
50 000 +	1	1	115 000	35·2
	23	39	326 400	100%

Including the four county headquarters – Voinjama, Gbanka, Sanokole and Zwedru – there are now 25 settlements in the interior which, owing to their size and importance and in accordance with the definition in the 1962 census (which in this context defines a town as a settlement of at least 2000 inhabitants), could be considered as towns, bringing the total number of towns to 39, as against 23 reported in the 1962 census.

STEFAN VON GNIELINSKI

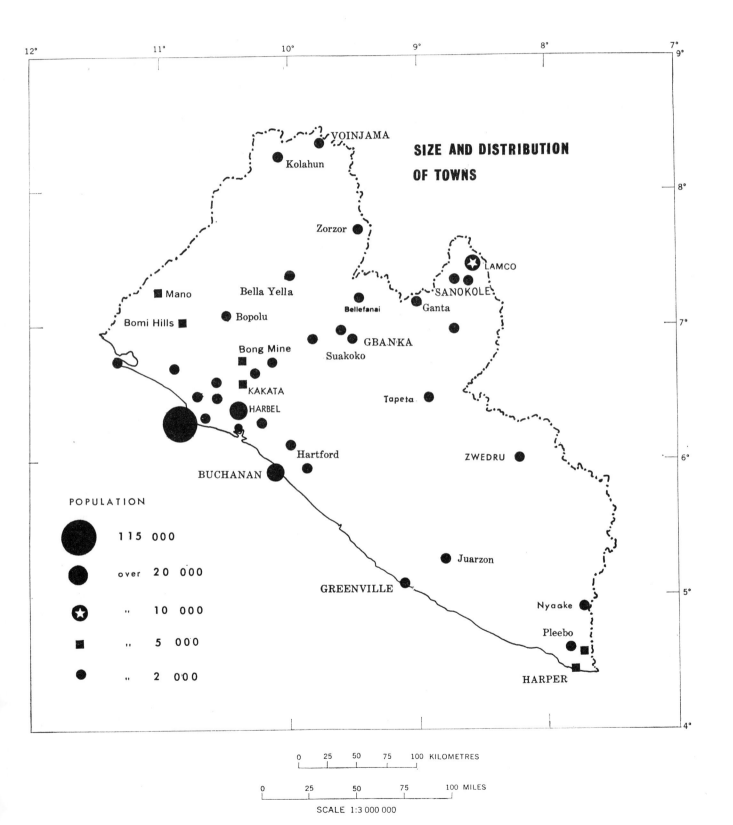

SIZE AND DISTRIBUTION
OF TOWNS

VOINJAMA

Kolahun

Zorzor

LAMCO

Mano

Bella Yella

SANOKOLE

Bellefanai

Ganta

Bomi Hills

Bopolu

GBANKA

Bong Mine

Suakoko

KAKATA

HARBEL

Tapeta

Hartford

ZWEDRU

BUCHANAN

POPULATION

115 000

over 20 000

" 10 000

" 5 000

" 2 000

Juarzon

GREENVILLE

Nyaake

Pleebo

HARPER

0   25   50   75   100 KILOMETRES

0   25   50   75   100 MILES

SCALE 1:3 000 000

One of the most striking features in modern Africa is the rapid growth and expansion of urban communities. This is also true in Liberia. Here urban settlements have been growing at a rate of approximately 7 to 8% per annum principally because of migration from rural areas. The upward trend of the economy, the increasing industrialization, the growing rate of foreign capital investment have all provided greater employment opportunities which have in turn accentuated the influx of the rural population to cities, mines and large plantations. The extraordinary expansion of the larger towns and urban centres can be expected to continue to grow disproportionately in relation to a relatively stable rural populace.

There are essentially two types of urban settlement in the country; towns which have been consciously designed, and towns which have emerged without planning. The first group is represented mainly by the towns within the coastal areas, established by the early settlers, e.g. the capital city Monrovia, Buchanan, Greenville, Harper, Robertsport and others. At the time of their foundation little was known about modern town-planning techniques. The lay-out of these settlements was done in a typical grid-iron or chequer-board pattern because it lends itself readily to subdivision of property and traffic finds its way easily, and houses are built conveniently in rectangular blocks. The modern mining towns have also been well planned. According to the different and sometimes difficult environment and the technical requirements of the mining site, their design may vary, but the industrial function is most clearly discernible. Often a radioconcentric pattern prevails and the residential area is arranged harmoniously in concentric rings placed in a wide arc around the industrial site of the mine. (See map on p. 89.)

In contrast to these, towns which have emerged in the interior are unplanned. This progression from village to town is a spontaneous and gradual one, but sometimes speeded by a newly established industry in the district. A well chosen village site on a major trading route may form the base for the development of a market centre which gradually grows into a town (Gbanka, Kakata, Sanokole, Voinjama, Zorzor). Trade increases and leads to the improvement of roads, houses, schools and other infrastructural facilities. Traders – mainly Lebanese – open up their stores and establish collection centres for the purchase of cash crops. Tradesmen settle to serve the needs of the inhabitants whose purchasing power is increasing. However, the extent of the retail market and trade is only one element supporting the growth of a town. Its administrative, medical and cultural functions are of equal importance. Most of the towns in the rural areas have developed by accretion. They sprawl or expand from a single nucleus without any particular plan, making roadway and utility improvement difficult and expensive (Gbanka, Zorzor and Zwedru, for instance). Only rarely has a town of the hinterland grown by fusion, absorbing smaller settlements nearby, whereas the coastal towns very often grew by engulfing smaller settlements (Monrovia, Buchanan, Harper, Greenville). Public utilities such as water supply and sewerage are not available in most country towns. While the nucleus of the town still shows its initial pattern of a Liberian village with narrow lanes and the irregular and often circular arrangement of houses, its core has been usually dislodged by a commercial centre. This central business district (CBD) includes shops and stores, petrol stations, markets, etc., occupying the most advantageous places. CBD's have grown alongside the busiest streets in a linear pattern, in a web-like pattern, or in T-shape, depending on the general lay-out of the town.

The town-plans opposite have been designed to show the functional complexities of several Liberian towns and their land use patterns. Residential, commercial and administrative sections can be differentiated while industrial sites in most of the towns of the interior are generally non-existent. Other ecological features include education, religion, health, transport and recreation.

1. *Harper*. Coastal promontories have been significant town sites as in the case of Monrovia, Robertsport, Marshall, and Harper (Cape Palmas). Harper is one of the early coastal towns. Rather isolated until a few years ago, it is now linked by an all-weather road to Monrovia via Zwedru, but because of the large detour the distance to the capital is over 430 miles (690 km.). The chequer-board pattern of the town is framed by the coast in the south, Hoffman River in the west, and a wide swamp in the north. The CBD stretches parallel to the coast some 550 yds (500 m.) from the port. (Port facilities are described in Chapter 49.) Administrative offices, several schools and the hospital are located near Lake Shepherd in the vicinity of the airport road. The town has expanded towards the north, absorbing by fusion Hoffman station and Gbenelu. Across the river an army camp was set up not far away from Puduke, a small fishing village. As the capital of Maryland, Harper has many administrative and cultural functions. Several missions and educational centres have been established including the College of Our Lady of Fatima.

2. *Voinjama*. The capital of Lofa County is an old market town and trade centre. Situated on the old Mandingo trading route leading from Guinea to Bopolu via Belle Yella, it has become one of the busiest towns in the Liberian hinterland. The soils within the district are especially fertile, and the Liberian Produce Marketing Corporation has established large plantations, a coffee and rice mill, and a large collection centre for coffee, palm kernels, kola and other important cash crops. The business centre has grown linearly along the main road, but the market formerly within the CBD has changed its position to the periphery although remaining within walking distance. The administration compound including the power plant, telecommunication offices and guest house are also located peripherally. The Catholic Mission is outside the township.

3. *Zorzor* owes its importance to several factors. It lies on the highway to the north-west linking Sierra Leone with Liberia. The surrounding countryside supports a fairly concentrated population so that the town has thrived as a marketing centre. The triangular-shaped CBD follows the most important streets, embracing the old town centre like a wedge. The better

class residential area is found in the outskirts. Here the rectangular-shaped bungalow prevails. Zorzor has become an important mission point of the Lutheran Church. The mission established not only a modern and well equipped hospital but also an elementary and secondary school. A Teachers Training College opened in 1964. The mission and hospital as well as the Teachers Training College and several schools are located away from the centre of town.

STEFAN VON GNIELINSKI

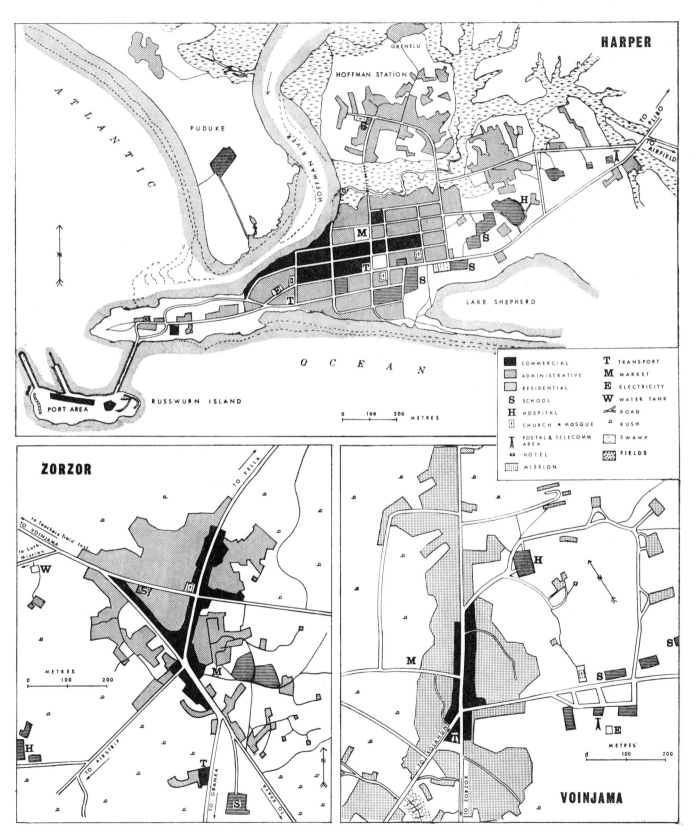

51

4. *Gbanka*, the capital of Bong County, is an industrial and busy town. Its commercial function is fundamental. Its nodal position is ideal because it is located on the main highway to Nimba and Zwedru with a road junction to Zorzor and Voinjama. The well developed CBD situated along the highway has cut a wide gap into the residential area. The administration offices including the government hospital are found just off the commercial ribbon within walking distance of each other. Only the power station is peripheral. The town's hinterland, its collecting and distribution area, has a radius of more than 30 miles (50 km.). The large experimental station of the Department of Agriculture in Suakoko some 9 miles (15 km.) south of Gbanka has been an impetus for the production of many cash crops which are collected and marketed in the town. The activities of several missions have stimulated the cultural life. They have established churches and schools, including Cuttington College, a well known institute of higher learning, and the modern Phoebe Hospital (both outside the town). The Moslem population, represented mostly by Mandingo traders, is served by a fine mosque.

5. *Zwedru*. In 1964 this town, which had only some 900 inhabitants, became the administrative headquarters of the newly created Grand Gedeh County. Since then its population has more than doubled, and its cultural and economic life has become very active. Several missions, schools and a well equipped government hospital have been established. A further incentive for the growth of this town was the completion of the roads to Greenville and Harper, furnishing a connection to Monrovia. Better transport facilities stimulated agricultural production within the surrounding area, and Zwedru serves as a collection centre for several cash crops. Two timber mills have started to operate in the district. Consequently, the importance of Zwedru as an administrative, market and traffic centre has greatly increased, and it has emerged as a central place of the first order. The possible exploitation of the iron ore deposits in the Putu Range by the Bong Mining Company would certainly have positive effects on the growth of this town.

6. *Nyaake*, a district headquarters of Grand Gedeh County is situated on the Cavalla some 40 miles (64 km.) north of the coast. It was once an important ferrying point and much of the trade was carried out across the border. The completion of the Harper–Zwedru road which leads through Nyaake did not advance the urbanization of this town but resulted in higher geographical mobility and as a consequence led to the migration of many inhabitants towards the coast in search of employment. The proposed hydro-electric Cavalla River Scheme a few miles north of Nyaake will perhaps end this state of stagnation and bring new life to this moribund town.

7. *Robertsport*, the capital of Grand Cape Mount County, is one of the oldest settlements in Liberia. Situated beautifully on a promontory which rises to 1068 ft (347 m.) above sea level, it overlooks the Atlantic Ocean to the south and Lake Piso in the north. This geographic location makes Robertsport a rather idyllic place; however, its isolation is a chief barrier to its urban growth. Since there is no direct road connection, visitors have to cross the lake by ferry or charter a plane. This explains the small volume of business turnover. The number of stores has declined during the past years, and there are only some 20 cars registered in town. Cultural life on the other hand is flourishing. Cape Mount has long been recognized as one of the major centres for education. There are a number of excellent public and mission schools, a training centre for nurses and a fine hospital. In 1964 the William V S Tubman Centre for African Culture was inaugurated, serving as an institute of research.

Future prospects for business might be enhanced when the Wologisi iron project materializes and plans for development projects such as a new port and a railroad are implemented to lead Robertsport out of its present isolation.

STEFAN VON GNIELINSKI

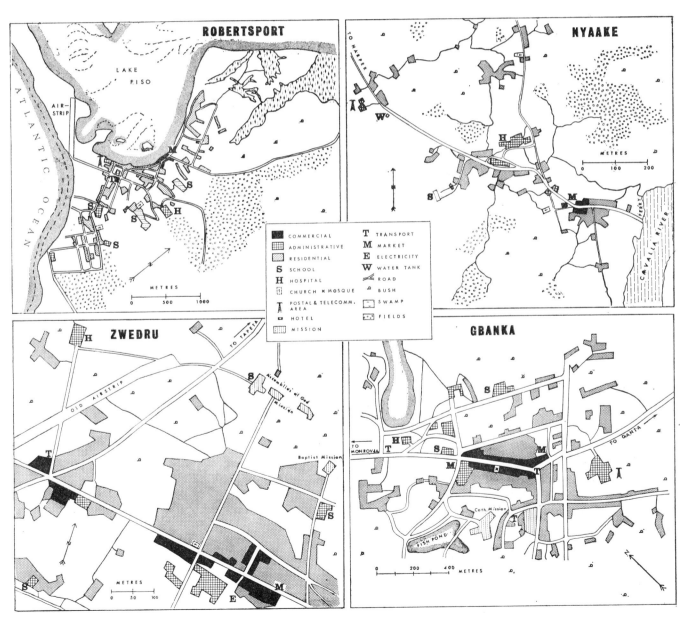

ROBERTSPORT

LAKE
P.ISO

AIR-
STRIP

ATLANTIC OCEAN

S
H
S
S
S
M
H

METRES
0   500   1000

NYAAKE

TO HARPER

S
W
H
S
M

METRES
0   100   200

CAVALLA RIVER
FERRY

	COMMERCIAL	**T**	TRANSPORT
	ADMINISTRATIVE	**M**	MARKET
	RESIDENTIAL	**E**	ELECTRICITY
S	SCHOOL	**W**	WATER TANK
H	HOSPITAL		ROAD
	CHURCH ✕ MOSQUE		BUSH
T	POSTAL & TELECOMM. AREA		SWAMP
	HOTEL		FIELDS
	MISSION		

ZWEDRU

H

TO TAPETA

S
Assemblies of God
Mission

OLD AIRSTRIP

T

Baptist Mission

S

S
METRES
0   50   100

M

E

GBANKA

S

TO MONROVIA

H
T
S
M
M
T
M
TO GANTA

I

Cath. Mission

T

FISH POND

0   200   400   METRES

53

Monrovia (6°19'N, 10°49'W) is situated on Cape Mesurado, a peninsula separated from the mainland by a broad lagoon at the mouth of the Mesurado River. Mamba Point, the highest spot of the Precambrian dioritic promontory ascending from the edge of the lagoon, reaches an elevation of approximately 300 ft (90 m.). South-east of Cape Mesurado the peninsula widens and the township extends along the coast for several miles. On the northern side of the Mesurado lagoon another wide stretch of land – Bushrod Island – is cut off from the mainland by the wide meanders of the Stockton Creek. Its tidal waters reach the mouth of the Mesurado River connecting it with the St Paul River simultaneously. The large sandbar in front of its estuary is known as Providence Island. The land east of the Stockton Creek consists mainly of sandy marshes and mangrove swamps and is at present unsuitable for settlement.

The first settlers from America gained a foothold in 1822, which they later expanded to establish the republic. Decimated by fever and continued attacks from the tribal people the settlement barely survived the first year, until matters began to improve under the leadership of Jehudi Ashmun. He first named the settlement Christopolis, but on 20 February 1824 it was renamed Monrovia, in honour of President James Monroe of the USA. Cape Mesurado was chosen because of safety, easy access to the sea and the natural waterway connecting the region with the interior.

Although Monrovia had only about 10 000 inhabitants at the beginning of the Second World War, it has been transformed in a few years from a quiet West African coastal trading post into a dynamic and burgeoning city. The change started with the 'Open Door Policy' enunciated and consistently pursued by President Tubman. This policy brought foreign capital and investment into the country. Since the construction of the Free Port of Monrovia the growth has been rapid. By 1962 the population exceeded 85 000 with some 12 000 households. Today the population of Monrovia is estimated to exceed 115 000 persons and the urban area is continuing to experience a boom in construction and expansion. Industrialization burst the frame of the old settlement. However, the geographical position slowed down the process of urbanization, marked by the increasing lack of space as a result of this 'island position', so that today an urban belt more than 10 miles (16 km.) long stretches as a narrow chain of new settlements from the north to the south-east, the area comprising Bushrod Island, Monrovia proper, Sinkor and Congo Town.

The oldest section, the nucleus of the town, begins on the eastern slopes of Mamba Point. Next to Fort Norris and the old lighthouse the luxurious, eight storey Ducor Intercontinental Hotel overlooks the city and the Atlantic Ocean. From here Broad Street follows the downsloping ridge and constitutes the backbone of the chessboard-like network of roads in the city centre, the most important of which are Randall, Ashmun and Benson Streets. Although the centre of the city still shows some buildings of the early settlers, most of them have made room for modern offices and commercial buildings reflecting new investment and technical advance. Several government offices, churches, schools, the post office and the old government hospital are also situated here.

United Nations Drive follows the wide arc of the southern coast. Here is found the most exclusive residential area, harbouring several embassies and many elegant villas. Running in an easterly direction the road passes the Barclay Military Training Centre and the Antoinette Tubman Stadium. Farther on the peninsula narrows and gently rises to Capitol Hill. Here in accordance with contemporary city planning the administration is concentrated. The Executive Mansion, an impressive edifice, is the office and residence of the President of Liberia. The copper-domed Capitol Building opposite to it is the seat of the Liberian Legislature. Along the same side are the Temple of Justice, the Department of Information and Cultural Affairs (which houses the radio and television station), the Chamber of Commerce and the Bureau of Natural Resources. Tubman Boulevard leading past the University and the City Hall connects the city with the eastern suburbs and Roberts International Airport located 35 miles (56 km.) farther inland. Beyond the City Hall the residential area of Sinkor has developed. Here many fine houses and bungalows fringe the coast as far as Congo Town. The two largest hospitals, the Catholic Hospital and J F Kennedy Hospital, several churches and schools are also situated here.

The larger settlements of the tribal people are found in the northern parts of the peninsula along the Mesurado River banks. Westpoint, the big sandbar north-west of Mamba Point, has become a large and overcrowded fishing village. Waterside presents an old and busy commercial centre with the largest local market, the offices of many shipping agents and importers, and many Lebanese retail and wholesale dealers. Nearby a large concrete bridge links Monrovia with Bushrod Island, the centre of industrialization. The busy freeport, many plants and factories, the brewery, saw-mill and other commercial enterprises have attracted many tribal people seeking employment. Typical tribal settlements of high population density and low building standard are Clara Town, Vai Town, Kru Town and Logan Town.

Owing to the special geographic position and limited area of expansion the vast growth of Monrovia today presents a set of major problems. With the construction of the Mount Coffee hydro-electric plant and the water purification system in White Plains on the St Paul River some of them have been solved already.

STEFAN VON GNIELINSKI

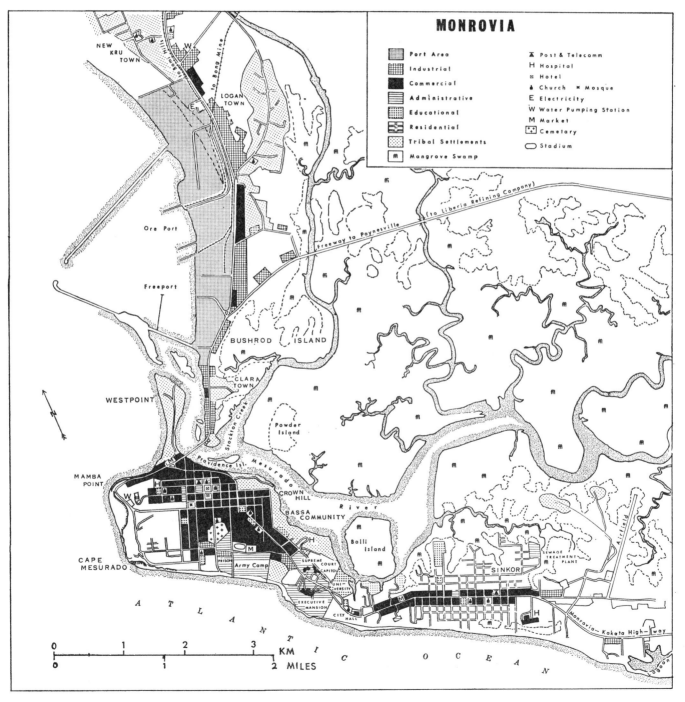

MONROVIA

Port Area
Industrial
Commercial
Administrative
Educational
Residential
Tribal Settlements
Mangrove Swamp

Post & Telecomm
H Hospital
Hotel
Church Mosque
E Electricity
W Water Pumping Station
M Market
Cemetary
Stadium

NEW KRU TOWN
LOGAN TOWN
to Bong Mine
Ore Port
Freeport
Freeway to Paynesville
(to Liberia Refining Company)
BUSHROD ISLAND
CLARA TOWN
WESTPOINT
Stockton Creek
Providence Isl.
Mesurado River
Powder Island
MAMBA POINT
CROWN HILL
BASSA COMMUNITY
Balli Island
CAPE MESURADO
PRISON
Army Camp
SUPREME COURT
CAPITOL
UNIVERSITY
EXECUTIVE MANSION
CITY HALL
H
SINKOR
SEWAGE TREATMENT PLANT
Monrovia—Kakata High-way
Lagoon

A T L A N T I C   O C E A N

0   1   2   3   KM
0   1   2 MILES

25 FORMS OF RURAL SETTLEMENT

Similar factors determining the distribution of settlements in Liberia have also influenced the form and size of the villages. Primarily the physical conditions of the location played an important role. While extensive swamps, rugged mountains and dense forests imposed limitations, settlements were placed as advantageously as possible with respect to natural features on protected spots, near arable land and sources of water and fuel, but otherwise the importance of physical agents is overshadowed by the emphasis placed on various social and economic considerations. The explanation for the form and size of settlements is therefore found mainly in the human factor, e.g. historical setting, tribal practice and the state of economic development.

Tribal wars and slavery left strong impressions on the form of the villages, which had to be hidden and well protected in the forest. In order to escape slavery and the pressure of stronger groups the tribal people were bound to the forest regions where they lived in their traditional surroundings. Especially the Gola and Kissi but also the Belle and Gbandi inhabit small circular villages of closely clustered huts protected by a wall of stockades and by the encircling forest. The dwellings are located in family groupings of three to seven and occasionally as many as a dozen huts. They are usually joined together by mud block walls – sometimes reed fences – to form a compound. This custom, however, is going out of existence as danger from wild animals has diminished and intertribal warfare has been stopped for many years.

In more recent times the form of the villages is largely governed by agricultural land-use. Shifting cultivation still prevails, and the size of the village varies according to the farmland available. The settlement consists of an irregular arrangement of family compounds, rotation farmlands, woodland and palm-forest, and interconnecting paths. The inner farmlands comprise the vegetable garden with some fruit trees, and the outer farmlands are cultivated on a rotational basis for producing staple food and cash crops.

The increasing economic activity of the village, e.g. its growing administrative, commercial and traffic functions naturally influenced its form and size. The extension of the road network into the interior has certainly had the greatest impact and although the nucleated village remains the predominant form of settlement, linear realignment starts as soon as the village is connected to the road system. The land adjoining the road becomes extremely valuable. New houses and shops will be erected because of the better market position and transport facilities, and the nucleated settlement will gradually change its pattern. Even a few scattered farmsteads, completely absent during the past, have since appeared alongside some roads.

Baila, a village near the St John River is one typical example. The once circular shape of the village has given way to a re-alignment along the road. This structural change can be observed in many settlements. People even leave their original villages and settle along the roads, utilizing the better market and transport facilities.

Lomboba is a typical Gola village with the circular protective lay-out and the cluster of family compounds of more than 6 huts. Mud walls formerly used have disappeared; so have the stockades. On the single footpath leading to the fields two rectangular houses have recently been built. These and the school located opposite the palaver hut show some modern design.

Bendaja shows a similar settlement pattern. Located close to the border with Sierra Leone, this village was once a stockaded 'siege town'. It has emerged as a fairly important market place since, and although the old kinship compounds are still noticeable, the traditional pattern is slightly disturbed and a few modern zinc houses have been constructed near the main road. The school is outside the village some 220 m. south of it.

The number of planned villages designed in a regular grid-pattern is very small. The National Planning Council initiated several community settlements throughout the country. Perhaps the best known attempt at improving living conditions of rural communities is the government low cost rural housing project of *Fisebu*. This village was destroyed by fire in 1959 and the rebuilding represents the first rural settlement laid out according to a definite plan. *Bilapo* is a Kru village halfway between Sasstown and Grand Cess. The Kru have their fishing villages aligned along the river estuaries or lagoons. Their huts are not clustered in the kinship groups but mainly at a short distance from each other along a sandridge. Usually small gardens are kept behind the houses fringed with coconut palms. A number of paths lead from the houses to the water.

Millsburg is one of the oldest settlements of the colonists from America along the St Paul River valley. The fields are near the river banks while the houses, some of them resembling the old American colonial style, are re-aligned along the road which runs parallel to the river. The smaller size distinguishes the houses and huts of tribal people from those of the immigrants.

Marshall is another of these colonial settlements. Because of its isolated position, Marshall, like many other of the old settlements, has experienced marked depopulation.

STEFAN VON GNIELINSKI

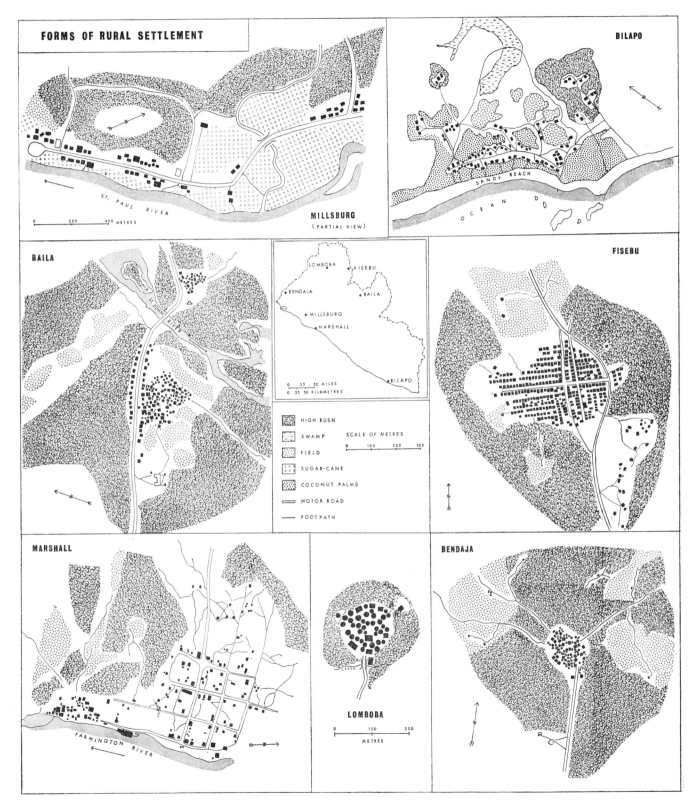

FORMS OF RURAL SETTLEMENT

MILLSBURG
(PARTIAL VIEW)

ST. PAUL RIVER

0   200   400 METRES

BILAPO

SANDY BEACH

OCEAN

BAILA

ST. JOHN RIVER

LOMBOBA   FISEBU

BENDAJA   BAILA

MILLSBURG

MARSHALL

BILAPO

0   25   50 MILES
0   25   50 KILOMETRES

HIGH BUSH
SWAMP   SCALE OF METRES
FIELD
SUGAR-CANE   0   100   200   300
COCONUT PALMS
MOTOR ROAD
FOOTPATH

FISEBU

MARSHALL

FARMINGTON RIVER

LOMBOBA

CREEK

0   100   200
METRES

BENDAJA

57

26 RURAL HOUSE TYPES

Originally house types in the rural areas varied according to the tribe. The construction of roads to the interior and the resulting higher geographical mobility, however, led to the adoption of modern ways of building. Therefore there has been a diffusion of tribal patterns of house building in recent years and the traditional types are only found in the most remote villages and are no longer characteristic for the economically more advanced settlements.

Traditional house types. The common house type for all interior tribes was the circular house (c), a structure of poles linked by vines and cross-ribs of palm leaves on a basis of loam some 3ft. (1 m.) high. This wall-structure is plastered with mud patches both outside and inside. The roofs are covered with raffia-palm leaves or grass, the eaves differing in length according to area. Very few octagonal or elliptical houses (j,3) are found in the interior. A more recent type is the rectangular house (d) with hip-roof and a central parlour from which the rooms extend on both sides; otherwise it is built in the same way as the one-roomed circular house. Many houses (2,4,6) have verandas, usually in front of the entrance. The interior of the houses, especially of the older round ones, is furnished with mud beds along the walls (1), the centre being occupied by the earthen hearth with an open fire for cooking. Chiefs of the Mande tribes build large round houses for all their wives and live separately. The coastal tribes build a rectangular structure with walls made of mats plaited out of the midribs of the raffia palm or sometimes the coconut palm (e,f). The mats are placed immediately on the sand (e) or on a platform forming the floor (f,7). Older authors – Schwab, Büttikofer – describe houses with two floors. The hip-roof consists of grass or palm leaves, the eaves extending over the edge of the platform which projects about 3ft. (1 m.) from the walls. The pitch of the roofs varies with the area: the traditional Kru-style house has a rather steep roof (e,f). In some coastal areas the rectangular mat house is not prevalent; De and Vai often have modern corrugated iron houses, which are gradually replacing the older type (b). The few round houses may be adopted from the Gola (c) who have penetrated into the territory. Some of the coastal Grebo also build circular mud houses. The American settlers and their descendants have a house style all their own. This is a two-or three-storied structure (a,m) built on stone pillars to protect it from rain and ants. The walls are either hard-wood or corrugated iron.

At various places even bricks are manufactured and used. The first floor of these houses consists of an open peripheral veranda leading around a core of living rooms. From here a stair leads to the bedrooms on the second floor. Characteristic are lattice shutters at windows and front verandas. The oldest houses of this type had shingled walls and roofs and no veranda. These houses, resembling the old 'southern' style in America, are only found in the original settlements of the immigrants along the coast.

Contemporary house types. Traditional house types still prevail in parts of the country, especially in settlements inaccessible by motor-road where modern building materials are unobtainable. However, even here the round house (c) or the house with mud walls (e,f) is increasingly replaced by the rectangular house (d) with mud walls and a thatched roof. In south-eastern Liberia, among Krahn, Sapo and interior Kru, the round house is obsolete, except among the Grebo (g).

In villages accessible by motor-road the large square house with walls of blocks and a low-pitched iron roof (b) tends to replace the traditional types, but often walls are still made of poles and sticks and daubed with mud. Roughcast is often lacking and the floor is still of mud rather than concrete. This house has a central parlour and an open porch in front of the main entrance (5, 6). Roof-trees, window-frames, doors and shutters are fabricated by a local carpenter rather than owner-made. Although the traditional house types still co-exist with the modern ones, once in decay they will be replaced by more spacious, zinc-roofed houses. Only the Gio (Dan) are still building large circular houses (h) with steep, high-pitched conical thatched roofs even in the larger villages along the highways.

In larger towns and administrative, commercial and traffic centres the large rectangular house (b) prevails. It is zinc-roofed, has a concrete floor and its walls are made of cement blocks. Windows often have screens, sometimes even panes. (Stores often have two floors and open towards the main street to attract customers. They are mostly owned by Lebanese merchants or Mandingo traders.) Even though modern houses are increasingly displacing the traditional types in economically more advanced locations and commercial centres, the majority of the tribes may still live in their traditional dwellings. The prevailing house types of the various tribes are listed below. Whereas the foregoing refers to dwelling houses only, a few other house types of importance are listed as well.

1. 'Palaver' houses. In these community houses all public matters are discussed by elders and chiefs. They are not found among the eastern tribes who prefer the open-air palaver yard.

House type \ Tribe	Vai	Gola	De	Bassa	Kru	Grebo	Krahn	Gio	Mano	Kpelle	Loma	Belle	Gbandi	Mende	Kissi	Mandingo
Round, thatch		x				(x)		x				x	x		x	
Square, thatch	x				x	x	x		x	x	x	x		x		
Square, zinc			x	x												x

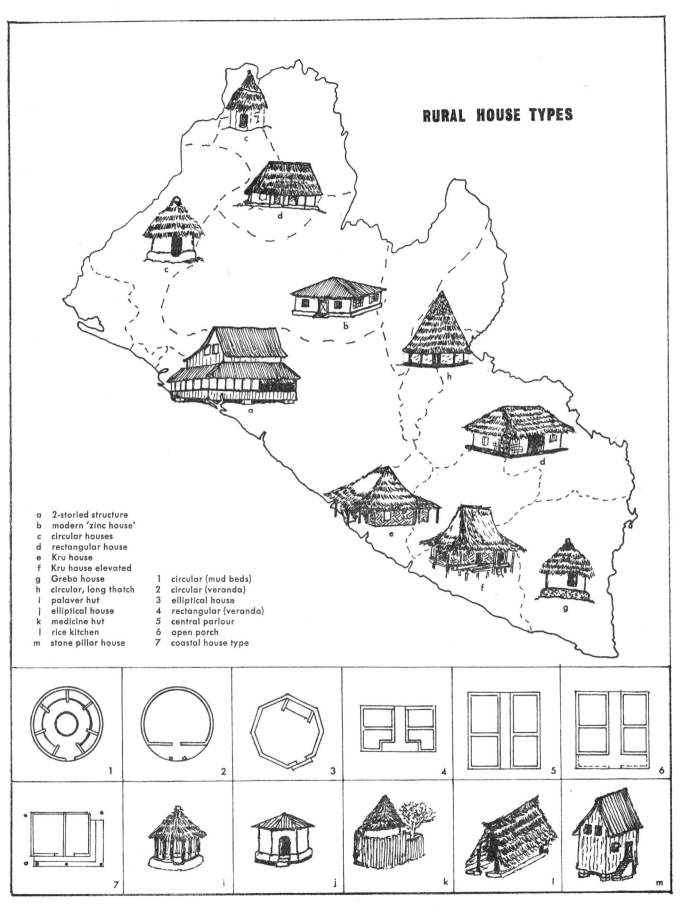

RURAL HOUSE TYPES

a   2-storied structure
b   modern 'zinc house'
c   circular houses
d   rectangular house
e   Kru house
f   Kru house elevated
g   Grebo house   1   circular (mud beds)
h   circular, long thatch   2   circular (veranda)
i   palaver hut   3   elliptical house
j   elliptical house   4   rectangular (veranda)
k   medicine hut   5   central parlour
l   rice kitchen   6   open porch
m   stone pillar house   7   coastal house type

The more elaborate type is a square open structure on a concrete platform with a roof supported by four strong corner poles. A balustrade often surrounds the platform leaving open the entrance and offering seats for the public. In the hinterland palaver-huts are usually smaller, round or rectangular in structure with thatched roofs, and floors and balustrades are made of mud (i).

2. 'Kitchen': small, rectangular structures without walls, but with a large attic and thatched roof. These serve as cooking shelters behind the dwelling house. In the field the 'rice kitchen' (l) is the almost permanent residence of the family throughout the farming season. It protects from the rain, serves as a sleeping and cooking place, and the rice stored in the attic is dried by the open fire below. In the villages small thatched round or square huts with daubed walls are built as granaries for rice and other foodstuffs.

3. Tribal medicines, fetishes, and sacrificial offerings are kept in special houses. Their construction corresponds to that of the dwellings, mostly rectangular in the east and circular in the west (k). These houses of acolytes, priests and country doctors often stand in an enclosure of palisades beside a young tree.

A MASSING

27 HEALTH SERVICES

The first organized Public Health Programme in Liberia, although limited to Monrovia, was initiated by President C D B King in 1928. President E Barclay realized the need to extend Monrovia's health programme to other parts of the country and, in 1930, he created the Bureau of Public Health and Sanitation with a staff of the country's three doctors. Although the scope was widened, the real problem remained unsolved for several years because of the nation's limited budget and lack of physicians and trained personnel.

In 1931 there were only 6 or 7 physicians and 1 government hospital in the whole country. Because of the absence of an adequate communication system, of roads and sufficient personnel and equipment, medical care was reserved for the inhabitants of Monrovia and nearby coastal towns. The Liberian Government Hospital was established in 1927, closed in 1935 and reopened in 1942. The Carrie V Dyer Memorial Hospital was opened in 1928; it closed for two years and was reopened in 1942 by the National Baptist Convention.

When President Wm V S Tubman took office in 1944, the Bureau of Public Health underwent dramatic improvements. In 1943, as President elect, he had appealed to the United States Government to send out a health mission. President Roosevelt himself appointed the advisory group of American experts headed by Dr J B West, who arrived late in 1944. A Five Year Development Plan in Public Health was drawn up and within three years there were doctors, trained nurses and technicians in every county and province of Liberia. In 1945 the Tubman National Institute of Medical Arts, School of Nursing was opened with lecturers and clinical instructors from the United States. The Public Health Mission from America functioned actively from 1944 to 1951, by which time it had trained second class laboratory technicians and nurses, made malaria and schistosomiasis surveys for Liberia and acted in an advisory capacity to the Bureau of Public Health. In 1951 the United States Public Health Mission was merged with the Bureau.

By 1950 the Bureau of Public Health had reached a budget of $325 000, which constituted 12% of the total government budget. The country then had 8 hospitals, containing 426 beds. Only two of these hospitals (130 beds) were operated by the Bureau, the rest being run by concessions and missions. Fifteen physicians were employed by the government out of a total of 32 in the country, including 2 Liberian doctors who had studied abroad under a scholarship programme.

In 1953 the President raised the status of the Bureau to that of a Department with a Cabinet Minister at its head. The 'National Public Health Service' has two main bureaux, one for sanitation and preventive services, and the other for medical services such as government hospitals and dispensaries. Eight hospitals were constructed, providing a total of 750 beds, and also a number of satellite clinics were established in the various counties and territories. By 1963 a total of 15 government hospitals had been established, 50 physicians were in full-time government service and the Tubman National Institute of Medical Arts was turning out paramedical personnel. The health budget had risen to $2·8 million. But against all suggestions of extravagancy President Tubman remained firm in his policy:

'I cannot compromise with any opinion, no matter how forcefully expressed, which holds, that funds used for public health are wasted. I am convinced that the progress of any nation is measured in terms of the progress and prosperity of its individual citizens, and if that citizenry is poverty-stricken, disease-ridden, unhealthy and illiterate, that nation is bound for failure, retrogression and eventual disintegration.'

In 1963, aware of the urgent need for the local training of many more medical doctors and technicians, the Government of Liberia through the aid of the Vatican State and the Italian Government made an agreement with the University of Turin to establish a medical school in Monrovia. The Monrovia–Torino Medical College opened a modern 250 bed hospital in 1966, and admitted its first class in 1968.

At present there are 33 hospitals and 156 out-patient clinics in Liberia; of these 95 clinics and 15 hospitals are operated by the government, 12 hospitals and 46 clinics by concessions, and 6 hospitals and 15 clinics operated by missions. A total of about 2200 hospital beds are available in the country as a whole, and about 100 physicians are employed, 25 of them being Liberian nationals who, after terminating their studies in USA, Germany, Israel and England, returned from abroad. Forty-six are employed by the government, 30 by concessions and 8 at mission hospitals. Apart from these, there is also a number of private practitioners and 14 dentists in Monrovia. In 1944 the ratio of doctor to population was 1:100 000, whereas in 1968 it was 1:10 000.

The $7·5 million John F Kennedy Hospital is nearing com-
pletion. For this hospital an easy term capital loan was obtained from the USA. This 300 bed medical centre will include also the Maternity Hospital and the Tubman National Institute of Medical Arts, with dormitory accommodation for 132 students. The Hospital is planning to begin operation in 1972.

There are two Institutes for Tropical Medicine—centres for medical research—in Liberia. One, the Liberian Institute of

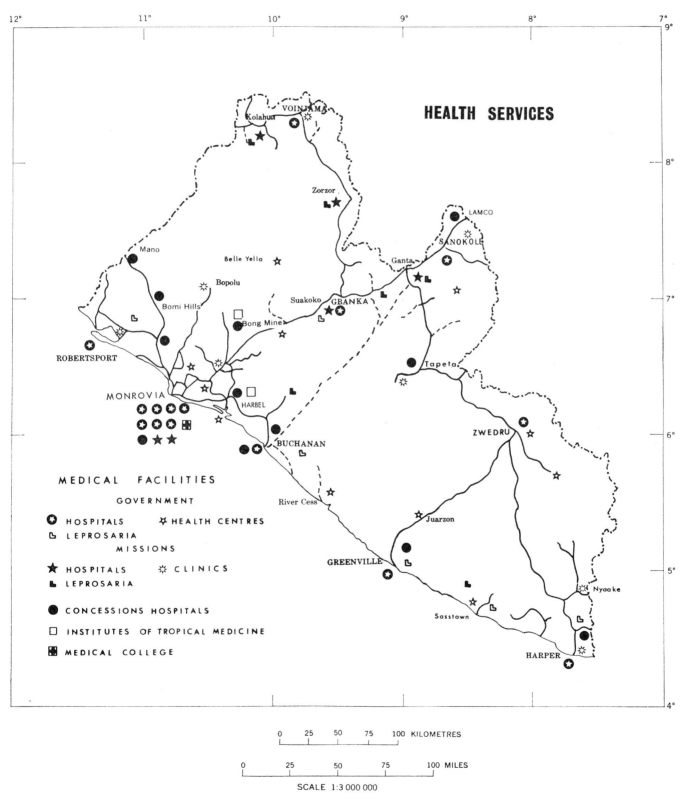

HEALTH SERVICES

MEDICAL FACILITIES

GOVERNMENT

⊙ HOSPITALS ✿ HEALTH CENTRES
ᘯ LEPROSARIA

MISSIONS

★ HOSPITALS ☼ CLINICS
ᘯ LEPROSARIA

● CONCESSIONS HOSPITALS

□ INSTITUTES OF TROPICAL MEDICINE

▦ MEDICAL COLLEGE

0   25   50   75   100 KILOMETRES

0   25   50   75   100 MILES

SCALE 1:3 000 000

Tropical Medicine, sponsored by the American Foundation for Tropical Medicine, was established in 1952 with the financial assistance of Harvey S Firestone on land donated by the government. The second, the Bong Range Tropical Research Institute with a scientific staff of 3 physicians and 3 technicians was established in 1968 as a field branch of the Tropical Institute of Hamburg, and is working in connection with the Liberian Government's Health Programme. The Institute is presently engaged in research on onchocerciasis or river blindness, a disease caused by the bite of the blackfly, from which an estimated 20 million people suffer, and the most serious foci of which are located in West Africa. The Volkswagen Foundation recently donated $300 000 for this young institution.

In the area of public health, yaws has been practically eliminated from the country and the eradication of smallpox with the control of measles is a present US Aid assisted programme in 19 West African countries. With the assistance of the World Health Organization (WHO) a project is under way for environmental health, maternal and child health, malaria control and health education. The infant mortality rate has been significantly decreased and mortality statistics have been improved. The modern water and sewerage systems for Monrovia have shown their first results, and schemes for 8 other urban areas have been developed.

M S KARPEH

28 EDUCATIONAL ESTABLISHMENTS

The early settlers, convinced that the success of their venture depended to a large extent on the education and training of their children, established public schools as early as 1826, and by 1847 sixteen primary, and several private and mission-operated secondary schools existed in the settlements. The schools were supported from public funds, but to a larger extent by religious and philanthropic organizations. Between the years 1862 and 1885 the educational system expanded considerably, and many new schools including some seminaries for the training of teachers and clergymen, as well as several vocational training centres were opened by the missions. The most significant event was the opening of the Liberian College in 1862. By 1900, the Bureau of Education was formed to establish and supervise a centralized school system which at this time encompassed the five coastal counties and served the need of the settlers. Very few schools were established beyond the coastal zone, and educational amenities in the interior were almost non-existent. Children of the indigenous population had at this time only limited access to education in some mission schools or through adoption by the families of the settlers. These conditions prevailed until 1944 when President Tubman was inaugurated. During his administration he put every emphasis on the need to intensify the educational programme in Liberia, and steady progress has marked this development.

In 1969 there existed in the country a total of 810 elementary, secondary and tertiary schools with a total of 147 110 pupils including some 15 680 secondary and high school and 1 230 college and university students.

The educational establishments of Liberia fall into two main categories: the government schools, and the private schools including those run by the concessions and missions. The map demonstrates their distribution over the different counties and shows the correlation between educational establishments and the degree of development as well as the distribution of the population. In general the elementary schools are widely scattered throughout the country, whereas junior high and senior

Distribution of Schools by Counties, 1969

Counties	Type	Elementary	Junior high	Senior high	Total	Grand total
Monrovia (City)	Public	42	5	2	49	
	Mission	3	3	7	13	
	Private	14	2	1	17	79
Montserrado	Public	79	5	1	85	
	Mission	14	1	3	18	
	Private	28	4	1	33	136
Bassa	Public	47	1	1	49	
	Mission	15	1	—	16	
	Private	3	1	—	4	69
Bong	Public	39	2	1	42	
	Mission	8	2	1	11	
	Private	3	—	—	3	56
Cape Mount	Public	14	—	1	15	
	Mission	8	—	1	9	
	Private	—	1	—	1	25
Grand Gedeh	Public	50	1	1	52	
	Mission	3	1	—	4	
	Private	3	—	—	3	59
Lofa	Public	44	4	2	50	
	Mission	12	1	2	15	
	Private	1	—	—	1	66
Maryland	Public	64	6	5	75	
	Mission	19	2	2	23	
	Private	7	—	—	7	105
Nimba	Public	69	1	1	71	
	Mission	13	2	—	15	
	Private	7	—	—	7	93
Sinoe	Public	85	4	1	90	
	Mission	21	3	—	24	
	Private	3	—	—	3	117
All Counties	Public	533	29	16	578	
	Mission	116	16	16	148	
	Private	69	8	2	79	805

high schools are concentrated in the larger settlements. The areas having the highest density of population – Monrovia and the coastal towns – also have the greatest number of schools. Outside the coastal lands the highest frequency of schools is found within the string of townships along the main highway from Monrovia to Nimba.

A continuous migration of students to Monrovia, the centre of the educational system, particularly from Sinoe, Grand Bassa, and Grand Gedeh Counties, has created a problem of great concern to the Department of Education. This phenomenon is not only explained by the general trend of population movement to the capital city, but by the comparable lack of adequate physical and instructional facilities, and the unsatisfactory calibre of teachers in parts of the interior. Students

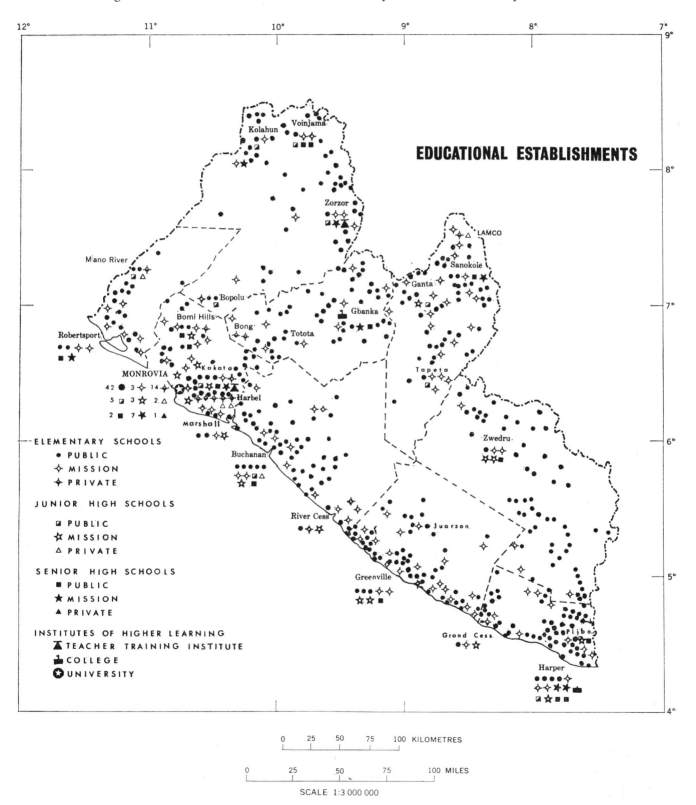

EDUCATIONAL ESTABLISHMENTS

ELEMENTARY SCHOOLS
• PUBLIC
✧ MISSION
✦ PRIVATE

JUNIOR HIGH SCHOOLS
◪ PUBLIC
✩ MISSION
△ PRIVATE

SENIOR HIGH SCHOOLS
■ PUBLIC
★ MISSION
▲ PRIVATE

INSTITUTES OF HIGHER LEARNING
▲ TEACHER TRAINING INSTITUTE
🏛 COLLEGE
✪ UNIVERSITY

MONROVIA
42 • 3 ✧ 14 ✦
5 ◪ 3 ✩ 2 △
2 ■ 7 ★ 1 ▲

0   25   50   75   100 KILOMETRES

0   25   50   75   100 MILES

SCALE 1:3 000 000

come to Monrovia in order to obtain an adequate pre-university education, thereby increasing the school population to such an extent that there are more than 6000 students on the waiting list of the Monrovia Consolidated School System, and most secondary schools work on at least a two-shift system.

The obvious remedy is to provide more well-trained teachers. Two rural Teacher Training Institutes have been set up, one at Zorzor and the other at Kakata. In 1969 those two institutes had a total of 359 students. Unfortunately for the educational system, the attraction of the capital city causes many of the graduates of these institutes to migrate into Monrovia, leaving the upcountry schools understaffed.

Vocational training takes place at the Booker T Washington Institute, Kakata, and also on concessions like Lamco, Bomi Hills, Bong and Firestone, etc., where about 800 students are trained at present in the knowledge and skills essential to satisfy the increasing demand for trained craftsmen on the labour market. There are three institutes of higher education: Our Lady of Fatima at Harper, with an enrolment of 20 students in 1969, Cuttington College, near Gbanka, with some 245, and the University of Liberia with 965 students in the same year. At present some 470 Liberians study overseas for higher degrees, mainly in the USA, UK, Germany and elsewhere in Europe.

The number of teachers and students has more than doubled since the last two decades. However, in spite of the great efforts of the government – the total public expenditure on education in 1969 amounted to $8·7 million – as well as international and US relief organizations, outside Monrovia and other larger urban places the majority of the population is still illiterate and many of them do not know English, the official language of the country. Nevertheless, the great number of students and the readiness of the government to mobilize a much larger force to provide the human resources necessary to fill the gaps, indicate that these problems will be solved in the not too distant future.

J B WILLIAMS

29 RELIGIOUS LIFE

Three major religions can be distinguished: traditional religion, Islam and Christianity, but there is a variety of religious expressions (like the Baha'i) which cannot be classified in the conceptual framework. Historically the Muslim Mandingos first influenced parts of the western tribes, and later people of the coastal tribes adopted Christianity. However, despite exterior influences for more than 150 years, the majority of the Liberian population are not formal members of either Islam or Christianity, and practise rites connected with the traditional religion, if any. Christians and Moslems, however, are constantly increasing in number. According to estimates in 1969, some 150–200 000 belong to the various Christian missions or churches and more than 200 000 confess the Islamic faith.

1. Traditional religion
All tribes in Liberia believe in a supreme being which has created the earth and everything in it. The idea is connected with the sky and the appearance of natural forces. The myth and the being itself differs from tribe to tribe. People confirm that one may pray individually to him, but there is no special cult of worship. The supreme being is said to be remote and does not interfere in the daily affairs of the people. Ancestor worship is predominant, ministered by the lineage elder. The deceased are believed to continue living as spiritual beings. They display the same behaviour towards men as they have done when living on earth. Therefore, the members of the lineage have to appease their mood by sacrificial offerings lest they disturb the daily life of their descendants. The spirits of the ancestors live in cotton trees, in rivers, or on mountains and could be incarnated in weaver birds or fish or be reborn in their grandchildren. In this case the children are given the names of their forefathers. Medicines (charms) are used against the spirits of the restless ancestors who might harm people because they have been witches. Each lineage has its food taboos. Breaking of the taboos may result in misfortune, sickness or death or barrenness of women. There is also a belief in spirits living under rocks, trees, in rivers or other places who are given food and offerings in order not to disturb the daily life or to help people in special undertakings. The Kru-speaking-people on the coast report special gods for their dakō (the residential and geographical notion of a number of patrilineal sibs which form a unity) ministered by trained priests. These gods (today spoken of as devils) are asked for help in all important matters concerning the dakō, especially in times of war, misery or suffering. Oracles among the Krahn, of which a permanent priest takes care, have similar functions. These priests conduct (sasswood) ordeals in cases where a person is accused of witchcraft. The belief in magic, witchcraft and sorcery is widespread among all tribes. In order to protect themselves against these forces, the people use medicines provided after divination by special medicinemen or women or 'native doctors'.

A main cultural difference between the eastern tribes and the western Mande and West Atlantic tribes is constituted by the secret Poro society for men and the Sande society for women, to which all adults belong after passing the initiation rites. The young boys are believed to experience a rebirth having been eaten by the 'bush thing' or gbeni = bush devil. This 'bush thing' or 'big zoo' appears in masks. Women and children are forbidden to see him when he enters a village after the 'bush school' or on the occasion of the funeral of an important man. Under him act other members in various ranks. The status of all 'zoos' is supported by the belief that they possess powerful medicines which can harm others. The Poro is at the same time an institution of native education and exerts a considerable influence on tribal politics. From the Kru-speaking-people parts of the Bassa have adopted this institution. There are also some secret societies among the Gio, Mano, Krahn, Grebo and Kru, but little is known of their function. Today most Grebo and Kru are members of Christian churches.

2. Islam

Islam was introduced by the Mandingo traders. Today, the Mandingo, Vai, larger parts of the Gola and Mende, some Kissi, Loma, Gbandi and Kpelle are Moslems. These tribes have been influenced by Islam for more than a century. One of the centres was the independent chiefdom of the Mandingos in Bopolu. The Mandingos are famous and influential traders, some of them displaying considerable wealth. They are mostly literate in Arabic, and speak some English. This makes Islam attractive to the illiterate poorer Liberian

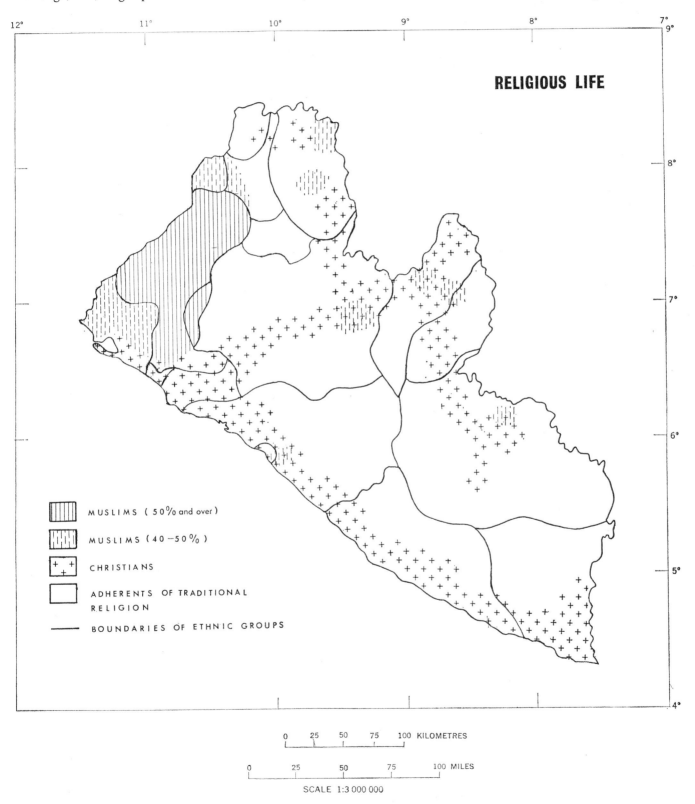

RELIGIOUS LIFE

|||||| MUSLIMS (50% and over)

MUSLIMS (40 – 50%)

+ + CHRISTIANS

ADHERENTS OF TRADITIONAL RELIGION

——— BOUNDARIES OF ETHNIC GROUPS

0   25   50   75   100 KILOMETRES

0   25   50   75   100 MILES

SCALE 1:3 000 000

peasants. Mosques can be found in Monrovia, and among the Vai, Gola and Loma also. Even as far as Zwedru, Gbanka, Bahn, Buchanan and Timbo the Mandingos form their communities centred on the mosque. They also have their own schools and other forms of social and cultural organization. The Amadiyya sect, a revival movement from the Far East, maintains a bookshop in Monrovia, but it exerts little influence.

The considerable attraction among the Liberian tribes towards Islam is explained by the adaptability to the traditional culture. Islam does not reject the belief in demons, spirits, magic and witchcraft and its formal ways of worship and the commonly known taboos facilitate conversation of the natives. Mandingo Moslems were respected 'sand cutters' (soothsayers) and medicine men in times before the Liberian Government controlled the hinterland. However, few members of the upper strata are Moslems.

3. Christianity

Christianity was introduced by the early settlers. From the beginning of mission work in Liberia, the American mother churches supported the immigrants. Their efforts were mainly confined to the coastal tribes around the settlements. The establishment of mission stations in the remote areas of the hinterland started only at the beginning of this century. The missions opened schools and dispensaries, and natives sent their children to school or came for treatment, so many of them became Christians. Today missions are obliged by law to run schools on their stations. With the increasing desire for education, the attraction of the churches does not cease, and social status is now correlated with church membership. Therefore, next to the descendants of the immigrant settlers, large parts of the Bassa, Kru-and Grebo-speaking-people, and minor parts of the Kpelle, Loma, Gbandi, Kissi, Belle, Gio, Mano and Krahn are christianized.

Since the Second World War, a number of independent churches have been founded, mainly by Bassa and Kru. They want to be free of foreign control and adapt the Christian message more or less to the needs of the people. The number of these churches is increasing, since more and more people move to Monrovia and other larger settlements, and the urban and rural societies are in steady process of differentiation. Even the tribal clubs and associations, organized for purposes traditionally satisfied by the lineage, are religiously influenced. Each of these clubs has an officer called a chaplain, who begins and ends the sessions with prayer.

Christianity has a very strong influence on Liberia. This can be seen very clearly in Monrovia, where nearly every mission or church has one or more congregations. The strength of the Christian churches is not only the result of their considerable achievements in education and social welfare, but due to the connection with the governing class, the majority of whom are descendants of the early settlers who brought the Christian faith to Liberia.

W KORTE

30 MISSIONS

Liberia is one of the few African states that had churches before the arrival of any missionaries. Very early the settlers, many of whom were clergymen, erected church buildings, and one of them, the Providence Baptist Church, dates back to 1822. In their struggle for survival they asked for help in religious and educational matters, and American Baptists, Methodists, Presbyterians and Episcopalians were the first to send out missionaries, whose activities began in Monrovia and surroundings, Robertsport, Edina, Greenville and Harper. From the beginning, apart from their spiritual work, the foreign missions have in great measure contributed to the educational, health and social welfare programme of the country.

Two main streams of missionary enterprises followed each other: one from 1822 to about 1900, the second starting at about 1908 with the arrival of the first pentecostal converts.

The first missionary group to begin work in Liberia were the *Baptists*, with the Rev. Lott Carey, one of the founding fathers, as their minister. The Baptist Foreign Mission Board founded the Rick's Institute in Brewerville, the Sueh Industrial Mission for girls, and the Lott Carey Mission, a co-educational school in Brewerville. They also founded and operated one of the first hospitals in the country, the Carrie V Dyer Memorial Hospital.

The second equally strong group were the *Methodists*, who began their work in 1833 with the Rev. Melville Cox as their first minister. The Methodist Episcopal Church (today United Methodist Church of Liberia) slowly extended its work to the tribes along the coast, and, despite the arrival of the African Methodist Episcopal Church and A M E Zion Church at the end of the last century, has remained the most influential Methodist Church. Locations of important educational and missionary activities include the College of West Africa, and the large mission at Ganta with a modern hospital and schools providing also agricultural and vocational training.

The *Presbyterians* received support from an American body, but help declined and the last ties were cut off in 1931. Their activities are confined to Monrovia and Greenville and to one mission in Todee near the Firestone plantation.

The *Protestant Episcopal Church* concentrated its work from 1835 in Maryland and spread very early to the Grebos. Its leaders and missionaries had a strong interest in literacy and translated the Bible into Grebo. The names of Bishop Payne and Bishop Ferguson are still well known today. This mission founded Cuttington College of Harper – now located near Gbanka – and several high schools, including a school for nurses at the St Timothy Hospital in Cape Mount.

The *Lutherans* established their first mission in 1860 at Muhlenberg near Mount Coffee. Later on the field of their activities widened towards the interior and they transferred their headquarters to Zorzor, where they operate a modern hospital as well as a co-educational school and a second hospital and nurses' school near Gbanka.

The *Roman Catholic Church* since 1842 made several attempts to establish a foothold in Liberia, but it was not until 1903 that it succeeded in building up some missions among the Kru, Bassa and Grebo. Since then missionary and educational work expanded rapidly, and in the 1930's mission stations were established in Gbanka, Sanniquellie and Zwedru. The Catholic Church founded the College of Our Lady of Fatima in Harper and several elementary and high schools. A $175 000 cathedral has just been consecrated in Monrovia, and the Catholic Hos-

pital or Medical College of Torino, financed by the Vatican State, were recent contributions to public health and education.

In 1927 the *Seventh Day Adventists* started their activities in Buchanan.

The second period of missionary effort is of another kind. The pentecostal and fundamentalist churches stressed evangelization and conversion more than education and went straight into the hinterland. Former Methodist missionaries were the first to teach pentecostal doctrines. Later they joined the *Assemblies of God*, beginning work among the Kru, Bassa and Krahn of the interior. Today the Assemblies of God represent

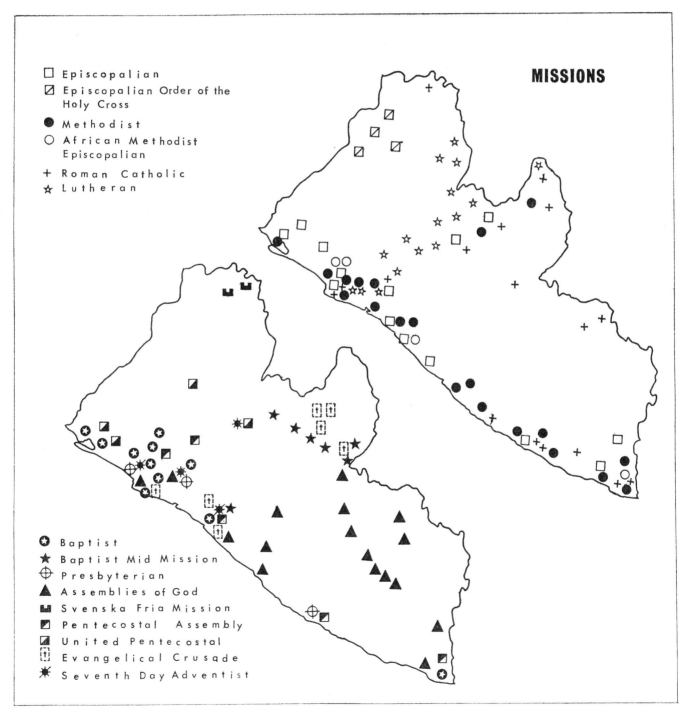

one of the largest churches in Liberia. Subsequently other pentecostal missions started work among the Gola, Belle, Gbandi, Mano and Gio; e.g. Pentecostal Assemblies of the World (1919), United Pentecostal Church (1938), Open Bible Standard Mission (1947), Svenska Fria Missionen (1944), etc.

Since missions are required by law to establish schools, most of them depend heavily on financial aid from the mother churches abroad. Most church organizations therefore have missionary status and only a few have succeeded in getting an autonomous status. The Liberian Baptist Missionary and Educational Convention and the First Presbyterian Church have been self-supporting for some time, the latter since 1868, but these comprise less than 15% of full members of Christian churches. The Methodist Church with the financial aid of President Tubman began an effort to achieve autonomy by choosing its own bishop in the mid-1960's. Some missionary groups have responded to the urge for Africanization, and have transferred some control to Liberians, even though the mother church continues to carry most of the financial burden.

The distribution of missions is shown on the two maps. Baptists, Methodists, and Episcopalians, the first denominations among the settlers, are still the three leading churches. They are found mainly in Monrovia and along the coast, since missionary work was done among the coastal tribes with whom the settlers were in constant contact. The work in the hinterland started later and mainly by American and Canadian missionaries, e.g. Baptist Mid Mission (Canada) for Mano and Gio, Order of the Holy Cross (Episcopal) for Gbandi and Kissi, and American Methodists among the Mano. Lutherans, Pentecostalists, Roman Catholics, and some other minor groups have mainly worked among tribal people and they represent the majority of their followers, the Lutheran mainly in the eastern and northern parts, the Pentecostalists in the northern and north-eastern parts and the Catholics in the south-eastern and to a lesser extent northern part of Liberia.

Christianity plays a rather important role in social life, and besides YMCA and YWCA there are many other Christian organizations. The radio station ELWA of the Sudan Interior Mission acts as a communication centre for religious news and instruction. Although none of the tribal groups is wholly Christian, traditional religion is clearly on the wane.

W KORTE

31 PEACE CORPS ACTIVITIES

The Peace Corps came to Liberia in response to a request of President Tubman to President Kennedy in 1961. The first project involved some 60 volunteers to take up assignments as teachers in both government and mission schools throughout the country. The second project provided for 30 elementary school teachers. Both projects began with the school semester starting in September 1962. During the last eight years some 1500 volunteers have served the Republic, each one for a minimum of two years (with some 35% extending for a longer period; that is, three years altogether).

The Peace Corps, a voluntary American aid programme, as it operates in Liberia today, has three basic aims: first, to provide Liberia with skills that are at present inadequately supplied; second, to increase the recipients' knowledge of America and its people, and finally to increase the understanding of Americans of developing nations by direct contact. These purposes are achieved by a Corps of volunteers of all ages who are carefully selected and intensively trained to carry out specific tasks and projects. This means that recruitment is highly specialized with a specific person filling a specific position under specific circumstances. Volunteers provide mainly 'middle manpower positions', in other words, they work in a purely operational capacity, being 'doers' rather than supervisors. Recruiting was previously directed to the white American college graduate, but more recently, Peace Corps is attracting more minority groups and at the same time providing volunteers with more technical skills.

In Liberia the Peace Corps programme in the majority of cases is geared to educational development. This involves direct teaching as well as teacher training programmes. In 1970, of the 250 volunteers operating, some 204 were involved in educational pursuits. The remainder are split into health schemes (17 volunteers) including the establishment of mothercraft centres and pre-natal clinics; pilot schemes (9 volunteers) primarily agricultural; and a further 20 volunteers are designated to public administration (a more recent extension). The Corps also participates in secondary activities, or 'self-help' projects, aimed at local community interests, frequently rendering invaluable service.

The volunteers are required to live in circumstances similar to their Liberian co-workers, obtaining no real salary, but receiving a living allowance of some 145 US dollars a month and having the same status as an American tourist. Married applicants are accepted if they have no children. For the immediate supervision of the volunteers, a Peace Corps director with a small staff is assigned to Liberia, residing in Monrovia, with a regional office in Gbanka. Gbanka is also the residence of the Peace Corps physician.

Initially, Peace Corps activities were solely in co-operation with the Liberian Education Department. Today, these activities are expanded into other directions since a number of volunteers work in fields which come under the respective control of the Department of Treasury, the Health Department and the Bureau of National Planning. A few volunteers may be found with the Power Authority, the Post Office, the Department of Agriculture, the Customs Office at the Free Port, the Liberian Information Service and the University of Liberia.

One of the main reasons for the presence of Peace Corps volunteers in Liberia, however, is to relieve a number of teachers for two years of additional training. By this arrangement the teacher who is temporarily replaced by the volunteer finds his position secured after his return to his school.

There is no doubt as to the success of Peace Corps in Liberia, and the basic aims of the scheme are being fulfilled. They have helped to fill many of the gaps associated with the lack of trained personnel. The aid-programme has been of particular value in supplementing the educational programme of Liberia. As for the future, there is no set period for the departure of the Corps, but numbers (250 in 1970, as against some 350 in 1966) tend to show a gradual diminishing as more and more Liberians take over their respective roles. Peace Corps pursuits have involved years of hard work and co-operation, but the results have proved both worthwhile and rewarding.

C PEARSON

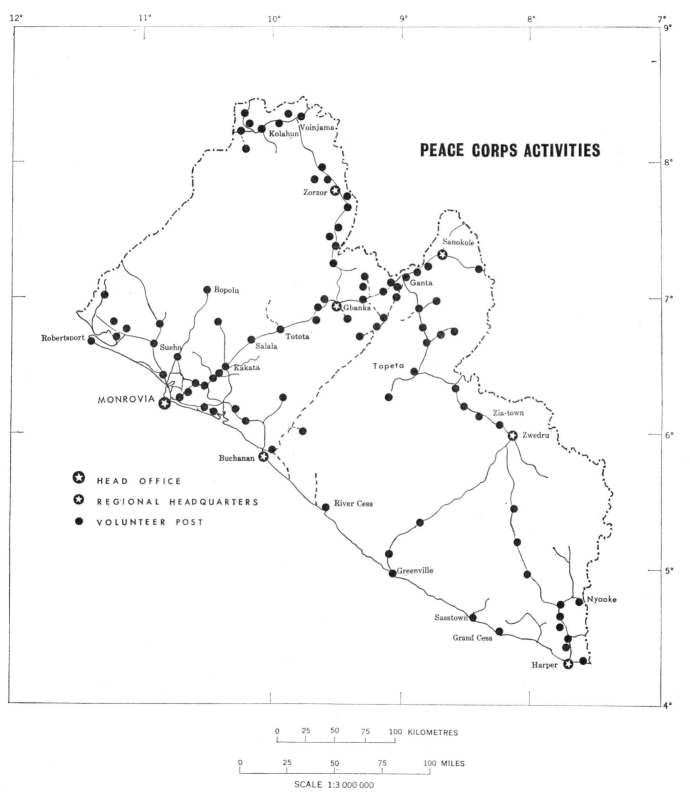

PEACE CORPS ACTIVITIES

✪ HEAD OFFICE
✪ REGIONAL HEADQUARTERS
● VOLUNTEER POST

0   25   50   75   100 KILOMETRES

0   25   50   75   100 MILES

SCALE 1:3 000 000

The early settlers from America who founded the 'Lone Star Republic' faced many grave problems from the beginning of their heroic task. They had to adapt to an environment unknown and unfavourable and also encountered a great many internal and external political difficulties. Their supporters were few, and they had to direct all efforts towards survival. However, the passionate desire for liberty and the endurance of the pioneers helped to overcome the period of consolidation. The settlers introduced many valuable crops like sugar-cane, tobacco, cotton, and also many different fruits and vegetables to the country, building up a substantial foreign trade at the same time. The main trading commodities were palm kernels from the Kru coast, camwood used for dyes, and fibres from the raphia palm.

After the proclamation of independence in 1847 the economy of the young republic started to thrive. By 1850 coffee and sugar plantations were flourishing and Liberian coffee was considered the finest in the world. Raw sugar and molasses were manufactured in large quantities for local consumption and export. Trade relations with England, Holland and Hamburg became especially intensive, and soon the ships of Liberian merchants, manned by skilled Kru men, carried the Liberian flag into American and European ports. In 1850 the first Liberian ship, the *Eusebia Roye*, sailed to Liverpool and New York with a cargo of palm kernels, the first to be exported from Africa. By 1855 more than 30 ships built in small shipyards near Monrovia sailed under the Liberian flag. Prosperity entered Monrovia and other coastal places, which was reflected in numerous mansions, public buildings, churches and schools in these towns. The Liberia College was founded in 1862 and became, next to Fourah Bay (Sierra Leone), the second institution of higher learning in West Africa.

However, owing to some far-reaching events of world-wide importance, Liberia was driven into isolation and underwent a grave economic crisis which lasted from the 1870's for more than 50 years. The road of the young republic was strewn with many obstacles and more than once the very existence of the country was at stake. Prices of many commodities, especially coffee, palm oil and sugar, dropped. Brazil, which had introduced Liberian coffee plants, soon dominated the American market. Sugar plantations in Cuba as well as the growing production of beet sugar in Europe proved to be too much competition for Liberian cane-growers. Oil and raphia palms were grown in many French and English colonies, and German synthetic dyes around 1900 finished off the camwood export. The development of the steamship was perhaps the heaviest blow and resulted in the complete disappearance of the Liberian sailing fleet from the ocean. Finally the outbreak of the First World War cut off the trade with Germany. Since government revenues fell below expenditures, Liberia, greatly to her own disadvantage, had to take several loans, the one in 1912 on condition that an American be appointed commissioner of Liberian Customs.

The first step out of this crisis was taken in 1926, when Firestone established the world's largest rubber plantation at Harbel. Large numbers of tribal people were recruited to work on the plantations and to build roads into the interior. The world depression in 1929 and the ensuing drop in rubber prices almost stopped this progress, and it was not until the beginning of the Second World War that rubber production proved to be the dominant enterprise within the country.

However, Liberia's economic growth really started with the beginning of the Tubman Era. President Tubman, the promoter of the 'Open Door Policy', opened the country to foreign investment and directed the republic through a period of astonishing progress. The rubber industry expanded and B F Goodrich, the African Fruit Company, and four other foreign companies started large plantations. This was in fact the first step in remodelling the system of subsistence agriculture because more and more Liberians, encouraged by the progress of Firestone, started planting rubber trees, and by the end of 1969 4000 private rubber farms were in production. With the opening of the first iron ore mine at Bomi Hills in 1951, the country experienced an exceptional investment boom. Three other iron ore mining companies started exploration during the following years and the production of iron rose from 3 million tons in 1960 to over 20 million tons in 1969 reaching an export value of 137·1 million dollars. The completion of the deepwater harbour at Monrovia shortly after the war facilitated this development. Since then a second port for the shipment of iron ore has been constructed in Buchanan. Four railway lines have been built and a number of new roads constructed. The government's strong commitment to a liberal trade and foreign investment promises a substantial future expansion and a gradual diversification of the economy, while the US dollar as circulating currency ensures stable monetary conditions.

The use of the Liberian flag as a 'flag of convenience' is another important economic factor. Shipowners the world over have taken advantage of the favourable registration rates offered, and since 1960, Liberia could claim to have the largest oil-tanker fleet in the world. In 1967 the Liberian fleet with 1 513 vessels (including 582 tankers) at 22 597 808 gross tons was named the second largest merchant shipping fleet in Lloyd's Register of Shipping. More than 20% of the state's income is now derived from shipping registration fees.

President Tubman's Unification Policy is also of far-reaching economic significance, because it has mobilized the human resources of the hinterland and paved the way for all segments of the population to participate in the economic development of the nation. The outlook for the future seems bright and the economy will continue to grow at a high rate. With growing exports revenues will increase which will render possible new investments and subventions on the public sector and development of new projects.

STEFAN VON GNIELINSKI

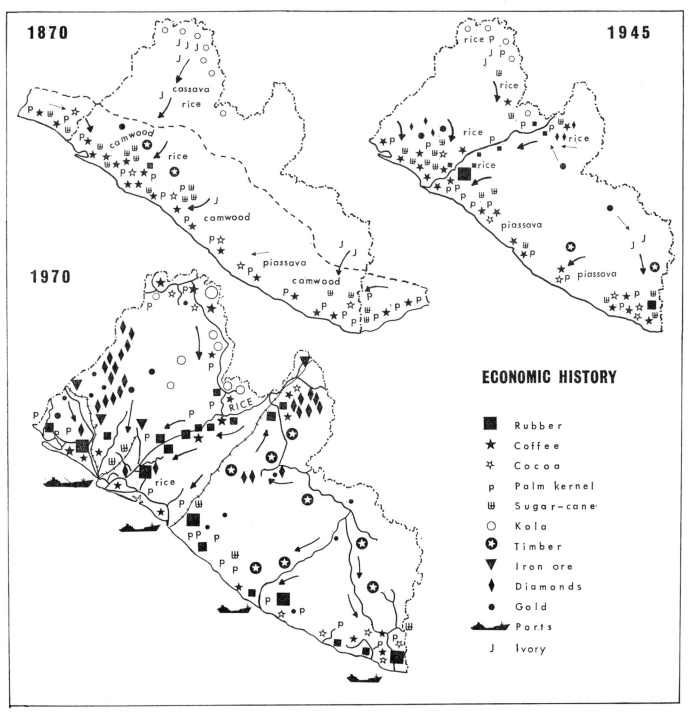

1870

J J J O
J O
J cassava
rice
O

P ★ ₩ P ☆
P ★ ₩
P ₩ camwood ✪
rice
P ☆ ★ p ✪
★ ★
₩ ★ ☆ ₩ ₩
p ₩
p ★ camwood
P ☆
★
☆ p piassava
P ★ ₩ ₩ P
J J
camwood
P ₩ P p ₩ P ★ ★ p
P p p ₩ P

1945

rice P O
J p
J p O
₩ O
rice
★
₩ O
P ■ ◆ ◆ rice
■ ◆ ◆
p ◆ ◆
★ p ● p ₩ ◆
₩ ★ ★ ■
★ ★ ★ rice
■ ■ rice
★ ₩ ₩ P
P P
p p ₩ ●
☆ ★
p piassava
★ ₩
★ p ✪
J J
★ p piassava ✪
₩ ☆ ★ P ₩
☆ P ■
☆ ★

1970

★
P ★ ●
☆ ★ P ●
O ☆ ◆
◆ ◆ ★
▼ ◆ ◆ O
◆ ◆ ◆ P ★
◆ ◆ ◆ O
P P ■ P ■ ■ ✪
p p ■ ▼ ■ ◆ RICE ☆ ◆
★ ₩ ■ ■ ◆
rice ★ ■ ✪
★ ✪ ◆ ◆
P ₩ ✪ ●
■ ■ ✪
P P p ●
P p ✪ ★ ✪
★ ✪ ●
P ■ ✪
☆ ● p
p
✪ ₩
☆ ★ ☆ ★ P
■ ★ p ☆
☆ ★ ■

ECONOMIC HISTORY

■	Rubber
★	Coffee
☆	Cocoa
p	Palm kernel
₩	Sugar-cane
O	Kola
✪	Timber
▼	Iron ore
◆	Diamonds
●	Gold
⛴	Ports
J	Ivory

33 AGRICULTURE

In spite of the rapid expansion of the iron ore mining industry, Liberia is basically an agricultural country. For more than 80% of the population agriculture is a way of life, and nearly half of the country – in fact all the land not covered by tropical rain-forest – is utilized, although only a small proportion is farmed each year because of the practice of shifting cultivation.

Liberian agriculture has a dualistic pattern; on the one hand are smallholdings, the majority of which are still cultivated in the old traditional ways of bush fallowing or shifting cultivation in order to plant food crops, and on the other hand are large commercial plantations using the most up-to-date techniques to produce rubber, coffee and palm kernels, and other export crops. In between there is an increasing group of Liberian farmers who, encouraged by the success and the assistance of foreign-owned plantations, have established smaller sized plantations of their own, generally in the vicinity of Monrovia, but also in other coastal areas and alongside the major roads leading into the interior.

Food Crops

Besides rice (see chapter 36), the most important staple foods – cassava, yams, sweet potatoes and other tubers – are planted next to many fruits and vegetables. None of these plants cultivated is indigenous, yet bananas and citrus trees as well as pawpaws, avocado, breadfruit, sugar-cane and pineapple are found in almost every village. Mango, soursop and guavas are also frequent. Most food crops are grown almost exclusively for local consumption, but a wide variety of vegetables and fruits is offered on the local markets for sale.

Cash Crops

Next to rubber and the oil palm (see Chapters 34 and 35), coffee, cocoa, and piassava are the principal export crops and the major sources of cash for the small farmer. *Coffee* is indigenous in Liberia and at the end of the nineteenth century *Coffea liberica* was the country's leading export. Thereafter production gradually declined, and by 1960 export dropped to less than $1 million a year. Only during the last five years has coffee – mainly *Coffea robusta* – regained some of its importance and in 1968 the annual production again reached 10·3 million lb. (4·7 million kg.) at a value of $2·9 million. The largest coffee plantation is managed by the Liberian Produce Marketing Company, LPMC, near Voinjama. The company also acts as the biggest buyer of all the crops in the northern parts of the country, including coffee, cocoa, palm kernels and piassava. To increase production in this area LPMC has established a model farm and some 20 village demonstration plots to provide training for the small farmers. The Episcopalian Mission in Bolahun has formed two co-operatives for the production and marketing of coffee. Coffee is also found in the coastal areas, mainly in the vicinity of Monrovia and Harper.

Cocoa is not so widely distributed, because the plant likes a relatively fertile and well drained soil. It was introduced in the 1920's by Kru people returning from contract work on the plantations of Sao Tomé and Fernando Po. Grown mainly along the south-eastern coast, cocoa was introduced farther inland some thirty years later by foreign concessions. Export values in 1968 reached $1·3 million.

Piassava, a swamp palm, is another cash crop which grows widely in most swamps of the country. From the plant such products as brooms, raffia bags, baskets and mats are made, but export of fibres is now of little significance. Other fibres like sisal and kenaf have been grown on a small scale only.

Sugar-cane is grown throughout the country and used mainly for the distilling of low-proof cane rum, the sale of which constitutes one of the major sources of money income. The factors limiting the commercial production of raw sugar are not the natural conditions, but the need for high capital investment and a secure market.

The commercial production of *bananas* proved to be a failure, and the plantation of the African Fruit Company near Greenville had to be abandoned and switched to rubber because of the Panama disease. Disease-resistant poyo bananas were introduced from Ivory Coast and are at present being tested on the University farm and other places.

Tobacco production started in 1963. The Liberian Tobacco Company and the Liberian Agricultural Company planted mainly Sumatra tobacco yielding high quality cigar wrapper leaf for export.

The ecological conditions warrant the commercial growing of *citrus fruits*: oranges, lemons and tangerines. Grape fruit grow especially well, and are more juicy and not as bitter as those grown in sub-tropical areas.

Pineapple, melons, tomatoes, cucumbers and other fruits as well as various kinds of vegetables, e.g. cow beans, soy beans, sweet corn and maize grow well in all parts of the country, while kola nuts, ground nuts and even cotton are found to some extent in the northern parts. The main bottleneck to increased production of all these crops is the lack of marketing facilities.

Recognizing that the status of progress of agriculture is of vital concern to the country, the Government in its 'Operation Production' policy has placed special emphasis on the production of food crops and given serious consideration to the development of subsistence farms. The Department of Agriculture has established an Agricultural Extension Service to provide technical and other assistance to the farmers, offering seeds for planting and advice on proper farming methods, the use of tools and fertilizers, etc. Many farmers have since started to grow cash crops and help to increase agricultural production.

A number of experimental stations have been established by the Government, FAO, and private concessions, and research is done in many fields. Both the University of Liberia and Cuttington College offer four-year degree courses in agriculture, while the Booker Washington Institute in Kakata offers agriculture within its vocational training programme.

The Government is determined to expand and intensify its agricultural programme to lead its population out of the stagnation of subsistence farming and enable them to participate in and benefit from the achievements of the economic growth.

STEFAN VON GNIELINSKI

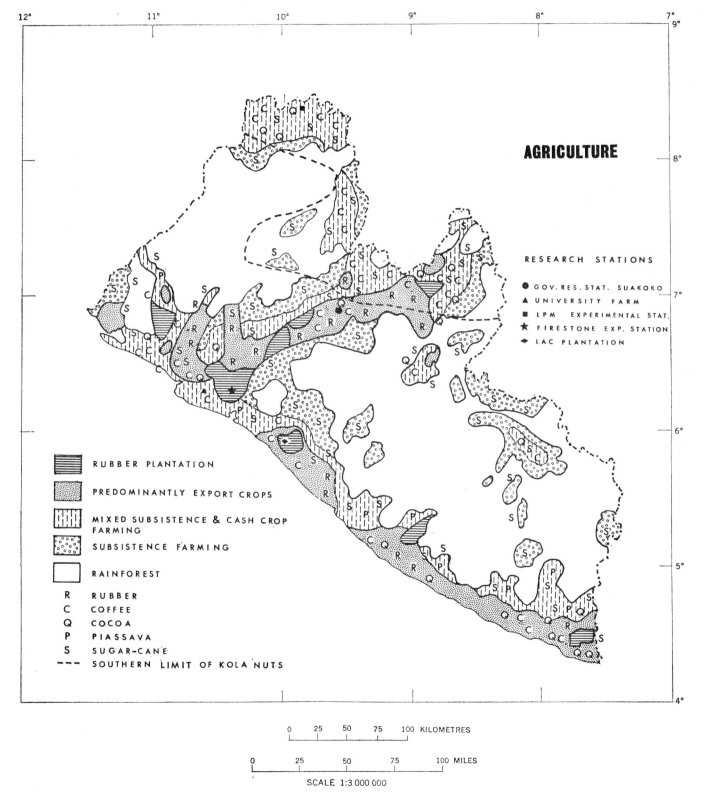

AGRICULTURE

RESEARCH STATIONS

● GOV. RES. STAT. SUAKOKO
▲ UNIVERSITY FARM
■ LPM EXPERIMENTAL STAT.
★ FIRESTONE EXP. STATION
◆ LAC PLANTATION

RUBBER PLANTATION

PREDOMINANTLY EXPORT CROPS

MIXED SUBSISTENCE & CASH CROP FARMING

SUBSISTENCE FARMING

RAINFOREST

R   RUBBER
C   COFFEE
Q   COCOA
P   PIASSAVA
S   SUGAR-CANE
--- SOUTHERN LIMIT OF KOLA NUTS

0   25   50   75   100 KILOMETRES

0   25   50   75   100 MILES

SCALE 1:3 000 000

Rubber, *Hevea brasiliensis*, is the most important export crop and has for many years dominated the economy of Liberia. Although there were several native species of latex-producing trees in the country, *Hevea* was introduced and adapted very well to climate and soil.

The history of rubber in Liberia goes back to 1910, when the first rubber plantation was established by a British company – the Mount Barclay Rubber Plantation Co. – which planted 2000 acres (800 ha.) at Mt Barclay 20 miles (32 km.) north of Monrovia. Before this time two other companies – the Liberian Rubber Company and the Monrovia Rubber Company – had been engaged in the export of rubber, but their activities were confined to the collection of wild rubber and its marketing.

After the First World War, the British abandoned the Mt Barclay plantation owing to falling prices on the world market. In 1924 Firestone, wanting to break the British rubber monopoly, started negotiations with the Liberian Government and in 1926 obtained a 99-year lease of a concession area of 1 million acres (405 000 ha.) near Harbel on the Farmington River. Firestone took over the Mt Barclay plantation, imported seedlings from Sumatra, and employed a Dutch specialist for bud grafting. By 1928 some 25 000 acres (10 000 ha.) were planted including 7000 acres (2800 ha.) on the Cavalla River, but it was not until 1935 that rubber was produced on a commercial scale. The Second World War stimulated production, especially after the Japanese had overrun Malaya; and Liberia, although minor among world producers, became the largest one in Africa. Firestone was the first to develop Liberia's human resources and has some 16 000 employees on the payroll. Over 13 000 skilled tappers tend some 10 million trees producing more than 90 million lb. (41 million kg.) of rubber each year. Today Harbel is the largest continuous rubber plantation in the world with more than 77 000 acres (31 000 ha.) of planted rubber. Virtually self-contained, Firestone operates a hydro-electric power plant, a brick factory, a saw-mill, a soft drinks factory and a plant manufacturing rubber cups, shoes and soap; and provides modern facilities including schools, clinics and hospitals, churches and club-houses. The second plantation at Cavalla has also more than 13 000 acres (5200 ha.) of rubber trees.

During the post-war period a number of concessions have been granted to other companies which include American, German and Dutch interests. B F Goodrich established a 12 500 acre (5000 ha.) plantation near Kle (Clay) along the Lofa River some 37 miles (60 km.) west of Monrovia; the German-owned African Fruit Company runs a 5000 acre (2000 ha.) estate on the Sinoe River 15 miles (24 km.) north-east of Greenville; while the Salala Rubber Corporation and several others have started operations farther inland. Their plantations cover in all about 50 000 acres (20 000 ha.), but they have so far not come into full production.

In addition there are over 4000 independent Liberian rubber farms, some of which date back to 1930. Among the pioneers of private rubber producers were the late Presidents C D B King, J F Cooper, E C Barclay and other notable citizens. In 1941 Firestone designed and organized a programme to help Liberian rubber planters and since then has distributed more than 10 million trees and valuable seedlings free of cost. Thus farmers were able to increase their production from 4% of the total rubber export fifteen years ago (1955) to more than one third at the present time, amounting to 40 million lb. (18 million kg.) in 1969. Since the independent farmers normally sell their rubber to the large concessions for processing, road accessibility is one of the principal considerations. Most of the farms are therefore situated along the main roads and preferably within a short distance from the concession areas. The smaller ones, consisting of narrow strips of land only, are locally known as 'curtain farms'. About two-thirds of the rubber sold is purchased by Firestone and processed at Harbel, the world's largest latex concentration plant. From here rubber and latex is shipped by shallow draught vessels down the Farmington River and along the coast to Monrovia, from whence it is exported to the United States.

The table shows the Liberian rubber production during the last decade. Although the volume of the rubber export has steadily increased, export value – owing to the fall in world market prices – declined during the periods 1960–1, 1962–3 and 1964–8. Since March 1968, rubber prices have recovered and prospects are that they will continue to be on a fairly high level in the near future. However, in anticipation of further price fluctuations on the world market, the major task of rubber farmers remains to increase output and reduce production costs. Higher-yielding varieties of trees are already showing beneficial results.

Hundreds of acres of rubber trees are approaching maturity, and the estimated production was 170 million lb. (77 million kg.) in 1971. Next to Nigeria, Liberia will remain Africa's largest producer of natural rubber.

Rubber Production 1960-1969
(million lb.)

	1960	1961	1962	1963	1964	1965	1966	1967	1968	1969
Firestone	80	80	77	73	75	80	84	90	90	88
Other concessions	—	—	—	1	2	6	6	12	13	16
Liberian farmers	14	16	17	18	19	24	32	36	40	43
Total production	94	96	94	92	96	110	122	138	143	147
Value: in mill. $	37·6	26·0	25·7	23·9	29·5	29·0	27·0	26·6	25·5	30·7

J B WILLIAMS

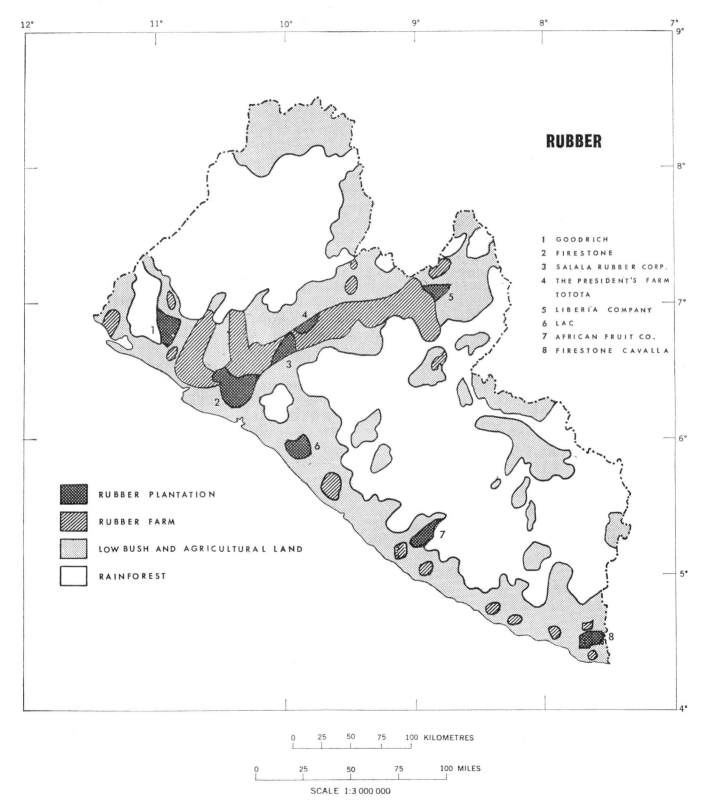

RUBBER

1 GOODRICH
2 FIRESTONE
3 SALALA RUBBER CORP.
4 THE PRESIDENT'S FARM
   TOTOTA
5 LIBERIA COMPANY
6 LAC
7 AFRICAN FRUIT CO.
8 FIRESTONE CAVALLA

RUBBER PLANTATION

RUBBER FARM

LOW BUSH AND AGRICULTURAL LAND

RAINFOREST

0   25   50   75   100 KILOMETRES

0   25   50   75   100 MILES

SCALE 1:3 000 000

35 OIL PALM

The oil palm (*Elaeis guineensis*) is indigenous to West Africa, being found wild in a great number of sites, often in extensive natural stands. The plant is extremely useful, because its clusters of fibrous, fleshy fruit contain a yellow brown oil, commonly known as palm oil. This oil is of basic importance in the daily diet throughout Liberia. In addition in the hinterland palm leaves are used for roofing, basket and mat-making, and the sap of the palm tree, obtained by tapping or cutting off the tree, is used for making the highly popular palm wine. The villagers extract the oil by traditional methods for home use, and it is estimated that over 10 000 tons of palm oil are produced and consumed locally each year. Next to the fruit or pericarp the inner kernel contains a high grade oil, too, but this is difficult to extract by primitive methods. It is therefore customary to export the kernels unprocessed to overseas manufacturing plants.

The oil palm is at least as suited to Liberian soils and climatic conditions as rubber and grows nearly anywhere, and wherever there are people living in the country the palm tree is found. It demands, like rubber, primarily a high rainfall, and is also adapted to the poor, leached soils associated with it. Earlier attempts to grow oil palms within the country on large plantations did not encourage greater efforts, possibly because inferior varieties were used. However, experiments to cultivate the tree by crossing varieties have been quite successful and yielded a much fleshier fruit. The improved oil palm planted today is therefore superior to the native tree.

In an attempt to diversify and modernize agriculture the Liberian Government through the National Production Council started an exploratory oil palm plantation in New Cess, Grand Bassa County, in 1963. Experiments with premium grade scions showed excellent results and indicate that improved oil palms grow well and promise good returns. The pilot plantation soon attracted the attention of private investors, and negotiations with the Getty Oil Exploration and the affiliated Liberian Operations Incorporated, LIBINC, led to the private take-over of the plantation at New Cess in December 1965. The Government agreed to the sale only after being assured that LIBINC would go into large-scale palm oil production. The company obtained about 40 000 acres (16 000 ha.) of land under concession agreement and expects to produce more than 5000 tons of palm oil annually by its peak production period in 1976. The company at present employs 450 Liberians and 3 expatriates. Since labour requirements are about half those needed for rubber and, moreover, the skill required to cut off an oil palm bunch is less than that needed to tap rubber, there should be no problems in obtaining the necessary farm hands, when the $3 million undertaking is scheduled to go into full operation by 1972. A pilot oil processing plant is already in operation and the assembly of a $600 000 plant from Belgium to meet increasing production has started. LIBINC is also fostering the growth and development of several Liberian-owned satellite plantations and smallholdings within the area, providing plants and scions from its large nursery. The oil palm may prove to be better suited to small-scale farms than rubber because production costs are lower, and less work and management skill is required. Since the new port of Buchanan is only 20 miles (32 km.) away from the processing plant, transportation costs within the country will be low.

Another major plantation of some 4000 acres (1600 ha.) was put in operation by the West African Agricultural Company in the vicinity of the Maffa River in Grand Cape Mount County, while a third large project is planned for Maryland County near the Firestone Rubber plantation covering some 7500 acres (3000 ha.). The three plantations will have about 16 000 acres (6500 ha.) under production and by 1981 some 6000 tons for the local market and approximately 15 000 tons of palm oil will be available for export.

The government also sponsors and encourages the private sector to invest in this industry with a view to entering the export market for palm oil. Up to 1968 the Department of Agriculture had distributed at cost 40 000 plants. More than 25 000 improved palm scions have been given to interested farmers alone during the last year. Several nurseries at state experimental farms and the University Farm cultivate high-yielding palms for this purpose.

Apart from palm kernels no oil is at present exported and most of what is produced comes from small farms with native palms. Although the price for palm oil is not encouraging at the present time, it is hoped that the increased world demand for vegetable oils will make the cultivation of oil palm a profitable venture. Exports of palm kernels decreased from 30 million lb. (14 million kg.) in 1967 to 26·6 million lb. (12 million kg.) in 1968. However, because of the changing world market prices the value of kernels exported rose to $1·9 million in 1968 as against $1·8 million during the previous year.

STEFAN VON GNIELINSKI

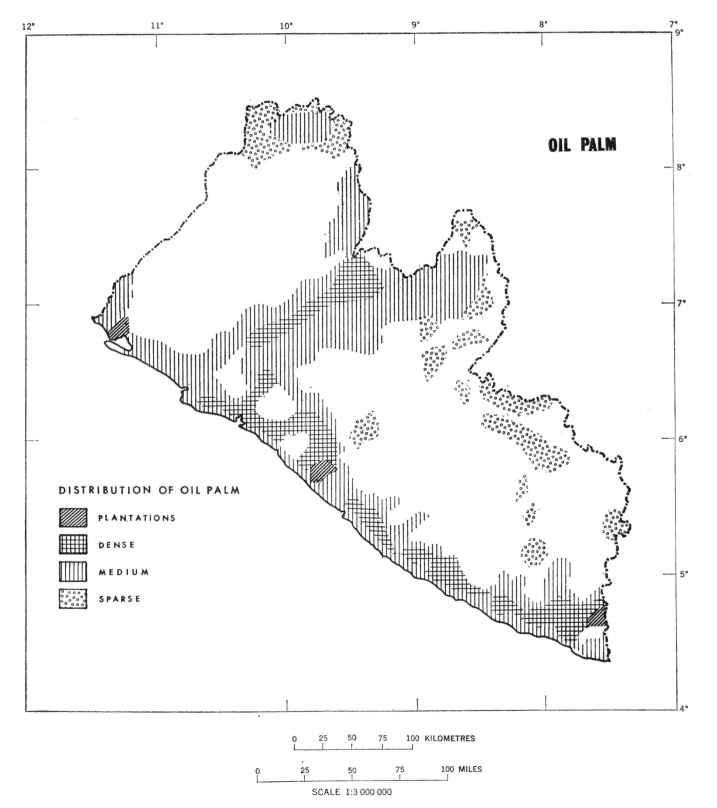

OIL PALM

DISTRIBUTION OF OIL PALM

PLANTATIONS

DENSE

MEDIUM

SPARSE

0   25   50   75   100 KILOMETRES

0   25   50   75   100 MILES

SCALE 1:3 000 000

Following directives issued by President Tubman in 1962 that the Republic of Liberia should be made self-sufficient in her staple diet, the Department of Agriculture made arrangements with the Food and Agricultural Organization (FAO) to formulate a scheme for increasing rice production. As more and more people are drawn away from subsistence farming by increasing opportunities to earn cash by working in the mines and rubber plantations, annual rice production cannot keep pace with the increasing demand. This necessitated greater imports of rice amounting to 50 000 tons at a cost of approximately $8 million during 1969. To offset the annual increase in rice imports, which are estimated at 2000 tons, the authorities are anxious to increase production and thus save foreign exchange for internal development.

Rice, *Oryza sativa*, is by far the most important food crop in Liberia and has been grown here for generations. Rice has many advantages over other crops. It has a high yield, is tasty and nourishing, keeps well, and is easy to store and transport. Rice also tolerates compact and acidic soils and grows in otherwise useless swamps. At present most of the rice grown in the country is of the upland variety planted on dry soil and hilly ground using the bush fallowing system. By this method new fields are cleared year after year, and after the bush is cut, burned, and cleared rice is planted by broadcasting. Only few fields are used more than two years because the soil is quickly exhausted, forcing the farmer to move to another area, and the abandoned plot is allowed to lie fallow for 8 to 10 years to regain its original strength. In many areas hill rice is intercropped with cassava, which is a heavy feeder and exhausts the soil even more.

The existing method of cultivating rice on uplands is considered unproductive and wasteful because every year large areas of high forest are destroyed by it. Since swamp rice has much higher yields and is not accompanied by wasteful agricultural practices such as cutting and burning valuable timber, the Department of Agriculture with the assistance of the FAO and other sources are introducing methods to grow swamp rice in Liberia. Nearly 720 000 acres (288 000 ha.) of fresh-water swamps exist within the country which could be converted into productive rice fields. Provided the right varieties of rice are used, production in these swamps can continue indefinitely with negligible loss of soil fertility. Even more than one crop per year could be obtained, depending on the variety of rice used.

Rice extension programme

The rice extension programme was initiated in 1962. With the help of two FAO experts, the Department of Agriculture conducted field surveys in several areas. The FAO approach was to establish a large number of small simple swamp rice schemes which the farmers can plant and maintain with simple hand methods and tools they are already used to. Several demonstration plots were established, and teaching and on the

job training were carried out. Furthermore, rice production zones in areas that seemed suitable for mechanized rice cultivation were established at the following locations:

1. Bo, Mani and Fandoh in Grand Cape Mount County
2. Korliema near Voinjama in Lofa County
3. Zleh Town (Gbarson District) Grand Gedeh County.

The Central Agricultural Experiment Station in Suakoko placed great emphasis on swamp rice cultivation, and under the supervision of a FAO rice expert more than 200 local and exotic varieties have been tested for comparative yield and disease resistance. Some high yielders like Sokotera, Gissi and Bentoubala have been used for seed multiplication and were distributed to primary seed farmers, among them the President's own farm, as well as to the various rice zones and to private concessions. The University Farm is also engaged in swamp rice research and seed multiplication and many varieties have been grown and tested since 1969 on large, well kept demonstration paddies.

Gbedin Land Development and Rural Improvement Project

This project, also known as the Gbedin Rice Project, was opened up in co-operation with a team of National Chinese rice experts from Taiwan. Their aim is to develop an area of some 3000 acres (1200 ha.) for irrigation agriculture and improved upland farming by training and resettling some 600 families in improved communities. The farmers form co-operatives and work their fields together. Heavy machinery was used for clearing, levelling and dam building. Mostly Chinese rice varieties, but also varieties like Indica and IR8 have been planted, and during 1968 on 140 acres (57 ha.) of paddy 404 700 lb. (182 700 kg.) of rice were harvested, and it has been shown that yields could be increased 50–100% by using these varieties and applying irrigation. Fifty-six farm families have been resettled and trained by the Chinese experts to grow swamp rice and manage their co-operative in processing and marketing their own crops. Similar to the Gbedin project resettlement schemes in Kpain, Nimba County, and Philadelphia and Bonike, Maryland County, were established.

Private concessions

Private enterprise also took an active part in the promotion of swamp rice production. The Firestone Rubber Company within its Community Development Service has grown rice for many years. At present two Chinese rice experts from Taiwan are stationed at Harbel plantation to supervise the project. Next to Firestone, B F Goodrich near Kle, Liberian Industrial Development Company (LIDCO) near Marshall, and the Liberian Agricultural Company (LAC), in Grand Bassa, undertook rice projects of their own. LAC alone planted 104 acres (42 ha.) of swamp rice with varieties from Surinam. Even the Liberian Mining Company at Bomi Hills and the National Iron Ore Company at Mano River cultivate some swamp rice within their concession areas.

During the last two years the Liberian Produce Marketing Corporation (LPMC) started a fully mechanized swamp rice project in the Makona River valley, Lofa County. Since then 1500 acres (600 ha.) have been cleared and nearly 300 acres (120 ha.) stand under crop already.

In September 1969 the West African Rice Development Conference was held in Monrovia under the joint auspices of the UNDP, ECA and FAO. Thirteen states were represented, thus showing the great interest in rice development in West Africa. The conference affirmed its willingness to establish an association for further co-operation.

STEFAN VON GNIELINSKI

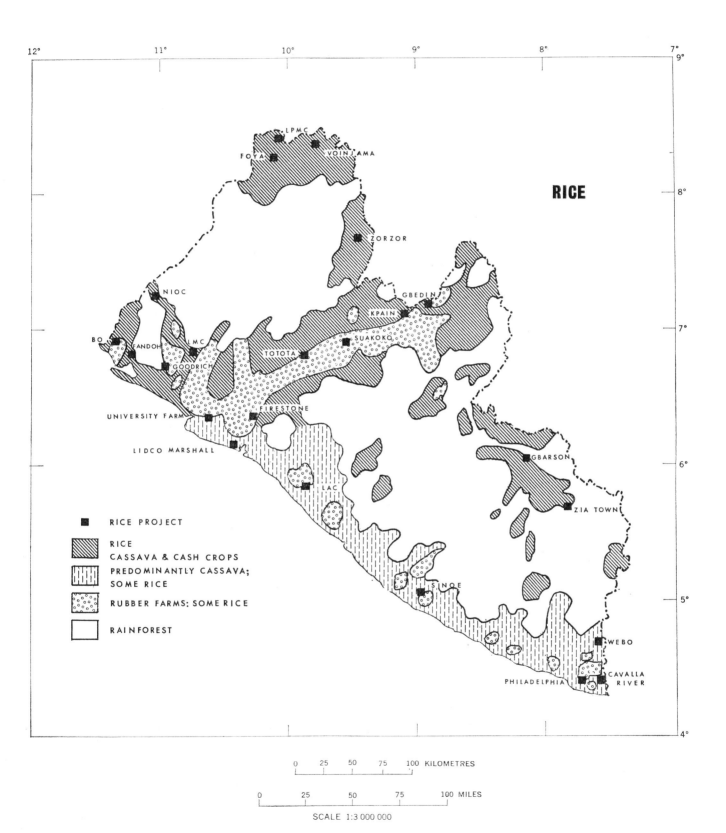

RICE

RICE PROJECT

RICE
CASSAVA & CASH CROPS

PREDOMINANTLY CASSAVA;
SOME RICE

RUBBER FARMS: SOME RICE

RAINFOREST

0 25 50 75 100 KILOMETRES

0 25 50 75 100 MILES

SCALE 1:3 000 000

37 LIVESTOCK

Livestock is found in most villages, and there is no actual lack of protein sources, but meat consumption is very low because cows, sheep, goats, pigs, even chickens and ducks are a traditional sign of material wealth. The acquisition of livestock in rural areas is of paramount importance and the farmer will seldom sell or slaughter his animals. However, the people have no tradition and knowledge of animal husbandry; fowl as well as goats and sheep run free in the villages or in the bush, and the herds of cattle are small in number.

Cattle

Most of the native cattle is of the West African shorthorn variety, or Muturu, and can be found chiefly in the coastal areas between Greenville and Maryland, but also in Bassa and to some extent near Monrovia. Muturu are black and brown dwarf cattle hardly over 4 ft (1·2 m.) tall. In the north the brown and larger longhorned N'dama cattle from Senegal and Guinea have been introduced by the Mandingos. The tsetse-fly precludes keeping other cattle except these dwarf species, which have very low weight – hardly over 500 lb. (225 kg.) – and are very poor milkers, but with proper selective breeding they might increase weight and milking yields. They are adapted to the climate, accustomed to natural foraging, and resistant to tropical diseases.

First research trials to improve herds by controlled breeding were successfully carried out by Firestone. They also conducted plant experiments with selective grasses suited for local conditions with good results. The College of Agriculture which took over the herd from Firestone two years ago is continuing this programme of herd development at the University Farm. Emphasis is placed not only on cross-breeding N'dama with Brown Swiss and Jerseys, but also on pasture development and ranch management practice. The Suakoko Experiment Station of the Department of Agriculture and the Liberian Agricultural Company (LAC) in co-operation with US AID are other bases of stock producing and distribution. They also provide practical training facilities to give on-the-job training in animal husbandry, sanitation and feeding, and pasture management.

A few leading farmers began building up herds of N'dama cattle and started pasture development as well, but all in all the total number of cattle is estimated to be only 4–5000 head. The northern savanna between Voinjama and Kolahun is particularly suitable for rearing cattle, but the south-eastern areas can also support cattle, and herds of some 100 000 head would seem a quite realistic proposition. At present much cattle is driven from Guinea and Mali across the border to the slaughterhouse in Monrovia.

Pigs

The native pigs are small in size and reach a maximum weight of little over 100 lb. (45 kg.). Experiments in Suakoko in crossbreeding native sows with imported hogs were quite successful. They could be raised profitably on locally grown feeds. Several farmers have gone into commercial production and have imported hogs of superior breeds – Duroc Jersey and Hampshire – to cross with native stock. The Department of Agriculture has listed 28 commercial farms with a stock of approximately 3500 pigs.

Poultry

Poultry farming has been established on a commercial scale using imported chicks from USA, Holland and Israel. The White Leghorn is the most common breed, but Rhode Island Red, New Hampshire, Light Sussex, etc. are also represented. The ubiquitous native breed is small and skinny, and a very poor layer. Early in 1960 there were only 5 poultry farms, but their number increased to over 30 in 1963 with about 45 000 layers and an average flock size of 1 500 per farm.

During the following years the commercial poultry population increased at a rate of 10 000 per annum amounting to some 110 000 laying hens in 1970. Egg production has doubled to an estimated 15 million eggs per year during the same time. A tendency for large-size farms developed and the number of farms decreased to some 20, with 7 farms having a 10 000 layer-unit or bigger. Firestone Plantation Company, once a pioneer in poultry raising and a major egg producer, has since abandoned activities in favour of independent farmers. The broiler production is the most recent phase of poultry-industry and several farms raise both layers and broilers. Most of the commercial poultry flocks are located around Monrovia within a radius of some 50 miles (80 km.), but several large farms are situated in the vicinity of other major towns and mining concession areas, and fresh eggs and poultry of high quality are available on the market throughout the year.

Sheep and goats

Next to poultry, sheep and goats have the widest distribution because they are hardy and can subsist on leaves and the limited grass pasture available. They are also small in size, some 25–35 lb. (11–15 kg.), and have short wool which is never shorn, but their possession is valued as exchange objects. LAMCO has introduced some rabbits, but so far only on a very limited scale, to supply workers with additional protein food.

Efforts are being made by the government to increase meat production. The Department of Agriculture, next to stockbreeding, is helping the farmers to increase and improve stocks by providing advisory and veterinary services, importing betteryielding strains of cattle, pigs and poultry, and making grants of equipment and initial stock. The veterinary services are engaged in an inoculation programme against endemic diseases and the Entomology Division has increased activities on insect control. The possibilities of providing animal feeds from locally grown plants are being investigated. The future will bring a potential supply from palm products (palm kernel cake), rice bran, bagasse, etc., because the production of concentrated feed containing protein, vitamins, minerals, etc. is an essential condition for increasing Liberian livestock.

STEFAN VON GNIELINSKI

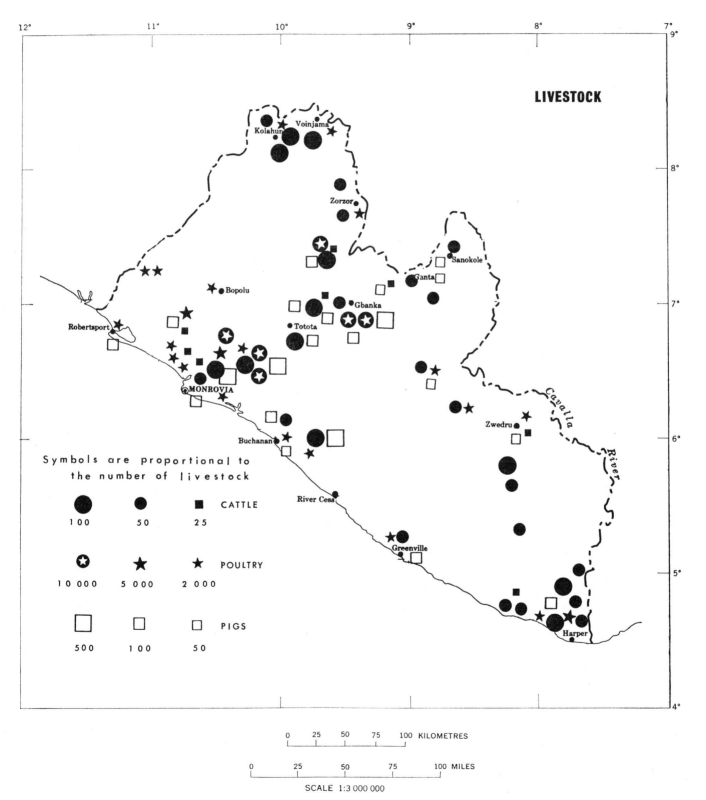

LIVESTOCK

Kolahun
Voinjama
Zorzor
Sanokole
Ganta
Bopolu
Gbanka
Totota
Robertsport
MONROVIA
Zwedru
Buchanan
River Cess
Greenville
Harper
Cavalla
River

Symbols are proportional to
the number of livestock

● ● ■ CATTLE
100 50 25

⊛ ★ ★ POULTRY
10 000 5 000 2 000

▢ ◻ ◻ PIGS
500 100 50

| 0 | 25 | 50 | 75 | 100 | KILOMETRES |

| 0 | 25 | 50 | 75 | 100 MILES |

SCALE 1:3 000 000

Hunting and fishing are among the oldest occupations of the Liberian people. They practise them wherever it is possible, and fishing especially is for many a chief occupation. Since game and livestock are scarce, fish provides the main source of protein food. Therefore, the development of the fishing industry and the adequate distribution of fish into all parts of the country must be a matter of concern.

Along the 350 mile (560 km.) coast of the country are many fishing villages mainly occupied by the Kru fishermen. The Kru still adhere to their traditional fishing techniques using hooks and lines and small dugout canoes capable of accommodating 1–3 men. The long-line fishing is conducted along the entire coast of Liberia. Species of fish caught are mackerel (*Scomber colias*), pike (*Sphyraena gauchancho*), barracuda (*Sphyraena* sp.), snapper (*Pagrus ehrenbergi*), gripper (*Lutjanus*), and cavalla (*Trachinotus*), etc. Because of their primitive methods and the large amount of bait needed, this type of fishery hardly exceeds the subsistence level. The Kru therefore often engage in farming, cultivating cassava, yams, rice and other crops to improve their living standard.

The Fante, the other large group of fishermen, first came to Liberia some 40 years ago. They originate from Ghana and can now be found all along the coast where they have established distinctive settlements of their own alongside the larger places like Monrovia, Cape Mount, Buchanan etc., next to the existing villages of the Kru and other Liberian people. They contribute to the indigenous fishery by introducing not only better craft, mostly fitted with outboard motors, but also improved techniques of fishing. The Fante always work together in groups. They use ali (ring) nets generally exceeding 200 yds (180 m.) in length, corked at the top and leaded at the base, which reach to a depth of over 25 ft (8 m.). Their canoes are often 30 ft (9 m.) long, stable and seaworthy and accommodate 6–12 men. Their catches include bonga (*Ethmalosa fimbriata*), herring (*Sardinella aurita* and *Sardinella cameronensis*) – in Liberia called 'bony' – butternose (*Larimus peli*), cassava fish (*Cynoscion senegalla*) – all in all 32 species. The majority of the catches are sold fresh directly to the consumer by the fish 'mammies', but some fish is also sun-dried, smoked or cured in salt and carried inland.

Another very small group of fishermen, the Popo, immigrated from Togo. They settled in the Monrovia area and probably introduced the method of beach seine fishing. Today it has become a general practice that some enterprising Liberians buy nets and boats, hire a crew of fishermen to do the work, and finally share the profit on a 50:50 basis. The best season for this type of fishing is from July to November. During this period fish is abundant in the muddy waters near the estuaries, and catches ranging up to 600 lb. (270 kg.) per net are not uncommon.

Freshwater fishing is carried out in all parts of Liberia. However, only in few rivers is fishing more than a small-scale enterprise serving more than local needs. Unlike sea-fishing, river-fishing is done almost as much by women as it is by men. It is practised by using small nets, fish weirs and traps, baskets, as well as hooks and lines. Many rivers are overfished, and catches are generally small and fish is expensive in village markets, except where frozen fish has become available. In order to increase the protein food of the rural population the Department of Agriculture has introduced fish 'farming'. At present over 60 fish ponds stocked with mangrove perch (*Tilapia*) and red bellies (*Pelmato chromis*) have been established throughout the country, but particularly in the Bong, Lofa and Nimba counties, and their annual yields exceed 50 tons of fish.

First efforts to start fishing on a commercial scale were made during the late thirties, but not until 1962 was the first commercial fishery enterprise, the Mesurado Fishing Company (Mesufish), established by the former Secretary of Agriculture, Stephen A Tolbert, and other Liberian and foreign shareholders, and promoted by the Liberian Government. Since 1964 the company has owned a modern cold store with a fish processing plant with a capacity of 1500 tons located next to the freeport of Monrovia. A small, but effective fleet of modern trawlers, equipped with freezing and packing facilities, chartered by the company, land more than 10 000 tons of fish per year, not including the large quantities of tuna which are landed for transhipment overseas by Japanese, Korean and, since November 1969, Nationalist Chinese fishermen. These vessels are able to reach the better fishing grounds which lie over 150 miles (240 km.) from the Liberian coast, and even sail as far as Las Palmas and Spain to participate in the catch of crustaceans, such as crayfish, crab, prawns and shrimps, which are usually exported to the United States of America and Europe. As soon as road conditions permitted, Mesufish erected 15 smaller cold stores in the hinterland with a total capacity of 500 tons, which are regularly supplied with frozen fish by refrigerated trucks.

Exact production figures of the fishing industry are not available, but estimated figures for 1968 were 18 000 tons. The landings of Mesufish amounted to 10 000 tons, while the subsistence fishery produced about 5–6000 tons, leaving some smaller enterprises with some 2–3000 tons. Since its establishment the Liberian commercial fishing industry has developed remarkably; consequently it becomes increasingly difficult for the Kru people to compete with the modern motorized fleet, and even for the Fante the margin of profit has been narrowing in recent seasons. To overcome this competition they will be forced to adapt new methods, use better gear and craft, and organize co-operatives. With the active help and guidance of the Bureau of Fisheries this can be achieved. The combined efforts of the commercial and subsistence fishery will provide the means to supply the people of Liberia with the required protein food from the sea.

STEFAN VON GNIELINSKI

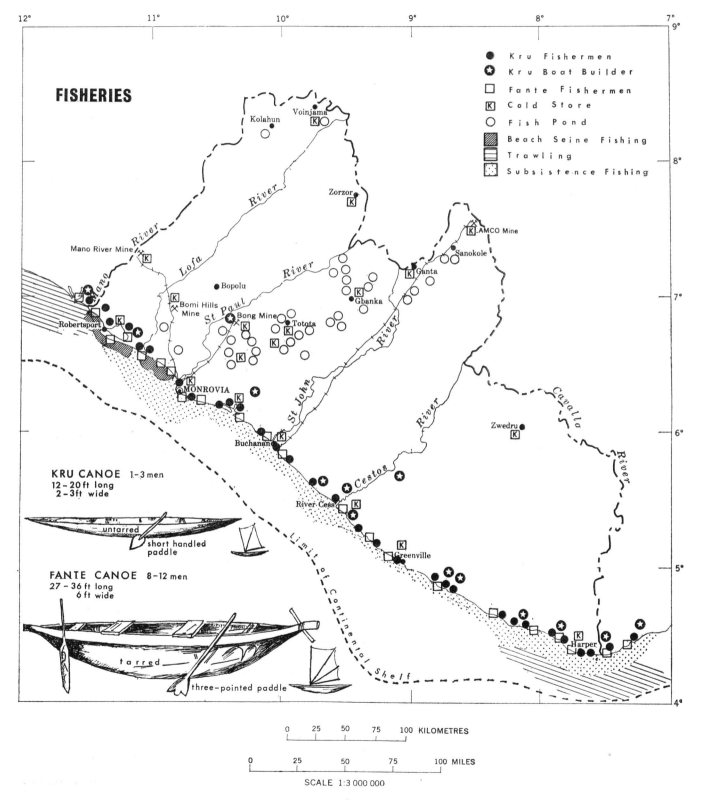

FISHERIES

Legend:
- ● Kru Fishermen
- ★ Kru Boat Builder
- □ Fante Fishermen
- K Cold Store
- ○ Fish Pond
- ▨ Beach Seine Fishing
- ▤ Trawling
- ⣿ Subsistence Fishing

KRU CANOE 1–3 men
12–20 ft long
2–3 ft wide

untarred
short handled paddle

FANTE CANOE 8–12 men
27–36 ft long
6 ft wide

tarred
three-pointed paddle

Kolahun
Voinjama
Zorzor
AMCO Mine
Mano River Mine
Sanokole
Bopolu
Ganta
Bomi Hills Mine
Gbanka
Robertsport
Bong Mine
Totota
MONROVIA
Buchanan
Zwedru
River Cess
Greenville
Harper

Mano River
Lofa River
St Paul River
St John River
Cestos River
Cavalla River

Limit of Continental Shelf

```
0    25   50   75   100  KILOMETRES

0      25      50      75      100  MILES

SCALE 1:3 000 000
```

39 THE FOREST ESTATE

The entire land area of Liberia was probably once covered with virgin high forest; however, because of shifting cultivation, dry season fires and other reasons this virgin high forest has disappeared. Nowadays the estimated area still covered with high forest is only one-third of the country; the rest is occupied by farms and settlements, lagoons, rivers and swamps, savannas and young and old secondary forests. An estimated 50 000 acres (20 000 ha.) of useful timber have been destroyed by farmers year after year. The Liberian Government has for some time realized the value of the timber resources and has tried to protect them. However, because of the inaccessibility of the country, no control was possible to enforce rules and regulations concerning the use of forests. It was therefore only recently that effective measures could be taken. In 1953 the Liberian Forest Conservation Act was passed. This act was followed by a supplemental act in 1957. Section IV of the Forest Conservation Act empowers the Government to control and manage the publicly owned lands 'to their most productive use for the permanent good of the whole people, considering both direct and indirect forest values, and to stop needless waste and destruction of forest and associated resources'.

Immediately after the Forest Conservation Act was passed, the Bureau of Forest Conservation was established in the Department of Agriculture. In 1959 a number of National Forests were established.

The Liberian National Forests

North Lorma	=	233 000 acres	(1 acre = 0·4047 ha.)
Lorma	=	107 500 ,,	
South Belle	=	164 300 ,,	
Nimba	=	110 000 ,,	
Gio and Gio North	=	93 000 ,,	
Gbi	=	150 700 ,,	
Grebo	=	643 300 ,,	
Sapo	=	378 000 ,,	
Krahn-Bassa	=	1 270 000 ,,	
Kpelle	=	432 000 ,,	
Gola	=	511 500 ,,	
Gola (Yoma)	=	36 700 ,,	
Total area	=	4 130 000 ,,	

The National Forests have a total area of 4·13 million acres or roughly 6500 sq. miles (16 835 sq. km.). Initially there was the Vai National Forest in Cape Mount County comprising an additional area of nearly 200 000 acres (80 940 ha.), but this forest project has since been abandoned.

The National Forests are administered by the government and will be used for industrial development. No agriculture is allowed within their boundaries, which have been surveyed and are regularly patrolled. Some mining companies like Lamco in Yekepa (Nimba National Forest) and the Liberian Mining Company in Bomi Hills (Gola-Yoma National Forest) have, by special arrangement with the government, been granted permission to utilize parts of these forests for necessary timber.

From 1960 to 1967 the Bureau of Forest Conservation in co-operation with the German Forest Mission made an inventory of all existing National Forests. During the seven years survey, field trips, botanical and utilization studies and inventories were made and gave an impression of the timber resources of the country and their exploitability. More than 235 species of trees have been classified. At least 60 are in marketable quantities, although only 11 of them are known on the world market, among them very valuable stands of mahogany, African walnut, makere, etc. The final results are laid down in the 12 volumes of the report of the German Forest Mission.

Commercial exploitation of timber resources outside the National Forests is a recent development. Concessions were granted to two timber companies in 1960, and the first export shipment of logs began in 1961. Thereafter, production gradually increased to some 15 to 16 million board ft per annum. During the last few years an increasing number of foreign and Liberian companies have become interested in utilizing the rich Liberian forests, since the remaining reserves of timber in other West African countries are becoming increasingly difficult to exploit.

Two recent developments offer promising possibilities of opening up the Liberian forest: the construction of the roads from the interior (Zwedru) to the ports of Greenville and Harper, and the LAMCO railway from Nimba to Buchanan. These improvements of the infrastructure provide outlets to the sea for timber products and will enhance the feasibility of large-scale commercial projects. At present an area of more than 5 million acres (2 million ha.) of forest has been made available to timber concessions and 19 saw-mills are in operation, 5 of which produce 75% of the total output in sawn timber. In 1968 more than 20 million board ft were produced with a total export of 10 million board ft and about 11 million board ft used for sawn timber. The export value of logs and timber rose from $1 461 200 in 1968 to $6 940 397 in 1969. The total revenue amounted to $487 465 in 1969 as against $243 000 in the previous year.

The lumber companies are mostly working in the eastern parts of the country using the ports of Greenville and Harper; so far only a small proportion of timber is shipped from Buchanan, but an increase is expected this year. Furthermore, the Maryland Logging Company is planning to extend its operation in the Harper area by establishing a wood-processing factory with facilities for producing plywood and hardboard.

Forestry development needs trained people and those people are available in Liberia. In 1955 the College of Forestry at the University of Liberia was founded with foreign assistance. Since 1959, 56 students under the supervision of FAO experts have completed the four-year courses in forestry and silvi-culture and related fields, including some practical training at the University Forest and Nurseries, and have received a Bachelor of Forestry degree. Several graduates have since been awarded higher degrees in the USA, Germany and the United Kingdom. The rest were taken up by the Department of Agriculture and by private firms. They are all serving their country and help to make optimum use of nature's fortune in Liberia.

J W A JANSEN

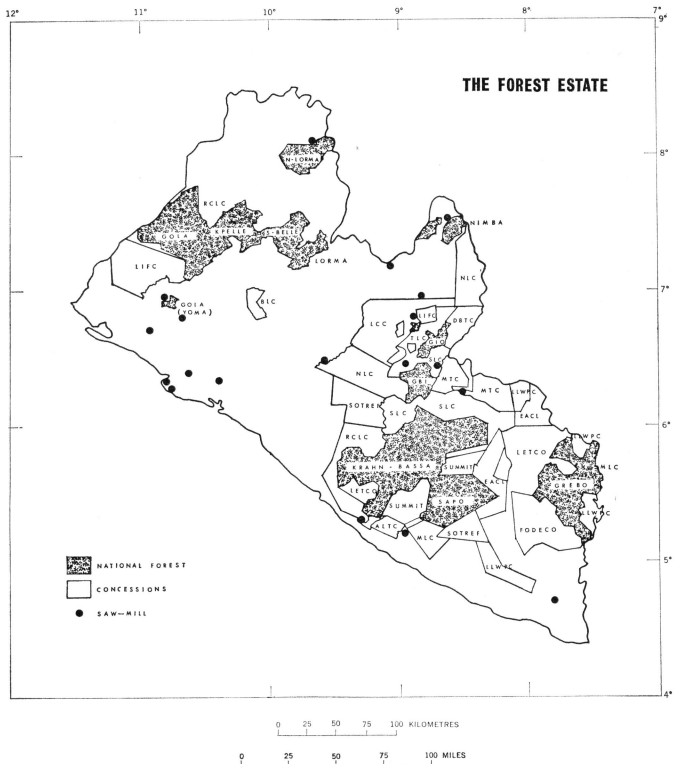

THE FOREST ESTATE

N-LORMA

RCLC

GOLA   KPELLE   S-BELLE

LIFC   LORMA

NIMBA

NLC

GOLA
(YOMA)

BLC

LCC   LIFC   DBTC

TLC   GIO

SLC

NLC   GBI   MTC

MTC   LLWPC

SOTRER   EACL

SLC   SLC

RCLC   WPC

KRAHN - BASSA   SUMMIT   LETCO   MLC

LETCO   EACL   GREBO

SUMMIT   SAPO   LLWPC

ALTC   SOTREF   FODECO

MLC

LLWPC

NATIONAL FOREST

CONCESSIONS

● SAW—MILL

0   25   50   75   100 KILOMETRES

0   25   50   75   100 MILES

SCALE 1:3 000 000

85

40 MINERAL RESOURCES

A large portion of Liberia's wealth is derived from its mineral resources. In addition to iron ore, diamonds and gold, a variety of other economic minerals have been discovered and evaluated by geological surveying teams from Liberia, the USA, and the United Nations while implementing a joint programme of geologic mapping and mineral exploration. Mineral discoveries have also been made by the W H Mueller Company within their concession area in south-east Liberia.

Those minerals which have been appraised and are indicative of good prospects include the following:

Barite – More than 13 vein deposits in the Gibi area, Salala District, with an estimated reserve between 1 and 2 million tons.

Kyanite – Estimated reserves of 2·66 million tons exist in deposits at Mt Montro, Grand Bassa County.

Ceramic Clay – Approximately 8 million tons exist in the New Georgia area near Monrovia.

Silica sand – Estimated reserves of 110 million tons are found in the Monrovia region.

Manganese is found near Zorzor, Lofa County.

Bauxite is found near Kolahun, Lofa County and Kaloke, Maryland County.

Cassiterite (tin) has been discovered in the railroad area about 62 miles (100 km.) from Buchanan.

Chromite has been discovered near the Nimba Range.

Beach sands and stream concentrates contain important amounts of heavy minerals including ilmenite, monazite, zircon, chromium-bearing minerals, magnetite, rutile, kyanite, sillimanite, and corundum.

Gold and diamonds are being mined for local use and for export. Individual miners are engaged in extracting these minerals by hand methods from streams and river beds in various parts of the country.

Several diamond concessions are employing more systematic and productive methods of alluvial mining by mechanical means. Kimberlite, the source rock of most diamonds, has been discovered in three different areas in western Liberia.

There has been a decline in gold production in recent years as increasing numbers of small miners engage in the diamond industry which yields more profits. In 1969, miners sold approximately 1135·77 ounces of gold to the Bank of Monrovia and to local jewellers. During the same period a total of 745 948·45 metric carats of diamonds were produced at a value of $8 168 974·34.

Interpretation of data resulting from the recent airborne geophysical survey of Liberia has indicated the presence of off-shore sedimentary basins which may contain petroleum. Liberia's coastline is one of the missing links in the offshore oil chain of West Africa. The Government of Liberia has granted concession rights to several interested foreign oil companies for detailed exploration of certain areas on the continental shelf.

A E NYEMA JONES

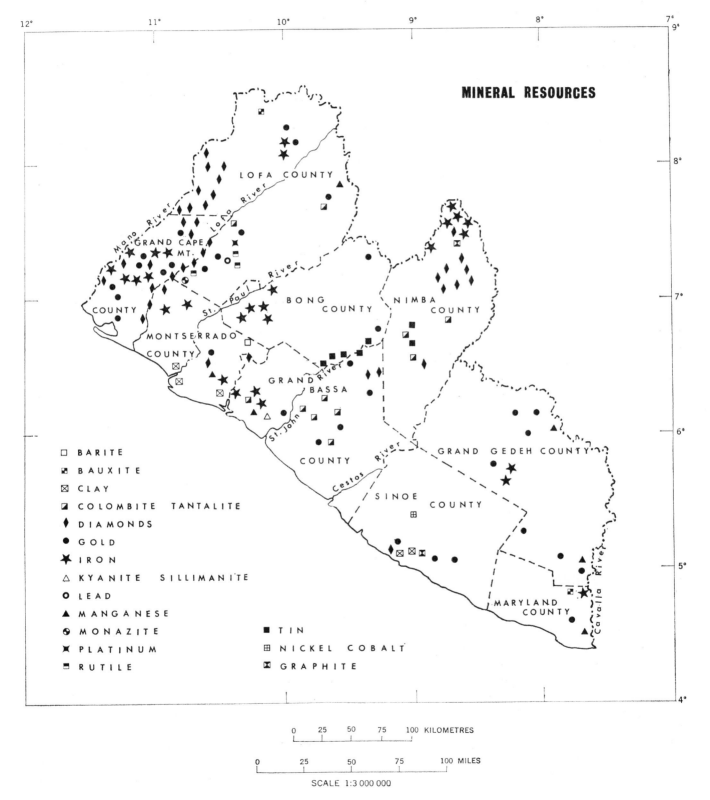

MINERAL RESOURCES

LOFA COUNTY

GRAND CAPE MT.

COUNTY

MONTSERRADO COUNTY

BONG COUNTY

NIMBA COUNTY

GRAND BASSA

COUNTY

GRAND GEDEH COUNTY

SINOE COUNTY

MARYLAND COUNTY

Mano River
Lofa River
St. Paul River
St. John River
Cestos River
Cavalla River

☐ BARITE
▧ BAUXITE
⊠ CLAY
◩ COLOMBITE TANTALITE
◆ DIAMONDS
● GOLD
✶ IRON
△ KYANITE SILLIMANITE
○ LEAD
▲ MANGANESE
✹ MONAZITE
✻ PLATINUM
▤ RUTILE

■ TIN
⊞ NICKEL COBALT
⊠ GRAPHITE

0   25   50   75   100 KILOMETRES

0   25   50   75   100 MILES

SCALE 1:3 000 000

41 IRON ORE

The mining of Liberia's iron ore deposits contributes substantially to its economy. This country produces approximately 40 % of Africa's output of iron ore, thus rating it the largest producer on the African continent and the fourth largest in the world production of iron ore.

The Liberian iron ores consist mainly of haematite, magnetite and itabirite with pure iron content varying from 35 to 70%. The average high grade ore contains approximately 66% pure iron. Total reserves of ore deposits near the coast and the interior of the country are estimated to be in the neighbourhood of one thousand million tons.

Located about 50 miles (80 km.) north-west of Monrovia is the Bomi Hills deposit which was the first iron ore deposit to be discovered. The first shipment of iron ore from this mine was made by the Liberian Mining Company in June 1951. Since then a total of about 40 000 000 tons of processed ore has been shipped to Holland, Great Britain, West Germany, Italy, France, Japan and the United States of America. A beneficiation plant (concentrator) completed in April 1958 accounts for over 10 000 000 long tons of concentrates included in the above figure.

The largest iron ore deposit in Liberia is located at Mount Nimba, 214 miles (342 km.) from Monrovia, near the Guinea and Ivory Coast border. This deposit is being mined by LAMCO (Liberian American-Swedish Minerals Company). At the time LAMCO made its first iron shipment in April 1963, total reserves were estimated to be 250 million tons of high grade haematite ore yielding 65 to 69% pure iron. In addition, there is a considerable amount of low grade ore.

Other iron ore deposits of lower grade occur in the Mano River Hills near the Sierra Leone border and in the Bong Range, 50 miles (80 km.) north-east of Monrovia. The estimated reserves of iron ore at the time production began were 50 million tons in the Mano River Mine, and about 250 million tons in the Bong Mine yielding 35 to 45% pure iron. The National Iron Ore Company, which is partly Liberian owned, is mining the Mano River deposit, while the Bong Range, which went into production in April 1965, is being developed by DELIMCO (German Liberian Mining Company).

Extensive iron deposits also exist in the Putu Range of Grand Gedeh County, the Bea Mountains in Grand Cape Mount County and the Wologizi Range in Lofa County. Detailed appraisal of these deposits has been undertaken by the Bong Mining Company, the Liberian Mining Company, and the Liberian Iron and Steel Corporation (LISCO), respectively.

In 1969 the four giant mining companies with highly sophisticated processing complexes exported a total of 21 337 421 long tons of iron ore as follows:

Liberian Mining Company (Bomi Hills)	2 442 000 tons
National Iron Ore Company (Mano River)	3 926 832 ,,
DELIMCO – Bong Mining Company (Bong Mine)	4 050 439 ,,
LAMCO J V Operating Company (Nimba County)	10 918 150 ,,

Included in LAMCO's total export figure are 1 434 670 tons of pellets, produced by the company's $51 million pelletizing plant established in 1964. A second pelletizing plant in the country with a design capacity of 2 million tons a year is currently under construction by the Bong Mining Company.

Continued increase in production and export of iron ore is expected in future as other iron deposits such as those at the Putu Range, Bea Mountains and Wologizi Range enter the production stage.

A E NYEMA JONES

42 LABOUR FORCE

A primary factor determining the economic growth of a country is the availability of manpower for the increasingly complex tasks required by accelerated development. Since manpower in association with capital and natural resources forms the basis of all gainful activities, the government, recognizing the need to assess the available labour force, put up a manpower information programme during the last quarter of 1967. Early in 1968 the Department of Planning and Economic Affairs with the assistance of the National Labour Affairs Agency established a manpower survey. According to this survey 411 800 persons out of the total population of 1·1 million Liberians claimed to work. The economically active population comprises some 263 600 males and 148 200 females.

About 80% of the working population are engaged in agriculture and forestry, mostly on the subsistence level, and only a small percentage participates in the money economy. There is a great overlap between self-employment and wage labour because many of the farmers and fishermen seek temporary jobs to earn some cash for special purposes, while others who are primarily wage-earners engage in agriculture to raise some of the family's food requirements or to supplement their income.

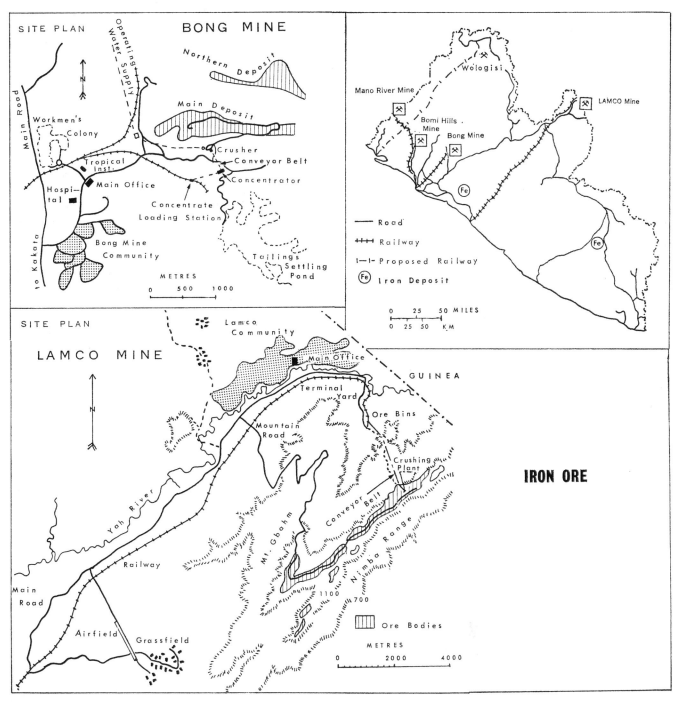

SITE PLAN

BONG MINE

Operating Water Supply

Northern Deposit

Main Deposit

Main Road

Workmen's Colony

Tropical Inst.

Crusher

Conveyor Belt

Concentrator

Hospital

Main Office

Concentrate Loading Station

to Kakata

Bong Mine Community

Tailings Settling Pond

METRES

0   500   1000

Mano River Mine

Wologisi

LAMCO Mine

Bomi Hills Mine

Bong Mine

Fe

Fe

Fe

——— Road

+++ Railway

ı–ı– Proposed Railway

(Fe) Iron Deposit

0   25   50 MILES

0 25 50   K.M.

SITE PLAN

LAMCO MINE

Lamco Community

Main Office

Terminal Yard

Mountain Road

GUINEA

Ore Bins

Crushing Plant

IRON ORE

Yah River

Railway

Conveyor Belt

Mt. Gbahm

Nimba Range

1100

700

Main Road

Airfield

Grassfield

Ore Bodies

METRES

0   2000   4000

89

The first table shows the established number of salary and wage-earners in the various counties of Liberia:

Employment by Counties 1968

Public and Private Sector

County	No. of workers	%	Private Sec.	Public Sec.
1. Montserrado	47 873	64·2	34 409	13 464
(Monrovia)	(27 954)	(37)	(15 632)	(12 322)
2. Maryland	5 539	7·4	3 961	1 578
3. Grand Bassa	5 223	7·0	4 389	834
4. Nimba	4 860	6·5	4 042	818
5. Bong	3 312	4·5	2 743	569
6. Sinoe	2 378	3·2	1 381	997
7. Cape Mount	2 283	3·1	1 882	401
8. Lofa	1 862	2·5	1 011	851
9. Grand Gedeh	1 242	1·6	854	388
All Counties	74 572	100	54 672	19 900

Source: Department of Planning and Economic Affairs

In June 1968 a total of 74 572 persons were full time employees on wages or salary, 54 672 in the private sector and 19 900 for the government, including the police force and some 1300 persons in the foreign service. This represents a large increase over previous years, as compared to the probably not much over 30 000 wage-earners of the 1950's, most of whom were employed by the Firestone Plantation Company. The survey also revealed that 37% of all people employed work in Monrovia and 64·2% in Montserrado County. Maryland followed with 7·4%, Grand Bassa with 7·0% of the labour force, while employment opportunities in the remaining counties were still lower.

Again the largest number of wage-earners were found in the field of agriculture with some 24 000 employees, mainly working with private concessions like Firestone, Goodrich, African Fruit Company, Liberian Agricultural Company and others, or working for the timber concessions and saw-mills. Approximately 14 500 persons work in mines and quarries, more than 11 035 of whom have found employment in the four iron ore mining companies. Other trades like services, industry, general trading and commerce, transportation as well as building industries, including road construction, account for the rest.

The opening of the iron ore mines constitutes, next to the Firestone Rubber Plantations, who made the first attempt to develop Liberia's human resources, the second large-scale industrial enterprise in the country. The impact on society was marked and can best be recognized by the study of the ethnic differentiation of the labour force employed at the different mines, as shown in the table below.

The occupational structure of the work force is as follows: the bulk of manpower is unskilled or semi-skilled and of a high mobility. There is actually no acute labour shortage; on the contrary, there is large unemployment of unskilled male and female labour, especially in Monrovia. On the other hand, there is a growing demand for many kinds of high-level manpower and the shortage of engineers, agronomists, accountants, scientists, educators, etc. has been recognized as a major obstacle to the progress of the country. Here employment opportunities are quite good. The same is true for the qualified competent middle-level workers, including primary school teachers, foremen, the technical aids supporting the high-level skills, and the whole corps of the 'white collar workers': draughtsmen, laboratory technicians, nurses, clerical and sales workers, and many tradesmen. At present, the professional people are still mainly aliens working in the country.

In order to meet the growing demand, a long range scholarship programme should be intensified for the high and middle level manpower. Vocational training and apprenticeship training should be encouraged as well as careful selection of workers for on-the-job training schemes. Here the co-operation of the industrial enterprises with the education system has already proved to be most beneficial in the preparation and development of highly skilled labour.

Number and ethnic origin of people employed in the Iron Ore Mines (March 1970)

	LMC	BONG	NIOC	LAMCO	LAMCO (Port)	Total
1. Bassa	210	133	168	191	773	1475
2. Belle	30	18	20	6	4	78
3. Dei	15	5	12	—	—	32
4. Gbandi	118	97	96	22	27	360
5. Gio	32	38	34	215	18	337
6. Gola	365	73	397	43	28	906
7. Grebo	165	167	117	228	85	762
8. Kissi	245	133	180	59	28	645
9. Kpelle	305	512	96	211	98	1222
10. Krahn	63	29	42	101	24	259
11. Kru	226	125	212	96	188	847
12. Loma	326	202	88	142	43	801
13. Mandingo	28	84	28	82	15	237
14. Mano	41	34	41	635	55	806
15. Mende	62	41	11	7	7	128
16. Vai	149	102	214	88	57	610
17. Others	15	19	17	208	22	281
18. Other Africans	30	52	13	24	5	124
19. Expatriates	132	310	131	312	240	1125
Total:	2557	2174	1917	2670	1717	11 035

STEFAN VON GNIELINSKI

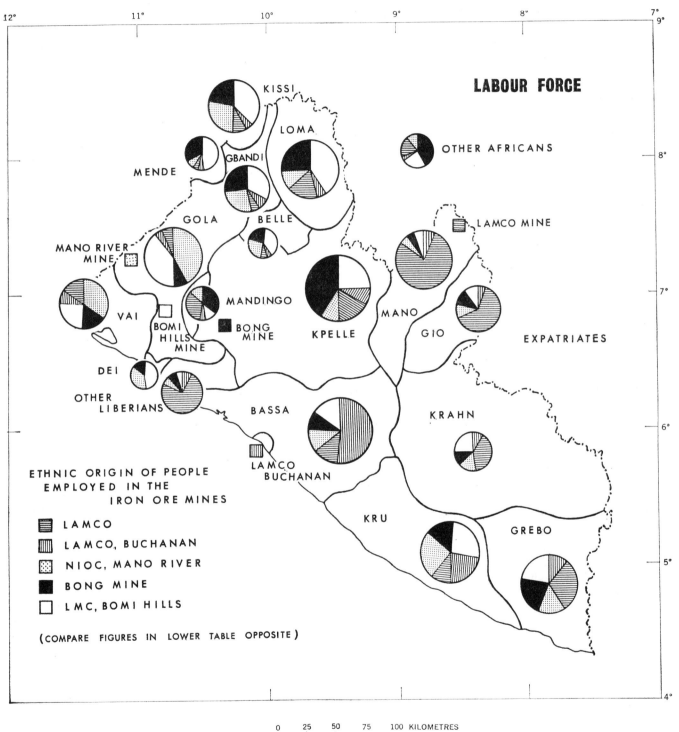

LABOUR FORCE

KISSI

LOMA

OTHER AFRICANS

MENDE

GBANDI

GOLA

BELLE

LAMCO MINE

MANO RIVER
MINE

MANO

VAI

BOMI
HILLS
MINE

MANDINGO

BONG
MINE

KPELLE

GIO

EXPATRIATES

DEI

OTHER
LIBERIANS

BASSA

KRAHN

LAMCO
BUCHANAN

ETHNIC ORIGIN OF PEOPLE
EMPLOYED IN THE
IRON ORE MINES

KRU

GREBO

LAMCO

LAMCO, BUCHANAN

NIOC, MANO RIVER

BONG MINE

LMC, BOMI HILLS

(COMPARE FIGURES IN LOWER TABLE OPPOSITE)

0   25   50   75   100 KILOMETRES

0   25   50   75   100 MILES

SCALE 1:3 000 000

43 ELECTRIC POWER AND WATER SUPPLY

For some time the Government of Liberia has considered an abundant, economical and reliable supply of electric power and water as a most significant condition for economic development. The shortage of energy and water has been the main obstacle to industrial expansion. Therefore, the extension of public utilities has occupied top priority in the overall development programme. The country's wide and well-branched river system provides an impressive hydro-electric potential that has been estimated at several hundred thousand kW.

Electric power

Since 1959 the Public Utilities Authority (PUA), an autonomous public corporation, has been responsible for generating and supplying electricity to Monrovia and the larger towns. Initially the PUA ran three diesel generating plants in Monrovia with an installed capacity of 6280 kW and one small plant each in Robertsport, Buchanan, Harper and Greenville. The larger concessions, such as the iron ore mines and rubber plantations, provide their own generating facilities. The first hydro-electric power plant with a capacity of 4200 kW was constructed by the Firestone Plantation Company on the Farmington River at Harbel. Apart from this, more than 320 private diesel generators are operated throughout the country by saw-mills, plantations and missions. The total capacity of these private plants far exceeded that of the Power Authority; in fact, until 1963, two of the mining companies sold electricity to the PUA when it was unable to meet public demand. During 1965 the total generating power of all plants exceeded 75 000 kW; today the seven diesel generators of the Bong Mine alone have a capacity of over 60 000 kW.

In 1966, a significant increase in the power production took place when the Mount Coffee Hydro-electric Scheme was completed in its initial stage and started to operate. The construction of this $29 million project started in mid-1964 on the St Paul River at Mount Coffee, 25 miles (40 km.) north-west of Monrovia.

The project was financed by a loan provided by the US Agency for International Development amounting to $24 300 000, while the balance was paid by the Government of Liberia. The scheme consists of four reinforced earth and rock dams and a one-gated spillway. With a drainage area of 8260 sq. miles (21 400 sq. km.) it has an impounded water reservoir of over 2000 acres (800 ha.), the main dam having a length of 2030 ft (620 m.) and a height of 73 ft (22 m.). The powerhouse has an intake of six turbines and generating units. At present two turbine generators with a total maximum capacity of 34 000 kW are installed, but the project will eventually include four additional turbo-generators, each with a 17 MW rating, and the total maximum capacity envisaged will be over 100 000 kW. Cross-country 69 000 volt transmission lines carry power to sub-stations at Bushrod Island and Capitol Hill in Monrovia, Bomi Hills, Goodrich Plantation in Kle, Voice of America at Careysburg, Paynesville and Buchanan. During 1968 a new out-station was installed at Zwedru, Grand Gedeh County, increasing the total of independent PUA outstations to six – Robertsport, Harper, Greenville, Gbanka, Sanokole and Zwedru in addition to the Monrovia complex.

In order to provide adequate peak-hour capacity for Monrovia, a 15 MW gas turbine was installed near the PUA diesel generating sub-station on Bushrod Island, at a cost of over $1·25 million. This advantageous development enabled PUA to reduce electricity rates for all consumers in July 1967. During the last three years the total output of PUA was as follows: 146·8 million kWh in 1967, 181·2 million kWh in 1968, and 214·3 million kWh in 1969. The total installed capacity of all power plants in Liberia in 1969 exceeded 213 MW and production reached 560·7 million kWh.

Next to the Liberian Mining Company in Bomi Hills and the National Iron Ore Company in Mano River, the Bong Mining Company became an important consumer of electric power. At present the PUA will supply the Bong Mine with a minimum of 1 440 000 kWh per annum. The feasibility of a joint hydroelectric scheme on the Cavalla River is at present being investigated by geologists from both the Republic of Ivory Coast and Liberia.

Water supply

Until 1954 Monrovia did not possess a central water supply system and needs were met by using cisterns, wells, etc. The rapid growth of the city increased the demand for water steadily, and the development of sources of drinking water and the construction of a drainage system became imperative. In mid-1957 work started on the construction of a 16 in. (400 mm.) pipeline to carry treated water from White Plains to Monrovia. A one million gallon (4·5 million litres) concrete storage tank was built at Mamba Point, Monrovia. The treatment plant, a modified slow sand filter with a capacity of 1·5 million gallons (6·6 million litres) per day, started operation in December 1959. After the construction of the hydro-electric plant at Mount Coffee, the extension of the White Plains purification plant became inevitable. This $7·8 million project, designed to pump 8 million gallons (36 million litres) of drinking water daily into Monrovia and its environs, was completed in 1968. An $8 million sewage system is nearing completion. This system will dispose of 6 000 000 gallons (27·3 million litres) of waste water per day.

Private concessions supply water at Bomi Hills, Bong Range, Harbel, Mano River, Nimba, Robertsfield, Marshall, Kle and Buchanan, but in the rural areas water supplies are inadequate. The Federal Republic of Germany has granted technical assistance to establish drinking-water systems in Greenville and Harper. In Greenville the construction of a system supplying roughly 180 000 gallons (818 000 litres) of water per day was completed in 1970. It consists of underground water collection facilities, a treatment plant, and a large water tower with a capacity of 135 000 gallons (614 000 litres). The construction of the Harper water system, which will be somewhat larger than that of Greenville, began late in 1970.

STEFAN VON GNIELINSKI

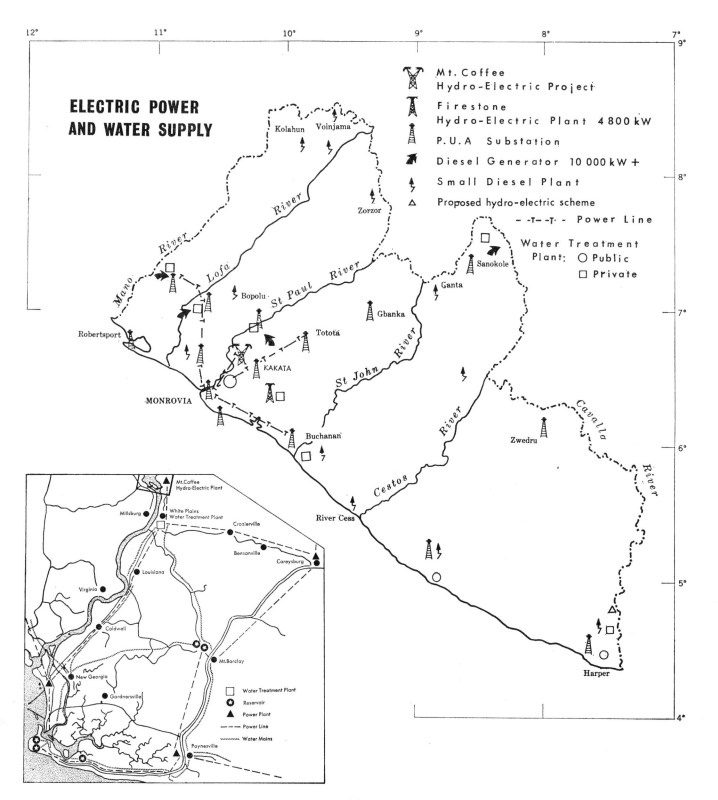

ELECTRIC POWER AND WATER SUPPLY

Legend:

- Mt. Coffee Hydro-Electric Project
- Firestone Hydro-Electric Plant 4800 kW
- P.U.A Substation
- Diesel Generator 10 000 kW +
- Small Diesel Plant
- △ Proposed hydro-electric scheme
- – ⊤ – ⊤ – Power Line
- Water Treatment Plant: ○ Public □ Private

Kolahun
Voinjama
Zorzor
Bopolu
Tototá
Gbanka
Ganta
Sanokole
KAKATA
MONROVIA
Robertsport
Buchanan
Zwedru
River Cess
Harper

Mano River
Lofa River
St Paul River
St John River
Cestos River
Cavalla River

Inset map:

Mt. Coffee Hydro-Electric Plant
White Plains Water Treatment Plant
Millsburg
Crozierville
Bensonville
Careysburg
Louisiana
Virginia
Caldwell
Mt. Barclay
New Georgia
Gardnersville
Paynesville

- □ Water Treatment Plant
- ⊕ Reservoir
- ▲ Power Plant
- – – Power Line
- ···· Water Mains

As in many other developing countries, manufacturing in Liberia is still relatively unimportant. It is surpassed not only by agriculture – the basic industry in all low-income countries – but also by mining, which was the pacemaker of Liberia's economic growth during the 1960's. In the closing years of that decade, manufacturing (excluding rubber and iron ore processing) contributed 4–5% to gross domestic product, giving employment to a similar percentage of the total labour force in the monetary sector. Since land plays a distinctly subordinate role in manufacturing, factor returns in this sector go mostly to labour and capital, native or foreign. Of the $9·2 million labour share in 1967–8, $7·7 million accrued to Liberians and $1·5 million to others; of the $3·2 million return to capital, $1·9 went to Liberians and $1·3 million to others.

Nearly four-fifths of the wages for labour services were earned in workshops, food and beverage processing establishments, motor vehicle repair shops, and clothing firms. The remaining one-fifth was paid to workers in handicraft, cement block and chemical production. The return to capital (including direct taxes) was about $1 million in the food-and-beverages and repair shop branches, and $0·5 million or less elsewhere; the capital share relative to that of labour was especially small in the clothing and handicraft groups. (Only in repair shops did non-Liberians earn a larger share than Liberians of the return to capital.)

Given the small size of the country and its low population density, Liberia's manufacturing sector consists mostly of small firms, and these are located predominantly in the area of the capital city, Monrovia. The following table conveys an idea of the size and scope of existing manufacturing industries in 1969. Omitted for statistical or other reasons are clothing and garment 'shops', and establishments turning out such diverse products as nails, cosmetics and jewellery. Although rarely classified as an industry, makers of various artifacts – decorative art made mostly from wood – sell these direct or through independent traders ('Charlies') in Monrovia and other towns with a large expatriate population.

The completion of a 125 000 ton cement plant and a 10 000 barrel-a-day refinery (Sunray DX and Hydrocarbon Research) in 1968 added two major manufacturing industries. An explosives plant exports part of its production, and a sizeable rice mill was constructed in the Monrovia Free Port Area. The Liberian Bank for Industrial Development and Investment has played a growing role in helping Liberians to participate to a greater extent than hitherto in light industry. Over $2·7 million in loans have been approved, and loans of a similar order of magnitude are under consideration. Almost 70% of the Bank's loans have been to Liberians or Liberian-owned companies.

Several new manufacturing establishments have been proposed, including a tyre factory, a confectionary plant, a paper conversion factory, a brewery (in Harper), a battery plant and a wig manufacturer. However, none of these could be expected to make a major contribution to total employment. The importance which the government attaches to the growth of manufacturing is reflected in a wide range of policies, the most basic of which is the 'open door policy' intended to provide attractive conditions for foreign investors. In addition, the Investment Code of 1966 provides for the exemption of approved manufacturing enterprises from import duties on machinery, construction materials and equipment, and also for the exemption for 5–10 years from duties on imported materials and from taxes on income derived from a given project. By the end of 1969, about two dozen enterprises had been granted the incentives under the Code.

Of two related factors which militate against a rapid growth of manufacturing in Liberia, one is the small size of the domestic market. This is especially inimical to the setting up of capital-intensive industries requiring large-scale plant for most efficient operation. (Their output would be many times as large as the amount that could be absorbed domestically at this time.) The second is the difficulty of achieving regional economic co-operation in West Africa which would assure outlets in neighbouring countries for that portion of the output of a plant of economic size which exceeds Liberia's domestic requirements. It is for such reason that a proposed iron and steel plant to be built at Buchanan (the leading port for iron ore exports), as well as the establishment of agricultural implements, road-building equipment, and similar industries providing a market for fabricated steel products have never advanced beyond the discussion stage. Nevertheless, there may well be several unexploited opportunities for small to medium size manufacturing industries whose establishment would create a supply of materials, tools and other processed inputs for existing major industries.

Activities of manufacturing industries

Type of manufacture	Number of firms	Value of output in 1969 ($)	Employment
1. Footwear (plastic and canvas shoes, leather sandals)	1	434 000	116
2. Umbrellas and scarves	1	195 000	30
3. Bakeries	3	572 000	101
4. Distillery	1	210 000	41
5. Brewery	1	1 500 000	166
6. Soft drinks	2	1 812 000	111
7. Cement, etc.	1	1 980 000	62
8. Paints	1	98 000	26
9. Plastics	1	41 000	54
10. Explosives	1	3 000 000	102
11. Soap	2	300 000	56
12. Refinery (gasoline, jet & diesel fuel)	1	7 986 000	297
13. Furniture	2	695 000	433
14. Building materials	2	2 488 000	400
15. Fish	2	3 500 000	200

Source: *Annual Report of the Department of Commerce and Industry*, Monrovia 1970

W E KUHN

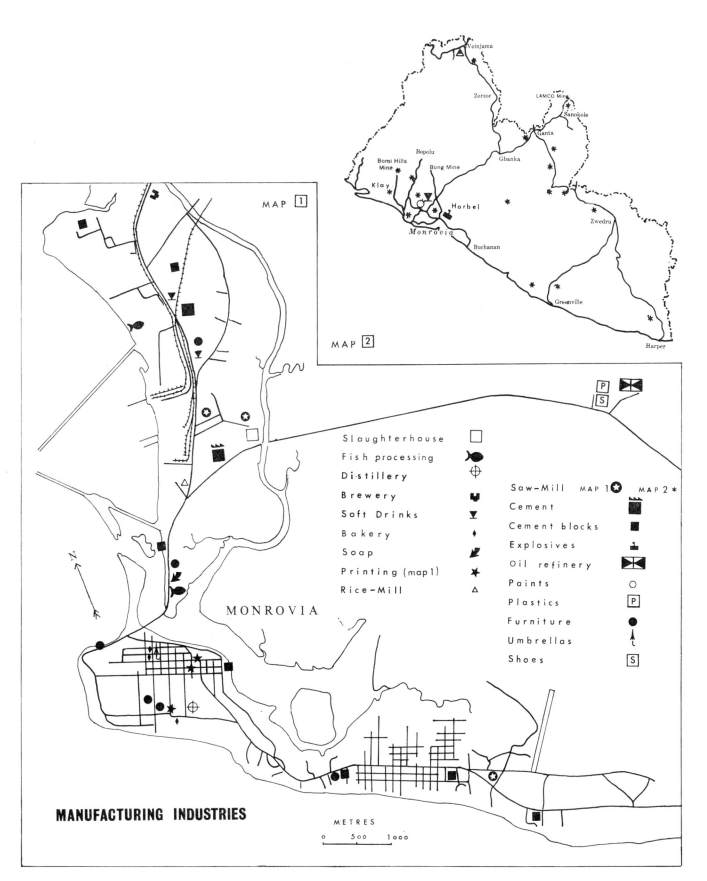

MAP 1

MAP 2

Voinjama

Zorzor

LAMCO Mine

Sanokole

Ganta

Bopolu

Gbanka

Bomi Hills
Mine

Bong Mine

Klay

Harbel

Monrovia

Buchanan

Zwedru

Greenville

Harper

Slaughterhouse	□
Fish processing	🐟
Distillery	⊕
Brewery	♉
Soft Drinks	▼
Bakery	♦
Soap	⚒
Printing (map1)	✴
Rice-Mill	△

Saw-Mill	MAP 1 ✪	MAP 2 *
Cement	▦	
Cement blocks	■	
Explosives	工	
Oil refinery	⋈	
Paints	○	
Plastics	P	
Furniture	●	
Umbrellas	↟	
Shoes	S	

MONROVIA

N

MANUFACTURING INDUSTRIES

METRES

0   500   1000

95

45 DOMESTIC TRADE

The rapid development of the Liberian economy, especially since the Second World War, has been reflected in a substantial increase in domestic trade. Up to that time the economy consisted of some hundred trading houses and a number of isolated trading communities situated along the coastline and serving as collection points for the export of rubber, palm kernels and other agricultural products and as centres for distribution into the hinterland.

President Tubman's 'Open Door Policy' provided an economic climate that attracted a large inflow of foreign capital, and numerous business and trading houses have since established themselves in Liberia, apart from many plantations, mining and lumbering concessions.

In 1970 some 1750 commercial and industrial enterprises were registered. These establishments are mostly general stores, but also include a number of trading companies engaged in selling imported machinery, motor vehicles, electrical appliances, textiles, general merchandise, groceries and the like. While trading on a large scale is done mainly by expatriates – American, West German, Dutch, British, Swiss and Lebanese nationals – the retail trade and small-scale wholesale trade is almost entirely run by Lebanese. Only a few Liberians participate in commerce so far, but they have made substantial investments in business and industrial enterprises, especially in transportation ventures and real estate, these activities being reserved for Liberian citizens by law.

The government itself has made great efforts to build an infrastructure, i.e., to provide basic facilities and utilities such as roads and bridges, communications, hospitals, schools and electricity. The expansion of the network of roads has connected formerly inaccessible parts of the interior with Monrovia. This has served to intensify domestic trade, drastically reducing the cost of transportation to and from all parts of the hinterland.

The retail trade throughout the country is dominated by Lebanese traders who own some 770 out of the 898 merchandise stores. Their many general stores in the interior make available all the necessities of daily living, e.g. imported foodstuffs, kitchenware, tools, etc. On the other hand they are the collecting stations for the bulk of agricultural products destined for export. Wherever the road leads to, the Lebanese shop will be nearby, since they depend on the roads as arteries of trade for bringing in goods and transporting collected crops to town.

The density of Lebanese shops is especially great in the mining areas. Here there is usually a large amount of money in circulation and imported goods are in greater demand. Places near Bomi Hills (Vai Town), Nimba (Grassfield, Sanokole), and Bong Mine (Vanne Town, Kakata) have usually more than 30 Lebanese stores. In Bahn, a small town in Nimba County, one of the diamond mining centres, 26 Lebanese shops are established. The map denotes the distribution of Lebanese stores. They are excellent indicators of trade activity within the country.

As in most African countries many people in Liberia are engaged in local trade. The tribal markets are colourful and busy scenes. Most of the market stalls are in the hands of women. For them trading is an important part of social life and from early childhood is a necessity combined with prestige and pleasure. They display much skill in petty trading in the markets, selling such diverse products as fruit, vegetables and other surplus foods from the farms; fish, baskets, brooms and other useful items. The earning on a single sale may be only cents, but the traders manage to arrive at a considerable profit by reinvesting part of it and gradually enlarging their business. In Monrovia, petty trade is carried out on Waterside, a number of markets, and along the roads. Tiny stores selling paraffin, matches, cigarettes, tinned goods, bottled palm oil, rice and fruit are found in abundance. Petty traders often purchase imported goods retail at Waterside and their prices may therefore be higher than in the big stores.

The trade activities of the Mandingos remain to be mentioned. They are well known in West Africa and started to infiltrate Liberia in the nineteenth century. Their trade routes are still known and used today. The main trading route led over Voinjama, Belle Yella to Bopolu and Monrovia. Many of the Mandingos have settled alongside this road and in the interior trading centres like Voinjama, Belle Yella, Foya Kamala, Kolahun, etc. Today the Mandingo trader deals in diamonds, gold, foreign exchange, ivory curios and artifacts, and many of them are quite wealthy.

STEFAN VON GNIELINSKI

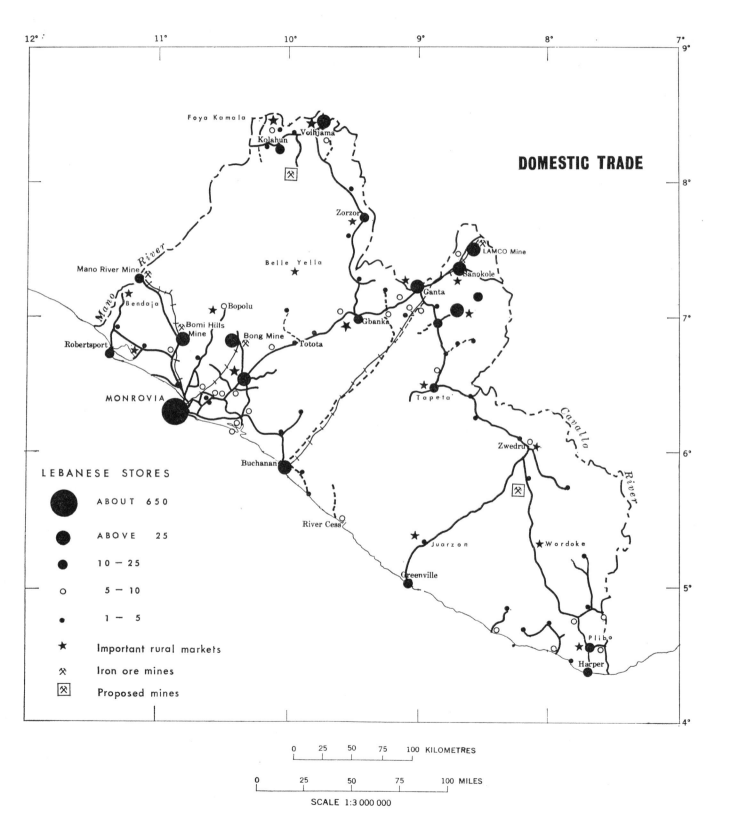

DOMESTIC TRADE

Foya Kamala
Kolahun
Voihjama
Zorzor
Belle Yella
Mano River Mine
Bendaja
Bopolu
Bomi Hills Mine
Bong Mine
Totota
Gbanka
Robertsport
MONROVIA
Ganta
Sanokole
LAMCO Mine
Tapeta
Zwedru
Cavalla River
Mano River
Buchanan
River Cess
Juarzon
Wordoke
Greenville
Plibo
Harper

LEBANESE STORES

ABOUT 650

ABOVE 25

10 — 25

5 — 10

1 — 5

Important rural markets

Iron ore mines

Proposed mines

0   25   50   75   100 KILOMETRES

0   25   50   75   100 MILES

SCALE 1:3 000 000

46 COMMUNICATIONS AND SERVICES

Planning authorities in the new and developing countries are becoming more and more aware of the basic importance of a well established infrastructure for national development. Apart from educational and health facilities, which are discussed elsewhere, transportation and telecommunication as well as banking facilities are considered essential for the overall development of the nation. Other important media for the educational and political emancipation of the people are radio and television. The increasing economic activity and social progress of Liberia is best reflected by the improved facilities of these services.

The overall development of the Liberian road system led to a rapid increase of motor vehicles in the private as well as in the public sector. During the last decade public transport ownership has expanded remarkably, especially in Monrovia, where now several transport agencies contribute to the nation's services, e.g. the YES Transport Service runs a fleet of taxis and buses and also some gasoline trucks. The Alfred Mensah Travel Bureau has a regular bus service to and from the airport at Robertsfield and provides taxis and buses especially for tourists, while Watco Transport Company specializes in school bus operation. Apart from these a great number of privately owned taxis and small buses, the so-called 'pick ups', frequent the roads and provide an unscheduled, but cheap and fairly regular service in the city and on the roads of the interior. The increased sales of petrol which almost doubled from 8·8 million gallons (39 million litres) in 1964 to nearly 16 million gallons (72 million litres) in 1969 indicate the growth of road traffic. The number of service stations has also increased markedly and apart from these, petrol is available in small quantities in most villages along the principal roads.

In 1910 Liberia was one of the first countries in Africa to introduce a telephone and radio-communication system. An automatic telephone exchange was installed in Monrovia in 1953, but at that time only 400 subscribers could be connected. The present telephone exchange, completed in 1965, had an initial capacity of 2000 lines with possible expansion to 10 000. A second exchange was installed in Sinkor with a capacity of 1000 participants with a possible expansion to 5000. All major towns have local telephone systems linked to this network. International communication facilities include air and surface mail services, and transatlantic cable services operated by the Government Cable Office and the French Cable Office. The Firestone Plantation maintains a commercial telegraph circuit between its office in Harbel and its headquarters in Akron, Ohio. Telephone connections and telex links to America, Europe, and to other African capital cities are also available. At present the country is served by 11 main post offices and over 25 postal agencies. A mobile post office made its inaugural trip in 1968. Mail is delivered twice weekly to stations in the various counties.

Radio and television have made a remarkable impact. Commercial broadcasting and television services are provided by the Liberian Broadcasting Corporation, ELBC* and ELTV studios in Monrovia. ELBC broadcasts in English and 13 tribal languages for 16 hours daily on 461·5 m. with short wave transmission at 92·2 m. It also relays the BBC African Service. ELTV started transmission in January 1964 with five hours of live and taped programmes nightly. The radio station ELWA was set up by the Cultural Missionary Broadcasting Section of the Sudan Interior Mission. Five main transmitters simultaneously broadcast news, music and principally educational, health and religious programmes to different areas of Africa in 43 languages and 13 Liberian dialects. The Voice of America, VOA, constructed at a total cost of 12 million dollars at Careysburg, is the largest relay station in Africa. A radio station at Yekepa operated by the LAMCO Mining Company in conjunction with the ELBC started transmissions in 1967. A new radio and TV station was set up in Harper, Maryland, in November 1970. At the end of 1969 there were approximately 200 000 radio receivers and some 6000 television sets in Liberia.

Eight commercial banks operate in Liberia, seven of which are foreign owned. While American banks hold major, if not complete interest in five of these banks, two are owned by Lebanese bankers. Only the Liberian Bank for Industrial Development and Investment (LBIDI), opened in 1965 by the Liberian Development Corporation, is an independant agency of the Liberian Government. Liberia has no central bank. The Bank of Monrovia, affiliated in 1955 with the First National City Bank of New York, is by far the most important banking institution in the country and acts as the government's agent for the supply of US currency notes, and since 1965 has performed clearing functions for the other commercial banks analogous to those of a central bank. The Bank of Monrovia has branches in Sinkor, Cape Mount, Harbel, Buchanan, Greenville, River Cess, Cape Palmas, Nimba and Bomi Hills.

TRADEVCO, the Liberian Trading and Development Bank, is affiliated with Mediobanca of Milan, Italy, and Bankers Trust Company of New York and has been in operation since 1955. In 1966, TRADEVCO opened a sub-branch in Bong Town. The Chase Manhatten Bank was established in 1961. As well as its head office in Monrovia, the bank recently opened a branch in Harbel (Firestone). Other banks are: the Bank of Liberia, founded in 1956 with branches in Ganta and Buchanan and one mobile branch; the International Trust Company, established as a bank in 1960 with one branch in Nimba; the Union National Bank, Monrovia, a subsidiary of the Union National Bank, Beirut, Lebanon, with a branch in Cape Palmas; and finally the Commercial Bank of Liberia. So far, the operations of commercial banks have been governed only by the General Business Law, but a Banking Law will be enacted soon.

Although the number of services is still limited and the distribution over the country is markedly uneven, improvements have been made over the last few years and there are plans for further extension in both public and private sectors.

A AMAGASHIE

* EL is the international radio code for Liberia.

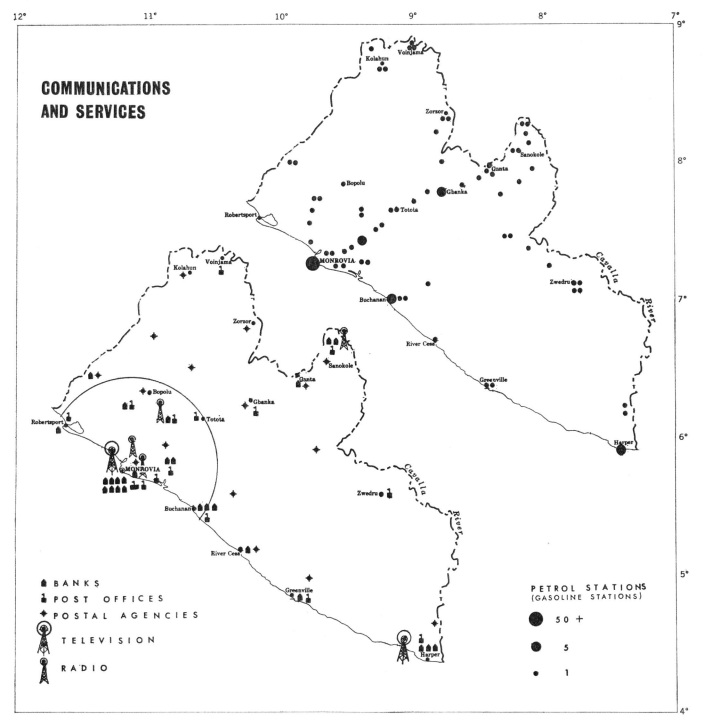

COMMUNICATIONS
AND SERVICES

Kolahun
Voinjama
Zorzor
Sanokole
Bopolu
Ganta
Gbanka
Totota
MONROVIA
Buchanan
Zwedru
River Cess
Greenville
Harper

Kolahun
Voinjama
Zorzor
Ganta
Sanokole
Bopolu
Gbanka
Totota
Robertsport
MONROVIA
Buchanan
Zwedru
River Cess
Greenville
Harper

BANKS

POST OFFICES

POSTAL AGENCIES

TELEVISION

RADIO

PETROL STATIONS
(GASOLINE STATIONS)

50 +

5

1

47 ROADS AND RAILWAYS

Roads

Some fifty years ago the first motor car, a model T Ford, landed in Monrovia, and by 1926 there were about five cars in the country. At that time there existed only one road in Liberia linking Monrovia with Careysburg, a distance of 27 miles (44 km.). People used to walk long distances over paths and bush tracks from the hinterland to town through dense forest and across hills, and under favourable conditions hammock-riding was possible. During the rainy season these paths were mostly submerged and traffic stopped completely. The road to Careysburg was extended by the Firestone Plantation Company a further 29 miles (47 km.) to Kakata with links to Harbel, the company's headquarters, in the vicinity of Robertsfield, the country's international airport. By 1941 the road had been pushed farther inland to Salala, and during the war units of the US Army constructed a further 86 miles (140 km.) to Ganta near the Guinean border.

President Tubman's administration realized the importance of a well defined road network for the opening up of the hinterland and for the economy of the country. An all-weather road system interlinking the principal towns has therefore been placed very high on the list of the priority projects to accelerate economic growth. From 1953 to 1960 road expenditure amounted to 10% of the total revenue collections. By 1964 there were over 1200 miles (2000 km.) of publicly constructed roads in the country, of which some 180 miles (290 km.) were paved and the rest surfaced with laterite. In addition at least 700 miles (1126 km.) of roads had been constructed within the concession areas.

Basically *primary* and *secondary roads* can be differentiated. Primary roads comprise all important long-distance roads and inter-urban highways. Secondary roads are farm-to-market roads and feeder roads of local character which are of minor importance to long-distance traffic. According to their type of construction primary roads can be subdivided into:

a. hard surfaced roads, sealed ⎫
b. laterite roads ⎬ all-weather roads
c. graded or improved roads. ⎭

Generally all primary roads are undivided two-way carriageways, which are quite sufficient, considering traffic conditions in the country. Nearly all public roads are main arteries connecting Monrovia with remote parts of the country with extensions to the neighbouring states. This road network is met by a great number of feeder roads and farm-to-market roads left to the responsibility and initiative of local authorities, using the labour and other resources at their disposal. With the completion of the road link to Maryland County in 1968 all nine counties have been made accessible by road. The expansion of the road network during the last 20 years is shown in the following table:

Public Roads in Liberia

1949	220 miles (354 km.)
1954	300 miles (482 km.)
1961	900 miles (1448 km.)
1967	2200 miles (3520 km.)
1968	2250 miles (3620 km.)
1969	2400 miles (3962 km.)

To accomplish this task, the Liberian Government spent more than $40 million on its road programme, and additional loans have been arranged with the USA and West Germany. German construction firms carried out major parts of the road building, including the paved highway to Buchanan, the Zwedru (Tchien) –Greenville Road, and the Capitol By-pass within the Monrovia metropolitan area. After the completion of the two roads from Zwedru to Greenville and Harper these coastal towns were connected with Monrovia, although by a circuitous route via the hinterland. The construction of a coastal road linking the capital city with Buchanan, Greenville and Harper with connections to the smaller coastal towns at River Cess, Bafu Bay, Sasstown and Grand Cess is proposed. Such a direct route would reduce the mileage from Monrovia to Greenville from 420 miles (676 km.) to 175 miles (282 km.) and to Harper from 470 miles (756 km.) to 310 miles (499 km.) as compared with the distance via Zwedru. The first section of this important east-west axis from Harbel to Buchanan was completed in 1966. In addition to public roads, private concessions have constructed some 1250 miles (2000 km.) of roads which also serve the public. Most recently roads have been built in order to explore iron ore deposits as well as to conduct timber operations. Here in the hinterland road construction and maintenance work faces great difficulties; it is complicated by the physical conditions of the environment, the dense vegetation cover, impassable terrain, such as swamps, deep and widely spread river courses and above all by the heavy precipitation during the rainy season. Therefore, road traffic is not very dense and headloading of crops to market along the road remains very common.

The extension of the road network led to a vast increase in motor vehicles. In January 1970 there were more than 16 000 vehicles in Liberia. About 9000 were private cars, 5600 commercial vehicles and 1400 public transport vehicles.

Railways

There are no public railways in Liberia. The existing railway lines in the country are all owned and operated by foreign iron ore mining concessions. These lines and their equipment were naturally designed primarily for the transport of ore from mines in the interior to ports for shipment.

The first narrow gauge railway line was constructed in 1951 by the Liberian Mining Company. It connects the iron ore mine at Bomi Hills with the port of Monrovia, a distance of some 43 miles (70 km.). By an agreement with the National Iron Ore Company this line was extended for 52 miles (84 km.) to the Mano River in 1961. To facilitate the use of this railway line by both companies an electric central traffic control system was installed during the same year. Two years later, in 1963,

LAMCO opened a railway up to its mine at Mount Nimba to connect it with the port of Buchanan. This railway has standard gauge track for a length of 168 miles (275 km.), four passing sidings and has become the most important line in Liberia. It is operated by a radio-centralized traffic control system with automatic block signalling between stations. By its concession agreement LAMCO is required to provide a small carrier capacity, and in 1967 provisions were made to carry other goods, mainly timber from up-country to the port. Arrangements have also been made to carry petroleum and other fuel inland. For a limited number of passengers, mainly guests and visitors to the mine, modern diesel rail cars are available.

Another 50 mile (80 km.) line between the German–Liberian Mining Corporation at the Bong Range and the port of Monrovia was completed in mid-1964. Like the LAMCO line the DELIMCO line is standard gauge track.

A fourth railway line leading from Robertsport, Cape Mount, up to the Wologisi Mountains is planned. It will serve a new iron ore mine which will be opened in the near future.

STEFAN VON GNIELINSKI

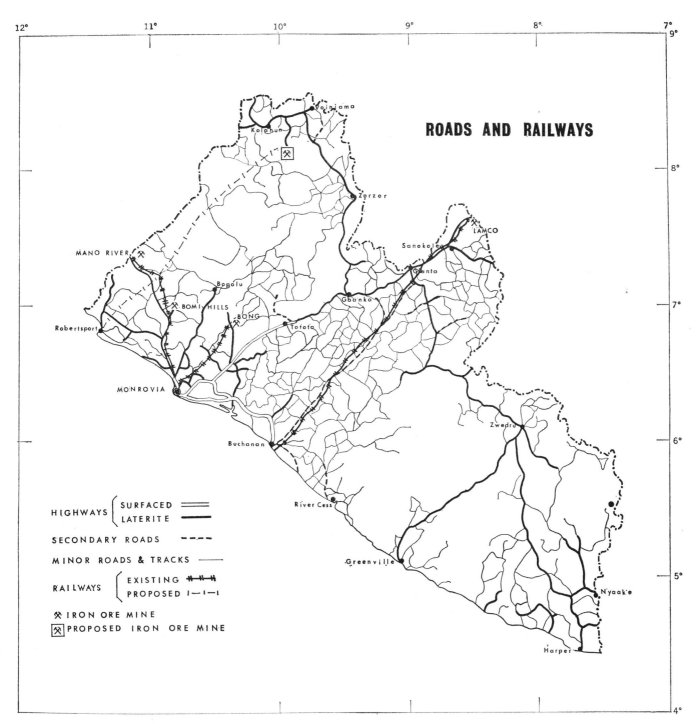

ROADS AND RAILWAYS

HIGHWAYS { SURFACED ═══
          { LATERITE ▬▬▬

SECONDARY ROADS ▬ ▬ ▬

MINOR ROADS & TRACKS ───

RAILWAYS { EXISTING ╫╫╫
          { PROPOSED ╎─╎─╎

✕ IRON ORE MINE
☒ PROPOSED IRON ORE MINE

48 AIR TRAFFIC

Roberts International Airport was constructed in 1941 by the United States Air Force and used as an air and military base during the Second World War. It was improved in 1960–61 to accommodate jet aircraft, and a contract was awarded to Pan American Airways to manage and operate the airfield for commercial purposes. Thus, a gateway was established for air traffic to other African countries, to Europe, North and South America and to the Middle East with links provided to all parts of the world. Robertsfield is built to international standards, with two central air-conditioned terminals – one is operated solely by KLM – a modern hotel and all the necessary air traffic control services including night landing facilities and modern navigational aids. The two runways are 9000 and 7000 ft (2700 and 2100 m.) in length equipped with high intensity runway edge lighting, but it is proposed to extend the runway length to 11 000 and 9000 ft (3300 and 2700 m.) respectively. Until 1968 the road from Monrovia via Firestone plantation to the airport was some 50 miles (80 km.). The construction of a new highway along the coast shortened this distance by some 15 miles (25 km.) so that Robertsfield can be easily reached in about 35 minutes drive from Monrovia. Next to Pan American Airways various other international airlines provide scheduled passenger, mail and freight services, mainly to Europe, namely Swiss Air, Union de Transport Aérien (UTA), Air Afrique, Royal Dutch Airlines (KLM), Scandinavian Airlines (SAS), and Middle East Airlines (MEA). Robertsfield is also connected with African air traffic, especially with the regional West African air network by the following African airlines: Ethiopian Airways, Ghana Airways, Air Guinea, Air Mali, and Nigerian Airlines as well as Liberian National Airways (LNA). Until 1968 direct connection with South America was provided by VARIG; however the route has been cancelled. Since May 1970 SABENA has had a regular service to Brussels. The West German airline Lufthansa proposes to join these airlines with scheduled flights to Frankfurt, Germany. Apart from this, during the summer vacation, Swiss Air and UTA usually arrange additional scheduled flights to Europe and back. Some mining companies also charter planes during the Christmas holidays and on special occasions to provide employees with cheaper air fares. At present more than 30 flights per week are scheduled from Robertsfield. The growth of international air transport during the last years is shown by Table 1.

Domestic air transport is carried out by LNA, air taxis and a few aircraft owned by mining companies and missions. The James Spriggs Payne Airfield on the south-eastern outskirts of Monrovia links the capital city with other West African countries, but it primarily provides a connection with the various towns in the interior of Liberia. The aerodrome is also managed by Pan American and next to Robertsfield is the busiest airfield in the country. Provided with modern ground facilities, communication equipment and meteorological observation facilities, it can serve 4 engined planes such as DC-6 and DC-7, and consideration is given to improvements which would enable the port to handle medium-range jets for regional international air traffic as well. Spriggs Payne Airfield is served regularly by the Liberian National Airways which provides scheduled services to Buchanan, Greenville, and Cape Palmas with their reliable DC-3 aircraft. In former years flights were provided to Tchien, Voinjama, Kolahun and other places in the interior, but with the construction of all-weather roads into the hinterland the service became less vital and was taken over by private air-taxi services, which offer small aircraft for charter at short notice for internal flights. While the activities of LNA slowly declined (see Table 2) those of the private air-taxis held their positions. Over the last twelve months more than 9500 aircraft movements have been recorded conveying some 60 000 passengers from Spriggs Payne Airfield alone. The official Liberia register kept by the Department of Commerce, Division of Civil Aviation, currently lists forty-five aircraft as being actively engaged in commercial aviation operating on 105 known airfields and airstrips, the most important being marked on the map. Six aircraft were newly imported during 1970. The Liberian Aero Club has several flight instructors, so that after successful training student pilots can obtain licences to navigate small aircraft, mainly Cessna 180, but also Maule, Tripacer, etc. The development of the hinterland will without doubt stimulate extensions of the domestic network of civil aviation.

Table 1 International Air Traffic 1965–69

Passengers	1965	1966	1967	1968	1969
Arriving	19 644	20 017	21 497	21 634	25 997
Departing	20 882	21 655	21 836	24 224	24 105
Cargo (kg)					
Landed	725 453	825 000	802 935	810 562	1 009 549
Loaded	257 950	300 000	209 133	236 427	329 513
Mail (kg)					
Landed	85 422	107 000	108 807	120 626	112 677
Loaded	40 615	50 000	44 389	51 622	54 182

Table 2 Domestic Commercial Air Traffic by L.N.A. 1965–69

Item	1965	1966	1967	1968	1969
Aircraft total miles	195 100	207 150	208 000	164 960	142 252
Total passengers	15 896	13 333	11 000	8 571	7 440
Freight (kg)	354 250	266 585	222 750	204 892	187 180
Mail (kg)	76 562	34 707	17 100	13 965	13 598

STEFAN VON GNIELINSKI

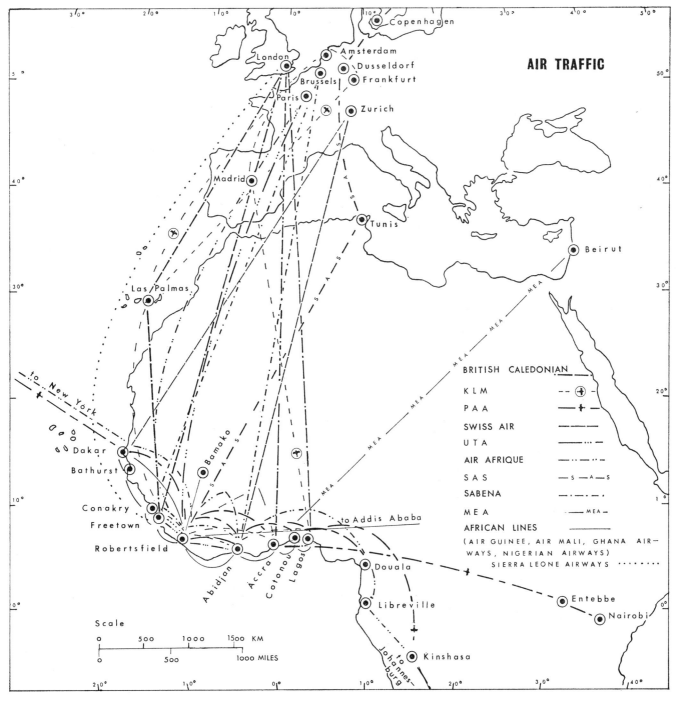

AIR TRAFFIC

Copenhagen

London
Amsterdam
Dusseldorf
Brussels
Frankfurt
Paris
Zurich

Madrid

Tunis

Beirut

Las Palmas

to New York

Dakar
Bathurst

Bamako

Conakry
Freetown

Robertsfield

Abidjan
Accra
Cotonou
Lagos

to Addis Ababa

Douala

Libreville

Entebbe
Nairobi

to Johannesburg

Kinshasa

BRITISH CALEDONIAN	
KLM	
PAA	
SWISS AIR	
UTA	
AIR AFRIQUE	
SAS	S — A — S
SABENA	
MEA	— MEA —
AFRICAN LINES	

(AIR GUINEE, AIR MALI, GHANA AIR-
WAYS, NIGERIAN AIRWAYS)
SIERRA LEONE AIRWAYS ·······

Scale

0   500   1000   1500 KM

0   500   1000 MILES

Liberia, with its fortunate coastal location, has learnt to rely on shipping as the vital link in communication and trade. There are no natural harbours, and those constructed vary considerably in size. By far the largest and easily the busiest of the four main oversea ports is the free port of Monrovia.

The construction of this port started in 1944 at Bushrod Island, about 2 miles (3·2 km.) from the city centre, as a result of a land-lease agreement with the USA at a cost of nearly $20 million. The artificial harbour is formed by two converging rock breakwaters extending over a mile into the open sea and embracing an area of 750 acres (300 ha.) of protected water with a width of entry of 850 ft (245 m.). The port has a 2000 ft (610 m.) wharf with a 35 ft (11 m.) draught, capable of handling 4 medium-sized vessels simultaneously, three separate finger piers for loading ore-carriers of up to 38 ft (10·7 m.) in draught, a tanker discharge berth for vessels of up to 25 000 tons dwt, and a special fishing pier with storage and processing facilities. Other facilities include five heavy cargo cranes, one with a capacity of 70 tons, a 150 ft (46 m.) drydock, several large warehouses and transit sheds, petroleum tank farms of the Liberian Refinery with 40 000 tons capacity and some latex storage tanks of Firestone. Opened in 1948, the port, under the terms of the agreement by which the USA furnished aid in its construction, is operated as a 'Free Port', e.g. within its area of about 500 acres (200 ha.) foreign merchandise may be stored, processed and repackaged free of duty as long as the goods are re-exported. Almost half of the port area is leased to the three mining companies, with large stockpiles of some half a million tons each.

Monrovia is served regularly by 18 shipping lines providing cargo and passenger services. Since 1966 more than 1600 vessels have called yearly. While freighters and other cargo vessels represent about 75% of these ships, tankers and ore-carriers make up the remainder. In 1968 over 10 million tons of cargo were handled, some 9 966 000 tons of iron ore for export and some 600 000 tons of general cargo as well as 200 000 tons of petroleum products were landed. These figures increased slightly during 1970.

Until recently the administration of the port was carried out by the Monrovia Port Management Company. In 1969, by Executive Order No. 11, all functions and obligations were transferred and assigned to the National Port Authority.

Port development in the last decade has been considerable, reflecting to a great degree associated development within the country as a whole. Improvements in warehouses and loading facilities have been completed, especially the installation of conveyor belts to expedite the loading of iron ore at 2000 tons per hour. The harbour basin has also experienced continued development with the acquisition of two new 400 hp ocean tugs, improved buoys and lighting aids and extension to the dredging programme. A loan of $3·5 million was secured by the World Bank to deepen the harbour basin to 45 ft (14 m.) to accommodate vessels of up to 90 000 tons to keep the port competitive for the loading of ore.

A second port built almost solely for the export of iron-ore by LAMCO was completed in 1963 at Buchanan, 60 miles (97 km.) south-east of Monrovia. The harbour is formed by two breakwaters and can accommodate ore-carriers of up to 45 000 tons dwt, with a draught of 42 ft (13 m.). It will eventually be deepened to enable vessels of up to 65 000 tons to be loaded. The ore-loading quay served with a 2300 ft (700 m.) conveyor belt permits loading at a rate of 6000 tons per hour. There are also two cargo quays with a length of 1100 and 450 ft (335 and 137 m.) respectively, for ships of up to 33 ft (10 m.) draught. 8·7 million tons of ore were loaded during 1968 as against 100 000 tons of general cargo, including 61 000 tons of petroleum products in bulk.

By comparison the port of Monrovia is larger, being the chief entrepôt of Liberia and its hinterland, and the port collecting and distributing area (PCDA) is consequently well established. On the other hand the existence of the LAMCO railway linking Buchanan with the interior induces the routeing of goods to Buchanan rather than Monrovia. The export of logs especially showed a gradually increasing trend, and for the first time a shipment of goods and equipment for Guinea was landed and transported by rail to Yekepa and taken by road across the border. Here the future development could result in a co-ordination of road-rail transport routeing Guinea traffic through Buchanan.

The port of Greenville 100 miles (160 km.) south-east of Buchanan was completed in 1963, but the traffic did not become significantly large until 1968 when a number of timber concessions operating in the hinterland started shipment of logs, some 30 000 tons per year. This increased activity will require extensions of the existing facilities to cope with the growth of demand, since the 600 ft (183 m.) quay can berth only one ship of 24 ft (7.3 m.) draught.

The facilities of the port of Harper, Cape Palmas, are still smaller. They consist of a stub breakwater and a 350 ft (107 m.) causeway connected to a 180 ft (55 m.) steel pier. The harbour behind the bar will accommodate ships up to 18 ft (5·5 m.) draught; larger vessels anchor in the open roadstead and have their cargoes lightered. The port has a reputation for severe tides which deter some trade. Main exports are logs, rubber and agricultural products.

Robertsport, Marshall and River Cess are also ports of call. Loading and unloading is done here with the help of surf boats.

Reliance on ports for essential imports and also especially for the exportation of local produce is paramount in Liberia as international road links are either poor or non-existent. The supremacy of Monrovia as the chief entrepôt for Liberia must continue simply because of location, the high density of consumer population, the existing momentum, the vital connection with the ore export, and finally the associated industrial complex which has built up in the immediate vicinity. No other port has all these attributes. Port development in Liberia has thus been closely associated with internal development and as future growth inevitably takes place, the ports of Liberia will likewise accommodate the expansion.

C W PEARSON

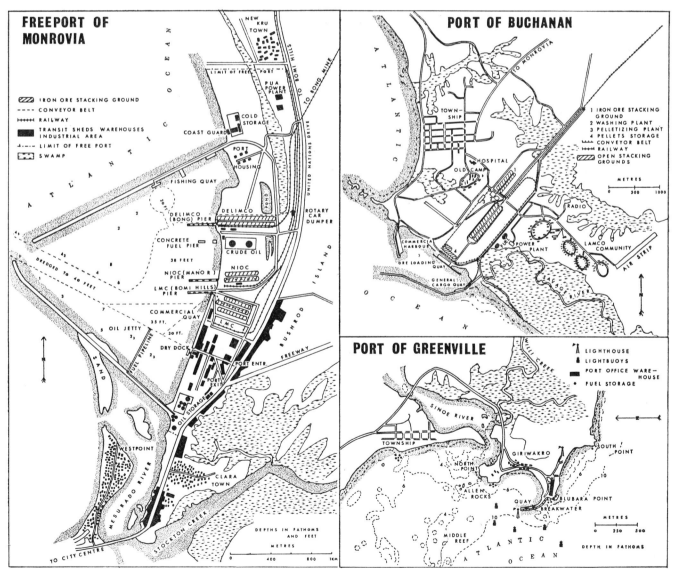

FREEPORT OF MONROVIA

ATLANTIC OCEAN

NEW KRU TOWN

LIMIT OF FREE PORT

PUA POWER PLANT

COLD STORAGE

COAST GUARD

PORT HOUSING

FISHING QUAY

DELIMCO (BONG) PIER

DELIMCO

CONCRETE FUEL PIER

CRUDE OIL

ROTARY CAR DUMPER

NIOC (MANOR) PIER

NIOC

LMC (BOMI HILLS) PIER

COMMERCIAL QUAY

35 FT.

LMC

OIL JETTY

20 FT.

DRY DOCK

FUEL PIPELINE

PORT ENTR.

PORT EXIT

FREEWAY

BUSHROD ISLAND

UNITED NATIONS DRIVE

TO BOMI HILLS

TO BONG MINE

DREDGED TO 40 FEET

30 FEET

38 FEET

SAND

OIL STORAGE

WESTPOINT

MESURADO RIVER

CLARA TOWN

STOCKTON CREEK

TO CITY CENTRE

Legend:
- IRON ORE STACKING GROUND
- CONVEYOR BELT
- RAILWAY
- TRANSIT SHEDS WAREHOUSES INDUSTRIAL AREA
- LIMIT OF FREE PORT
- SWAMP

DEPTHS IN FATHOMS AND FEET

METRES

0   400   800   1KM

PORT OF BUCHANAN

ATLANTIC OCEAN

TO MONROVIA

TOWN-SHIP

HOSPITAL

OLD CAMP

COMMERCIAL HARBOUR

ORE LOADING QUAY

GENERAL CARGO QUAY

POWER PLANT

RADIO

LAMCO COMMUNITY

AIR STRIP

ST. JOHN RIVER

1 IRON ORE STACKING GROUND
2 WASHING PLANT
3 PELLETIZING PLANT
4 PELLETS STORAGE
- CONVEYOR BELT
- RAILWAY
- OPEN STACKING GROUNDS

METRES

0   500   1000

PORT OF GREENVILLE

WELL CREEK

SINOE RIVER

TOWNSHIP

NORTH POINT

GIRIWAKRO

ALLEN ROCKS

QUAY

BREAKWATER

BLUBARA POINT

SOUTH POINT

MIDDLE REEF

ATLANTIC OCEAN

- LIGHTHOUSE
- LIGHTBUOYS
- PORT OFFICE WARE-HOUSE
- FUEL STORAGE

METRES

0   250   500

DEPTH IN FATHOMS

50 EXTERNAL TRADE

During the five-year period 1964–68 the total value of Liberia's combined exports and imports fluctuated between $237 million and $284 million. During the same span, her monetary sector gross domestic product never exceeded $322 million or fell below $266 million. Even if the estimated $30 million of gross domestic product generated in the subsistence sector is added to these figures, Liberia's foreign trade remains a relatively large fraction of her total output of goods and services, namely around four-fifths. This dependence of her economy on the world market became very pronounced in the 1960's, as shown by the figures in the table below. During the 10-year period from 1958 to 1968 imports increased by 180% and exports by 214%, well in excess of the rate of growth of domestic product and of global world trade. The most important contributing factors were the rapid expansion of Liberia's raw material (iron ore) exports and the growth of her imports of certain capital goods (especially machinery and transport equipment). It is clear that the two major components of foreign trade are not only closely related but have been mutually reinforcing; the building of ports and railways aided by the importation of specialized capital equipment enabled Liberia to boost sales abroad of her major natural resource products, while the products from these sales in turn gave new impetus to purchases of more investment goods. This would be true even in the absence of foreign aid, which Liberia used to pay for some of her imports.

During the 1965–69 period iron ore exports contributed upward of 70% of the total value of Liberia's exports, while rubber exports declined from 21 to 15%, but diamond sales rose from 1 to 5% of the total export value. In each of the five years, iron ore, rubber and diamonds combined, contributed at least 90% to the value of sales of Liberian export commodities. Among the minor ones accounting for most of the remainder are coffee, palm kernels, cocoa and timber. Rubber exports consistently declined in terms of value (from $29 million in 1965 to $25 million in 1968) in spite of their increasing volume (from 116 million lb. in 1965 to 144·7 million lb. in 1969). In 1969, however, rubber prices stabilized and export values climbed to $30·7 million.

Year	Imports (mill. $)	Exports (mill. $)	Excess exports over imports
1958	38·7	53·8	15·1
1959	42·9	66·9	24·0
1960	69·2	82·6	13·4
1961	90·7	61·9	—28·8
1962	131·6	67·6	—64·0
1963	108·0	81·1	—26·9
1964	111·2	125·7	14·5
1965	104·8	135·4	30·6
1966	113·7	150·5	36·8
1967	125·2	158·8	33·6
1968	108·5	169·0	60·5
1969	114·6	195·9	81·3

The USA has for many years been Liberia's major trading partner. Since the mid 1960's she has lost ground relatively as a buyer of Liberia's exports. The United States' share declined from 37% in 1965 to 27·7% in 1969. A similar development occurred vis à vis Germany, which bought 27% of Liberia's exports in 1965 but only 23·2% in 1969. Thus, while the United States and Germany combined absorbed nearly two-thirds of Liberia's exports in the former years, they took just over half in the latter. The Netherlands has become an important buyer (9% in 1969 compared with 5% in 1965) and to the same extent this is true of Italy (8·6% in 1969), the fourth in importance of Liberia's customers. Japan, although still far behind in absolute terms, has also advanced a great deal relatively; it may in time come to buy more from Liberia than such countries as Belgium, the United Kingdom and France.

Regionally, Liberia sold about two-thirds of her 1969 exports to Europe (especially the EEC, 53·8%) and only a little over one-fourth in North America. There are indications that the Common Market is rapidly replacing the United States as the most important buyer of Liberia's exports. The small remainder was exported to Asia (6·6%) and Africa (less than 2%).

On the import side an average of a little over one-half of commodity transactions in the late 1960's has been accounted for by a) machinery and transport equipment, and b) manufactured goods classified by materials. Food and live animals made up nearly another one-sixth. Most of the remaining one-third were imports of a) miscellaneous manufactured articles, and b) mineral fuels, lubricants and the like, c) chemicals, and d) beverages and tobacco, in this order. It may be noted from the table that imports fluctuate much more than do exports in the short run, climbing to great heights in some years (1962, 1967), only to fall off sharply in the next year. This phenomenon of 'overbuying' followed by retrenchment was caused by relatively meagre foreign exchange reserves coupled with tightening of foreign aid. In harmony with trends on the export side, imports from the USA declined from 50% in 1965 to 33·8% in 1969; while imports from Germany were much lower, they remained steady and climbed to 14·2% during 1969. Japan was able to increase her share from 5% in 1965 to 9·3% in 1969 and for the first time outflanked the United Kingdom as a seller of commodities to Liberia. Few long-time residents of Monrovia could have missed the 'invasion' of Toyota and Datsun buses and taxis in the second half of the decade! Besides USA, UK, Germany and Japan, only Sweden and Hong Kong provided more than 5% of Liberia's imports.

From a regional point of view, Europe and North America in 1968 were almost evenly matched (43%) as sources of Liberia's imports while in 1969 Europe contributed 44·8% and North America 36·6%. During the same time Asia climbed from 8% to 16% while Africa's share, about 2·3%, remained insignificant.

In 1969 Liberia had large export surpluses – varying from $29·2 million with Germany, $15·5 million with the USA, $15·2 million with Italy, $13·3 million with the Netherlands, $11·7 million with Belgium, to $9·0 million with France.

W E KUHN

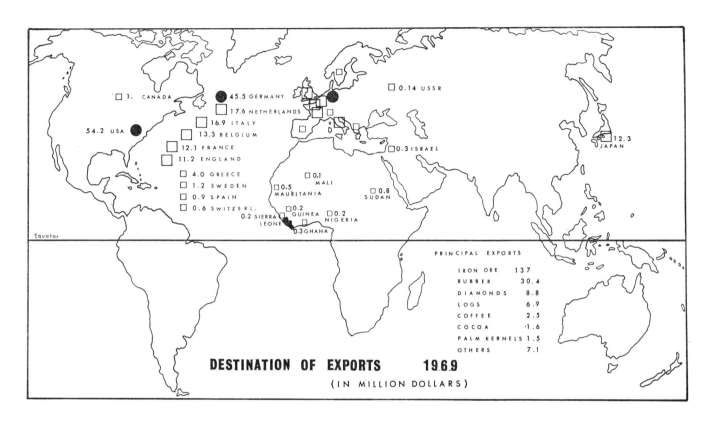

DESTINATION OF EXPORTS   1969

(IN MILLION DOLLARS)

1. CANADA
45.5 GERMANY
17.6 NETHERLANDS
16.9 ITALY
13.3 BELGIUM
12.1 FRANCE
11.2 ENGLAND
54.2 USA
4.0 GREECE
1.2 SWEDEN
0.9 SPAIN
0.6 SWITZERL.
0.14 USSR
0.3 ISRAEL
0.1 MALI
0.5 MAURITANIA
0.8 SUDAN
0.2 SIERRA LEONE
0.2 GUINEA
0.2 NIGERIA
0.3 GHANA
12.3 JAPAN

Equator

PRINCIPAL EXPORTS

IRON ORE	137
RUBBER	30.4
DIAMONDS	8.8
LOGS	6.9
COFFEE	2.5
COCOA	1.6
PALM KERNELS	1.5
OTHERS	7.1

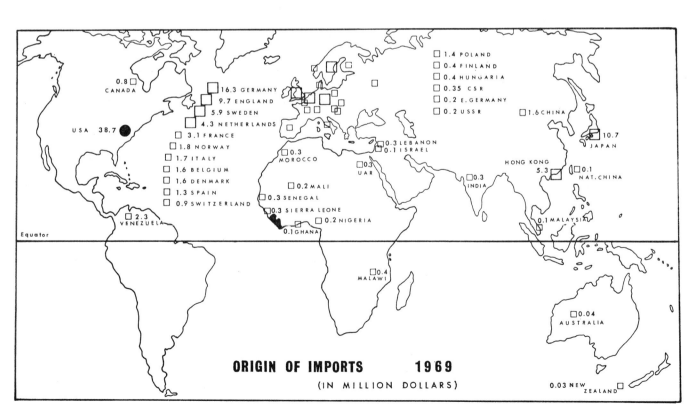

ORIGIN OF IMPORTS   1969

(IN MILLION DOLLARS)

0.8 CANADA
16.3 GERMANY
9.7 ENGLAND
5.9 SWEDEN
4.3 NETHERLANDS
3.1 FRANCE
1.8 NORWAY
1.7 ITALY
1.6 BELGIUM
1.6 DENMARK
1.3 SPAIN
0.9 SWITZERLAND
USA 38.7
1.4 POLAND
0.4 FINLAND
0.4 HUNGARIA
0.35 CSR
0.2 E.GERMANY
0.2 USSR
1.6 CHINA
0.3 LEBANON
0.1 ISRAEL
0.3 MOROCCO
0.3 UAR
0.3 INDIA
10.7 JAPAN
HONG KONG 5.3
0.1 NAT.CHINA
0.2 MALI
0.3 SENEGAL
0.3 SIERRA LEONE
0.2 NIGERIA
0.1 GHANA
2.3 VENEZUELA
0.1 MALAYSIA
0.4 MALAWI
0.04 AUSTRALIA

Equator

0.03 NEW ZEALAND

CONCLUSION

This volume describes and explains the complexity of Liberia in the past and present in terms of continuity and change and gives an account of the great transformation the country has undergone during the 123 years of its independence and particularly during the last 25 years. The synopsis of the physical, cultural and economic environment of Liberia gives a diversified picture, placed in the right perspective.

The physical conditions of the environment are described in the opening chapters. Environmental factors, especially climate and vegetation, have influenced and limited the economic activity. A comparison of maps demonstrates the connection between agriculture and physical features, between rice production and swamps, forest reserves and empty spaces. The bush-fallowing system adopted is conditioned by the fast diminishing soil-fertility caused by the leaching effects of the heavy rains.

According to size and population Liberia is one of the small states in Africa, but according to her history and her political and economic growth she deserves a different classification. Accounts of the history naturally centre on the settlers from America and their descendants, while ambiguity exists about the tribal population which comprises a much larger number and presents a great complexity of origin, language, and culture. The unification policy has been a major step towards uniting the entire nation. Despite differences in culture and social attitude, a mingling of the people and, in particular, inter-marriage is very common now.

Economically, Liberia is classed among the developing countries in the world. She faces the challenge of bringing to her people the advantages of progress. True, most of the country remains today at the level of a subsistence economy, but with the coming of Firestone and the establishment of large plantations the process of absorbing labour from sub-sistence agriculture into the market economy began, and many farmers started to produce crops of commercial value. The exploration for mineral resources began after the Second World War, and the export of iron ore soon took the lead in the country's economy. The 'Open Door Policy' of President Tubman encouraged foreign investment which stimulated the economic growth of the country significantly. The government has taken many positive steps to speed the process of eco-nomic and social development. The National Development Plan was designed to realize a rational assessment of all resources and lead the nation to prosperity. In this task Liberia has received substantial assistance from the United States of America and other foreign governments, the United Nations, mission groups, and private companies.

The increasing economic activity and social progress is best reflected by the improved infrastructural facilities of the land. The building of ports, roads, water and power plants are only a few examples. Opportunities have been offered to all Liberians to acquire an education at all levels, and the number of students is continuously increasing. So is the participation of the tribal population in the economy. Health facilities have been extended throughout the country.

Although prospects for the future seem to be good, various problems in the present economic structure merit close attention. Despite the overwhelming importance of iron ore and other mineral resources for export, agriculture will remain the base of the economy. These mineral resources should therefore help to provide the necessary capital to modernize and diversify agriculture and improve its productivity. More serious efforts must be made to encourage and support Liberian farmers to grow cash crops and participate in commerce, industry and service activities. The introduction of oil palms, coffee, cocoa and tobacco grown on a commercial scale would appear to offer promising possibilities. The increased exploitation of the country's considerable timber reserves has only just begun.

On the industrial side, several new ventures are under consideration: a plant to produce tyres from Liberian rubber, a textile mill, and several other projects will soon start operations.

In April 1968, the heads of state of nine African countries at a meeting in Monrovia formed the 'West African Regional Group' to discuss co-operation in various fields. This economic co-operation could open a potential market for some 80 million people.

Liberia looks toward the future with determination and confidence. The country's mineral wealth, its vast forest and agricultural land, its stable government, free movement of capital without currency restriction, and the 'Open Door Policy' guarantee the growth of investment and offer the promise of continued progress. This book is a contribution, however small, to that end.

STEFAN VON GNIELINSKI

BIBLIOGRAPHY

ANDERSON, R E Liberia, *America's African Friend*, Richmond, 1952.

d'AZEVEDO, W L 'Some Historical Problems in the Delineation of a Central West Atlantic Region,' *Annals of the New York Academy of Sciences*: XCVI, Art. 2, 1962, pp. 512–538.

—— 'Continuity and Integration in Gola Society,' Unpublished Ph.D. Dissertation, Northwestern University, 1962.

BATTELLE INSTITUTE 'City and Regional Planning, Monrovia, Liberia' *Report* Frankfurt-Main, Germany, 1964.

BATTELLE MEMORIAL INSTITUTE 'Study of Roads and Harbors for Development of Southeast Liberia', *Research Report*, Columbus, Ohio, 1967.

BLAMO, J B 'The Impact of Industrialization on Liberian Society,' unpublished Master's Thesis, International Graduate School, University of Stockholm, 1964.

BRASS, W *The Demography of Tropical Africa*, Cambridge, 1968.

BROWN, G W *The Economic History of Liberia*, Washington, 1941.

BUREAU OF NATURAL RESOURCES AND SURVEYS, *Annual Reports 1966–1970*.

CASON, J W 'The Growth of Christianity in the Liberian Environment,' Ph.D. Thesis, Columbia University, New York, 1962.

CASSEL, C A *Liberia, History of the first African Republic*, New York, 1970.

CLARKE, J I *Sierra Leone in Maps*, University of London Press, London, 1966.

CLAYTON, E S *Agrarian Development in Peasant Economies*, Oxford, 1964.

CLOWER, R W and DALTON, G & HARWITZ, M *Growth without Development*, an Economic Survey of Liberia, Northwestern University Press, 1966.

COLE, H R Ed. *The Liberian Yearbook*, 1962, Monrovia, 1963.

COOPER-DENNIS, A 'Marine and Freshwater Fishes of Commercial Value to Liberia', *The Liberian Naturalist*, June 1969.

DALBY, D 'The Mel Languages: A Reclassification of Southern West Atlantic' *African Language Studies VI*, 1965.

DEVELOPMENT AND RESOURCES CORPORATION, *Development of Southeast Liberia*, New York, December 1965.

EASTMAN, E *History of the State of Maryland in Liberia*, Monrovia, 1956.

FAGE, J D *An Introduction to the History of West Africa*, Cambridge University Press, 1961.

FAGG W *The Art of Western Africa*, UNESCO, 1967.

F.A.O. 'Fisheries in the Food Economy', *Basic Study No. 19*, Rome, 1968.

FRAENKEL, M *Tribe and Class in Monrovia*, Oxford University Press, London, 1964.

GARDLUND, T *Lamco i Liberia*, Stockholm, 1967.

GEOLOGICAL, MINING AND METALLURGICAL SOCIETY OF LIBERIA, *Bulletin*, Vol. I, II, and III. 1966–70.

GERMAN FOREST MISSION TO LIBERIA, *Technical Reports 1–9*, Monrovia, 1966 68.

GIBBS, J L jr. 'The Kpelle of Liberia' in: *People of Africa*, New York, 1965, pp. 197–240.

von GNIELINSKI, S 'Some Thoughts about the Geology of Liberia', *The Liberian Naturalist*, Sept. 1966.

—— 'Zuckerrohranbau in Liberia und seine wirtschaftliche Bedeutung', *Zeitschrift für Ausländische Landwirtschaft*, Vol. 7, Heft 3, Berlin, 1968.

—— 'Weather and Climate in Liberia', *University of Liberia Journal*, Vol. VIII, July 1967.

—— 'The Occurrence of Diamonds in Liberia', *Liberian Naturalist*, March 1969.

—— 'The Study of Geography at the University of Liberia', *Bulletin Geological, Mining & Metallurgical Society of Liberia*, Vol. III.

—— 'Internal Migration an Indicator of the Development of Liberia', *University of Liberia Journal*, Vol. IX, Jan. 1970.

—— 'Aerial Photograph, Monrovia', *Die Erde*, Berlin, 1970.

—— 'Die Intensivierung des Reisanbaus in Liberia', *Die Erde*, Berlin 1971.

—— 'Die Küsten-u. Flussfischerei in Liberia', *Africa Forum*, Munich, Nov. 1970.

GOUROU, P *The Tropical World*, 4th edition, London, 1969.

GREENBERG, J *The Languages of Africa*, Indiana University and the Hague, 1963.

HALLETT, R *People and Progress in West Africa*, Oxford, 1966.

Handbuch der Westküste Afrikas, Deutsches Hydrographisches Institut, Hamburg, 1960.

HARGREAVES, J D 'African Colonisation in the Nineteenth Century, Liberia and Sierra Leone', *Sierra Leone Studies No. 16*, (1962).

HARLEY, G W *Looking Back, Liberia, Trade, Industry and Travel*, Monrovia, 1962.

—— 'Notes on the Poro in Liberia', *Papers of the Peabody Museum*, Harvard University, XIX, No. 2, Cambridge: The Museum, 1941.

HARRISON CHURCH, R J *West Africa*, London, 1966.

—— *Africa and the Islands*, 4th edition, London, 1970.

HODDER, B *Africa in Transition*, London, 1967.

HOFF, A A 'Higher Education for a Changing Liberia', unpublished Ph.D. Thesis, Columbia University, 1958.

—— *A Short History of Liberia College and the University of Liberia*, Monrovia, 1962.

HOLSOE, S E 'The Cassava-Leaf People: An Ethno-historical Study of the Vai People with a Particular Emphasis on the Tawo Chiefdom', Ph.D. Thesis, Boston University, 1967.

HOLSOE, T *Forestry Progress in Liberia 1951–59*, Monrovia, 1960.

HUBERICH, C H *The Political and Legislative History of Liberia*, 2 vols, New York, 1947.

HUNTER, G. *The New Societies of Tropical Africa*, New York: Oxford University Press, for Institute of Race Relations, 1962.

JOHNSTON, B F *The Staple Food Economies of Western Tropical Africa*, Stanford, California, 1958.

JOHNSTON, Sir H H *Liberia*, 2 vols. Hutchinson and Co., London, 1906.

JONES, A E N 'Origin and Distribution of Elements in Laterites and Lateritic Soils', Ph.D. Thesis, University of Chicago, 1962.

—— 'Mineral Resources of Liberia', *Mineral Information Service*, California Division of Mines and Geology, Vol. 20, No. 2, 1967.

JONES, H A B 'The Struggle for Political and Cultural Unification in Liberia', Ph.D. Thesis, Northwestern University, 1962.

—— *Grand Cape Mount County*, Monrovia, Liberia, 1964.

JOSHUA, J P 'The Potentials of our Swamps, *University of Liberia Journal*, Vol. IV, January, 1964.

JÜRGENS, H W 'Beiträge zur Binnenwanderung und Bevölkerungsentwicklung in Liberia', *Africa Studies*, Springer, Berlin, 1965.

KARNGA, A *Topics from Liberian Geography*, Monrovia, 1955.

KIMBLE, H T *Tropical Africa*, 2 vols, New York, 1962.

KOELLE, S W *Polyglotta Africana*, London, 1854, reprinted Freetown and Graz, 1963.

KUHN, W E 'Growth without a Central Bank. Peculiarities of the Liberian Case', Nebraska, *Journal of Economics and Business*, Vol. 9, 1970.

KUNKEL, G 'The Trees of Liberia', *German Forestry Commission Report No. 3*, Munich, 1966.

LEE, D H K *Climate and Economic Development in the Tropics*, New York, 1957.

LIBERIA, REPUBLIC OF;

—— *Department of Agriculture, Annual Report 1965–1970*.

—— *Department of Commerce and Industry, Annual Report 1967–1970*.

—— *Department of Education, Annual Report, 1967–1970*.

—— *Department of the Interior, Annual Report, 1966–1970*.

—— *Department of Planning and Economic Affairs, Annual Report, 1966–70*.

LIBERIA, REPUBLIC OF;
—— *Department of Public Utilities, Annual Reports*, 1968–1970.
—— *Bureau of Natural Resources and Surveys, Annual Reports*, 1966–70.
—— Department of Planning and Economic Affairs, *Economic Survey 1968 and 1969*. Monrovia, 1969 and 1970.
—— Department of Planning and Economic Affairs, *A Study of the Social Situation in Liberia*, Monrovia, 1970.
—— Department of Planning and Economic Affairs, *Report on the 1967 Agricultural Survey in Bong County*, Monrovia, 1968.
—— Department of Planning and Economic Affairs, *Liberian Population Growth Survey*, Handbook, 1969.
—— Department of Planning and Economic Affairs, *Bulletin of the Population Growth Survey*, Monrovia, Nov. 1970.
—— Department of the Interior, *Traditional History and Folklore of the Glebo (Grebo) Tribe*, Monrovia, 1957.
—— *Summary Report of the 1962 Census of Population*, Monrovia, 1964.
—— Department of Information and Cultural Affairs, *Liberia, Open Door to Travel and Investment*, Monrovia, 1968.
—— Liberia Information Service, *Liberia, Story of Progress*, Monrovia, 1963.
LIBERIA AND FIRESTONE, *The Firestone Plantation Company*, Harbel, Liberia, 1962.
LIBERIAN SUGAR PROJECT, *Preliminary Feasibility Report*, Universal Sugar Project, Inc., New York, 1961.
LIEBENOW, G J 'Liberia', in: CARTER, G M Ed., *African One-Party States*, Ithaca, Cornell University Press, 1962.
LIEF, A *The Firestone Story*, McGraw Hill, New York, 1951.
LITTLE, K 'The Mende in Sierra Leone', in FORDE, C D *African Worlds*, London, 1954.
LUDIN, A & THOMA, E *Die Wasserwirtschaft in Afrika*, Berlin, 1943.
McCOURTIE, W D 'Traditional Farming in Liberia', College of Agriculture and Forestry, University of Liberia, *Research Bulletin No. 16*, 1968.
MANSHARD, W *Einführung in die Agrargeographie der Tropen*, Mannheim, Germany, 1968.
MARINELLI, L A *The New Liberia*, New York, 1964.
MAUGHAM, R C F *The Republic of Liberia*, Allen and Unwin, London, 1920.
MIGEOT, F W H *The Languages of West Africa*, London, 1913.
MILLER, G C *Marine Fishery Development in Liberia*, US Department of Interior, Washington, Sept. 1957.
MORGAN, R *World Sea Fisheries*, Methuen, London, 1956.
MURDOCK, G P *Africa: Its People and Their Culture History*, New York, 1959.
NATIONAL PLANNING ASSOCIATION, *The Firestone Operations in Liberia*, by Wayne Chatfield Taylor. (United States Business Performance Abroad: Fifth Case Study.) Washington, National Planning Association, 1956.
NATIONAL PLANNING COUNCIL, *Four Year Plan for Economic and Social Development*, Monrovia, 1967.
OSTERKAMP, H 'Ganta, ein Liberianisches Dorf im Wandel', *Zeitschrift für ausländische Landwirtschaft*, Vol. 4 No. 2, Berlin, May 1965.
PHILLIPS, H A *Liberia's Place in Africa's Sun*, New York, 1946.
PORTER, P W 'Population Distribution and Land Use in Liberia', Ph.D. Thesis London School of Economics and Political Science, London, 1956.
PRITCHARD, J M *Africa: A Study for Advanced Students*, Longmans, London, 1969.
PUGH, J C & PERRY, A E *A Short Geography of West Africa*, London, 1960.
QUERENGÄSSER, F A *Liberia*, Bonn, 1965.
QURESHI, M A, MIZOE, Y and COLLINGS F 'The Liberian Economy' *International Monetary Fund, Staff Papers*, Washington, 1964.
REED, W E *Reconnaissance Soil Survey of Liberia*, Washington, 1961.
Report on the Conference of the Liberian Research Association, Robertsport, Grand Cape Mount County, Liberia, June 1967.
RICHARDS, P W *The Tropical Rain Forest*, Cambridge University Press, 1964.

RICHARDSON, N R *Liberia's Past and Present*, London, 1959.
ROEPKE, H Ed. *Readings in Economic Geography*, Wiley, New York, 1967.
ROSENBLUM, S and SRIVASTAVA, S P 'Silica Sand Deposits in the Monrovia Area', *Liberian Geological Survey, Report MR-47*, Monrovia, 1969.
ROSENBLUM, S 'Preliminary Spectrographic Analysis of Monazite Concentrates from Western Liberia', *Liberian Geological Survey, Report MR-48*, Monrovia, 1969.
de la RUE, S *The Land of the Pepperbird, Liberia*, London, 1930.
SCHULZE, W O 'An Outline Geography of Liberia', Mimeographed Paper, Monrovia, 1963.
—— 'Early Iron Industry in the Putu Ranges in Liberia', *University of Liberia Journal*, Vol. IV, January, 1964.
—— 'Climate and Weather in Monrovia', *The Liberian Naturalist*, Vol. II, No. 2, April, 1964.
—— *Economic Development and the Growth of Transportation in Liberia*, Sierra Leone, Geographical Association, Freetown, 1965.
—— 'Liberia: Bevölkerungsstruktur und Bevölkerungsverteilung'. *Geographisches Taschenbuch 1966–69*, Wiesbaden, Germany.
—— 'The Ports of Liberia' in: *Seaports and Development in Tropical Africa*, edited by B S Hoyle and D Hilling, Macmillan, London, 1970.
SCHULZ-KAMPFHENKEL, R 'Im Afrikanischen Dschungel als Tierfänger und Urwaldjäger', Studentenexpedition in die Wildnisse der Pfefferküste (Liberia), Leipzig, 1934.
SCHWAB, G 'Tribes of the Liberian Hinterland', with additional material by G W Harley. (*Papers of the Peabody Museum of American Archaeology and Ethnology*, Harvard University 1947. Kraus Reprint, New York, 1968.
SEIBEL, H D 'Kuu- Eine Arbeitsgruppe bei den Kpelle in Liberia' in: *Urgenossenschaften in Afrika*, Freiburg, 1967.
—— 'The Adaption of Labour to Modern Economic Conditions', *University of Liberia Journal*, Vol. VII. No. 2, July, 1967.
SIDERIS, C P 'Report on Agricultural Research from 1957 to 59', unpublished report, Suakoko, Liberia, 1959.
SIEGMANN, W 'Report on the Bassa'. Ethnographic Survey of Southeastern Liberia. Tubman Center of African Culture, Robertsport, Liberia, 1969.
SMITH, R A *The Emancipation of the Hinterland*, Monrovia, 1964.
—— 'We are Obligated' *Hanseatische Druckanstalt*, Hamburg, 1969.
SMITH, W A 'Fresh Water Fisheries', Completion of Project Report, US AID, Monrovia, 1963.
SRIVASTAVA, S P 'Mineralogy of Phosphate Rock from Bambuta, Liberia,' *Liberian Geological Survey, Report MR-51*, Monrovia, 1970.
STANLEY ENGINEERING COMPANY, 'Hydrologic Data', *Republic of Liberia*, Monrovia, 1960.
—— 'Power Resources, Requirements and Development,' *Republic of Liberia*, Monrovia, 1960.
—— 'Mount Coffee Hydroelectric Project', *Feasibility Study*, Monrovia and Washington, 1962.
STANLEY, W R 'Changing Patterns of Transportation Development in Liberia', Ph.D. Thesis, University of Pittsburgh, 1966.
STAUDENRAUS, P J *The African Colonization Movement 1816–1865*. Columbia University Press, New York, 1961.
STILLMAN, C W (Ed.) *Africa in the Modern World*, University of Chicago Press, 1956.
STRONG, R P *The African Republic of Liberia and the Belgian Congo*, Harvard University Press, Cambridge, 1930.
SYMONS, L *Agricultural Geography*, London, 1967.
TANDON, O B 'Commercial Poultry Production in Liberia', *University of Liberia Journal*, Vol. IV. No. 2. July, 1964.
TAYLOR, W C *The Firestone Operations in Liberia*, Washington, 1956.
TEMPANY, Sir H and GRIST, D H *An Introduction to Tropical Agriculture*, Longmans, London, 1964.
THIENHAUS, R 'Die neuen westafrikanischen Eisenerzlagerstätten im Rahmen des Strukturwandels der Welteisenversorgung'. *Die Erde*, Berlin, Vol. 97, 1966.

THOMPSON, B W *Climate of Africa*, Oxford University Press, 1965.

TOWNSEND, R E *President Tubman Speaks*, London Consolidated Publication, 1959.

——— *The Official Papers of William V S Tubman, President of the Republic of Liberia*, London, 1968.

RADEVCO, Liberian Trading and Development Bank, *Liberia: Basic Data and Information 1968*, Monrovia, 1969.

TROWELL, M. *Classical African Sculpture*, Faber and Faber, London, 1954.

UNITED NATIONS, *Demographic Yearbook*, New York, 1966.

———*Economic Development in Africa 1956–57*, New York, 1958.

UNITED STATES, Operations Administrations, *Liberian Swamp Rice Production a Success*, Washington, 1955.

———Department of Agriculture Statistics, Washington, 1968.

———*Army Handbook of Liberia*. H.Q. Department of Army Pamphlet No. 550–38, Washington, 1964.

——— *Operations Mission to Liberia USOM.* 3rd Report on Forestry Progress in Liberia, Washington, 1960.

——— *Operations Mission to Liberia.* The Liberia Aerial Photographic and Mapping Project, Washington, 1969.

VARFLEY, J S 'The Role of the Foreign Retailers in Liberian Business' Unpublished Bachelor's Thesis, Cuttington College, Liberia, 1958.

VOORHOEVE, A G *Liberian High Forest Trees*, Wageningen, Holland, 1965.

WAIBEL, L *Die Rohstoffgebiete des tropischen Afrikas*, Leipzig, 1937.

——— *Vom Urwald zur Küste, Natur und Lebensbilder aus Westafrika*, Breslau, Germany, 1928.

WEBSTER, J B, BOAHEN, A A and IDOWU, H O *The Growth of African Civilization*, Longmans, London, 1967.

WEBSTER, C C & WILSON, P N *Agriculture in the Tropics*, Longmans, London, 1966.

WELMERS, W E 'The Mande Languages', *Georgetown University Monograph Series*, Washington, 1961.

West African Directory, 1968, London, Thomas Skinner, 1968.

WESTERMANN, D *Die Kpelle*, Göttingen, 1921.

——— and BRYAN, M A 'Languages of West Africa', (*Handbook of African Languages*, Pt. II) Oxford University Press for International African Institute, 1952.

WHETSTONE, H V 'Lutheran Mission in Liberia', Master's Thesis, Hartford Seminary Foundation. Board of the Foreign Missions of the United Lutheran Church in America, 1955.

WHITE, R W 'Sedimentary Rocks of the Coast of Liberia', *Liberian Geological Survey*, *Report MR-39*, Monrovia, 1969.

——— 'Stratigraphy of the Sedimentary Basins on the Coast of Liberia', *Liberian Geological Survey*, *Report SP-3a*, Monrovia, 1969.

——— 'Metamorphism of Iron Formation and Associated Rocks in the Wologizi Range, Liberia', *Liberian Geological Survey*, *Report MR-46*, Monrovia, 1969.

——— and LEO, G W 'Geologic Summary of Age Provinces in Liberia', *Liberian Geological Survey*, *Report MR-57*, Monrovia, 1969.

WHYTE, R O *Crop Production and Environment*, Faber and Faber, London, 1960.

WILLIAMS, G J 'The Fishing Industry of Sierra Leone', *Bulletin Journal Sierra Leone Association*, No. 10.

WILLIAMSON, R J *Activities of the United States Bureau of Public Roads during the years 1951–57. Liberia*. Department of Works, Monrovia, 1957.

WILLIS, J R ed. *Studies of the History of Islam in West Africa*, London, 1970.

WILSON, C M *Liberia*, W Sloane Association, New York, 1947.

WORRAL, G A *Soils of the Monrovia District*, College of Agriculture, University of Liberia, Monrovia, 1965.

——— *Soils of the University Farm*, College of Agriculture, University of Liberia, Monrovia, 1965.

YAIDOO, H W *Rural Development in Liberia*, Department of Planning and Economic Affairs, Monrovia, 1969.

YANCY, E J *The Republic of Liberia*, Allen and Unwin, London, 1959.

——— *Historical Lights of Liberia Yesterday and Today*, Tel-Aviv, 1967.